About the Author

THOMAS MOORE was a monk in a Catholic religious order for twelve years and has degrees in theology, musicology, and philosophy. A former professor of psychology, he is the author of *Care of the Soul, Soul Mates, The Re-Enchantment of Everyday Life, The Education of the Heart, The Soul of Sex,* and *Original Self.* He lives in New Hampshire with his wife and two children. Visit the author's website at www.careofthesoul.net.

The
Soul's
Religion

Cultivating a Profoundly

Spiritual Way of Life

Thomas Moore

 Perennial

An Imprint of HarperCollinsPublishers

A hardcover edition of this book was published in 2002 by HarperCollins Publishers.

HarperCollins books may be purchased for educational, business, or sales promotional use. For information please write: Special Markets Department, HarperCollins Publishers Inc., 10 East 53rd Street, New York, NY 10022.

First Perennial edition published 2003.

Designed by David Bullen

The Library of Congress has catalogued the hardcover edition as follows:
Moore, Thomas.
    The soul's religion : cultivating a profoundly spiritual way of life /
Thomas Moore.— 1st ed.
        p.   cm.
    Includes bibliographical references and index.
    ISBN 0-06-019286-0
    1. Spiritual life. 2. Title.
  BL624 .M66445   2002
  291.4'4—dc21   2001051446

ISBN 0-06-093019-5 (pbk.)

03 04 05 06 07 ❖/RRD 10 9 8 7 6 5 4 3 2 1

To my mother and father,
who are never far from the source

Acknowledgments

This book touches on everything I have ever lived or thought in my life, and so I owe a debt to just about everybody. But to limit the list I want to thank Satish Kumar, Redmond O'Hanlon, Christopher Bamford, and Pat Toomay each for their friendship and constant stimulation. In his own way, Father Patrick McNamara kept me thinking, though I know that I move in a different direction. A few key and intimate observations by Gurucharan Singh Khalsa stayed in my mind and influenced me considerably. I thank the religious order of Servites, with whom I have reconnected and who nurtured my religious life early on. JerriAnn Boggis has become an extension of myself and contributed at every stage. As always, Michael Katz and Hugh Van Dusen have kept faith in my imagination and brought this beast to pass, and Carol Williams kindly and expertly helped clear my muddled thoughts. Thanks, too, to Sioban Piercy for her artistic help. My continuing idiosyncratic practice of religion owes much to the inspiration of Joan Hanley, who is my companion every inch of the way, and to Siobhán and Abraham who make it all worthwhile. I have written this book in the presence of the unnameable, and my deepest gratitude is to the angel who inspired and allowed it.

Contents

"Out of the depths I cry to you, O Lord.

Lord, hear my voice."

Psalm 21

The
Soul's
Religion

Introduction

EVERY HUMAN LIFE is a profound mystery. Deep and invisible currents make us who we are, and the world around us is full of secret intentions and laws. One response to all this mystery is to treat it as a problem to be solved and to do everything possible to be informed and in control. But another way is to bow down in ignorance and confess our limitations. Religion and spirituality, for eons intimately connected, offer creative ways to become people of depth and compassion through embracing mystery.

The religions have a precious cargo, but they often fail in their job by moralizing, intellectualizing, and defending themselves to such an extent that their real purpose is obscured. Today people all over the world are abandoning the religions in disgust and anger. Still, everyone has an instinct for transcendence. People know intuitively that some kind of spiritual life is necessary, and so many are searching on their own or joining new churches and communities. They distinguish sharply between the personal spirituality they have found and the religious institution they have abandoned.

I was speaking with a woman recently about the craving for spirituality. I asked her what she thought it was all about. She became quiet for a moment and then slowly and carefully said, "We want more, more than what is." I've heard this response all over the world, and I believe that simple statement about wanting more expresses the need for transcendence. The object of this desire is unknown and open-ended. It isn't described in typical religious language, and yet I think it evokes the very essence of both religion and spirituality.

I have spent my entire life pursuing this desire for more than what is. At thirteen I left home to join a religious order. I didn't know exactly what I was doing, but I felt an overwhelming yearning to reach as high as I could. At twenty-six I left the order with the same yearning for more. I didn't feel settled again until I had become a professor of religion, but after a few years I was fired from that post. I read that dismissal as a sign, too, that life had more in store for me. When I was fifty and had no money, no position, and no prospects, suddenly one of my books became popular. Then I had work to do and the means to support a family. Looking back, I sense that all these turning points were moments of transcendence, mysteries that charted my spiritual progress.

In *Care of the Soul* I presented the ordinary human situation as full of mystery requiring a sense of paradox and deep acceptance. I recommended, as a response to our troubles, a shift from cure to care, from what my friend James Hillman calls heroic to what I might call foolish. In the human comedy we all fall on our faces. Sometimes we can laugh at ourselves, but often we take ourselves so seriously that we try to be perfect — healthy, we say today. The comic view is the spiritual one, and that's why throughout this book I speak of holy foolishness to deepen our intelligence about things spiritual.

I have been profoundly influenced by the religions of the world. From Zen I have learned never to believe that I have grasped the truth or have understood anything fully. From Taoism I have been taught to find strength in yielding and never to believe that my conception of the meaning of things is ever completely accurate. I have learned from

Christian mystics to be content in a cloud of unknowing, to risk the dark night of the soul, and to cultivate deep and ironic ignorance. Among the Sufis and Native Americans I find the image of the fool as a persona of holiness.

I sense a religious sensibility in all open minds and open hearts. It can be found in the religious institutions, in the new communities, in people searching and questioning, in skeptics, in the secular arts, and in the old traditional stories and rites. All of these things are part of my religion, but I realize that my use of the word is different from that of most people. They see the pomp and circumstance, the authority, and the emphasis on select morals. I mean the word differently, and one purpose of this book is to redefine religion, to grasp its soul, and to present it in such a way that spirituality is not an alternative to it, but part of it.

Care of the Soul addressed the deep soul as found in the emotions, relationships, and culture. In that book I also laid the foundation for a new approach to spirituality, but I gave little more than a taste. Here I focus directly on the spirit and explore its many aspects. I have a great love for religion and spirituality, as they are found in many different forms. Here I present the very core of my life experience and ideas—a way to be spiritual that is honest, close to physical life and emotion, and not arrogant by any means.

In this work I search for spirit in the tangled emotions, the impossible relationships, and the endless failures that come along in most lives. This is the opposite of spirituality as escape; it is an appreciation for the spirituality to be found down in the depths of experience, in the never-ending efforts to make sense of life, and in the ordeals that can be seen as spiritual initiations rather than failures to achieve a self.

This book may look simple, but it is not naïve. It doesn't coddle the ego. It offers the challenge to be a person fully in the flesh while developing at the same time an intelligent and deep-seated spiritual identity. It doesn't encourage gazing at your navel but finding the infinite in all that lies within and beyond the self. It defines transcendence as getting through a divorce and as offering service to your community. In this spirituality, justice is more important than enlightenment and humor holier than ambition.

Unlike many people I know, I am not antagonistic toward the religious institutions. My mother and father have lived graceful lives of good humor and community and are models to me of the spiritual life. Yet they have consistently found their inspiration in the Catholic Church. In recent years I have redefined Catholicism for myself and find unexpected riches there. But I am aware that the official church is largely in a state of retrenchment. It's frustrating to meet people all over the world who are desperately hungry for spirit, while at the higher levels the churches are becoming more defensive and authoritarian, losing the opportunity to feed themselves and the people of the world with the spiritual intelligence both crave.

In this book I write from my personal experience as a Catholic and former member of a religious order, as a psychotherapist, and as a specialist in religion. My own Catholicism has deepened and widened so much that I don't fit well in an official Catholic setting. I hope the reader will not find my personal background limiting but more a model of someone on a spiritual odyssey who has not completely abandoned his roots but has revisioned them. While I feel an innate and ineradicable Catholicism in me, I also feel a brotherhood with all sorts of spiritual seekers and explorers.

IN MY WORK I am always looking for spiritual depth, and I use that phrase carefully. As a therapist I know that people get into trouble when they separate their spiritual search from their emotional life and their relationships. I see it all as one piece and devote many chapters of this book to the deep spirit found in the ordinary travails of life. In each case I am looking for the link between soul and spirit.

When the situation is ideal, it is impossible to tell the difference between these two dimensions. But circumstances are rarely ideal, and then only for a passing, revealing moment. We can spend half our time enmeshed in the tangles of the soul—at work, at home, in dealing with our desires and fears. We devote the other half to cultivating a spiritual life that has meaning and is honest and well founded. These two dimensions feed each other. One without the other is inevitably neurotic.

This book is full of paradoxes and inversions: I stand many things on their heads as I look for spirit in the depths rather than the heights. I am in search of a religious and spiritual intelligence that has nothing to do with information or quantitative studies. I want to cut through to an incisive and substantive intelligence about the spirit, but I want to avoid the fantasy of being smart about it all, of knowing more than it is given to us to know. I want be intelligent about mystery and not defend against it with excessive explanations and theories. At the same time I don't want to slip into spiritual romanticism with a numb mind and an overactive heart.

This ironic foolishness is not literal stupidity. It is something infinitely subtle, like a mist or a ghost who colors our thinking and acting. As such it is compatible with clear thought and good judgment, which come from some other ghostly presence. Those who have written in praise of the fool, such as Plato, Erasmus, Jung, Yeats, Blake, Dickinson, and Lao-tzu, were all brilliant minds but they were aware of an entirely different kind of intelligence.

The point of spirituality is to find a way to break the boundaries of reason and ego. What we find on the other side is not wisdom but emptiness. The word fool originally meant an inflated ball or a bellows. The *American Heritage Dictionary* uses the telling word *airhead*. On the other side of ego is air, the possibility of breathing again instead of trying to outsmart existence. Similarly, Hildegard of Bingen speaks of being a feather on the breath of God.

It has taken me a lifetime to reach this beginner's appreciation of air and emptiness. All the arguments and examples in this book point to the last page, the empty one. Intelligence happens when you stop trying to be smart. A sense of self appears when you no longer have a need to be somebody. Transcendence arrives when you embrace the life that is given.

Having its own origins,

educated by no one,

without a mother,

calm,

nameless,

having many names,

living in fire:

that is God.

A mere portion of God

are we,

angels.

LACTANTIUS (A.D. 300)

I | Emptiness

To enter the area of the spiritual and the holy, the precinct of the sacred, requires a profound openness of mind and heart. We stand aware of our ignorance, willing to give up our agendas and follow the signs. Without this attitude of detachment, we may end up embarrassingly naïve and get tripped up by some of the common traps of spirituality: blind allegiance, runaway enthusiasm, and poor choice of leaders and teachings.

Many stories tell of the person in search of enlightenment, full of heroism, asking for a demanding task. The Zen master says work with me in the garden for a while. The Taoist says do nothing. Jesus says give up everything that is important to you. As a therapist, again and again I've observed people in their search for the right teacher, the excellent book, or the perfect community. Usually there is little emptiness in their ambition and no room for reflection, and they go from one enthusiasm to the next, getting nowhere.

And so I begin this book with traditional images of emptiness. Recently I attended a summer solstice ritual conducted by a Native American elder. Early in the ceremony he approached the other leaders and some of the crowd with a band of feathers shaped like a scoop. He gathered invisible impurities from each person in the ceremonial shovel and shook them out forcefully onto the ground. Of course we are always imperfect people, but we can make an effort to cleanse our intention as we enter the religious arena. This is the point of rituals of cleansing in many traditions, such as washing the feet or hands or dipping the hand in holy water before entering a holy place or performing a rite. Incense changes the air, a candle focuses attention, and a small sacrifice clarifies the will. We start by emptying.

Heraclitus, a mystical poet of ancient Greece, gave us the image of life as a river. "Panta rhei," he said — everything flows or, perhaps, everything rivers. To be spiritual, to have religion, is to be in this stream, empty and generous. The journey begins like the Fool of the Tarot cards, who in some versions stands at the edge of a cliff, dressed in his motley or looking impoverished, ready to take a leap into nothingness.

The early Christian theologian Tertullian is famous for saying, "I believe because it is absurd." I've always found inspiration in that statement, but at this point I would probably reword it: I believe in and trust absurdity. Any religious statement that doesn't twist your mind into a knot is probably too rational and off the mark. Therefore, it might be good to approach the spiritual life without the need for understanding and clarity. In this area it is appropriate to become less certain, to be forced into wonder about the central mysteries, and to keep moving along without a plan or a goal. Both the object of the quest and the process are saturated with mystery.

Now he thought,
There should be a sky over their heads,
So they can look up at it.

Seneca creation story

1. A Hole in the Sky

As PEOPLE WHO like to fill our minds with facts and our lives with things, we may find it difficult to cultivate emptiness, which is both an intellectual and an emotional openness. But spiritual emptiness is not literal nothingness. It's an attitude of nonattachment in which we resist the temptation to cling to our points of view. This kind of emptiness, confident but never certain, gives us the room to be flexible and self-aware. The religions are filled with symbols for it even if they don't always put it into practice.

It was raining the day I first saw the Pantheon in Rome. My wife and I stood in the cool, damp air and marveled at the oculus or "eye" in the top of the temple 140 feet above the plain stone floor. The emperor Hadrian is responsible for the current shape of the building. It is said that he wanted the hole in the top to reveal the sky so the temple could mirror the human condition of being both exposed to the infinite universe and enclosed in its own shelter. Nathaniel Hawthorne referred to the hole in the dome as "the pathway of heaven's radiance."

When I looked up at the circular opening in the roof, I thought I saw a key to the meaning of religion: a courageous, openhearted appreciation for the mystery that surrounds, permeates, and stands at the center of our lives. Our sciences and technologies approach life as a problem to be solved. Religion goes in the opposite direction: it grants mystery its eternal validity and, rather than solving it, looks for ways to contemplate it and give it honor. While science tries to fill in all the holes in human knowledge, religion celebrates empty spaces and makes them a model and an ideal.

The oculus of the temple, focusing the divine eye that is the sky, mirrors a certain emptiness in our intelligence. Without it, all is lost, because mystery is the heart of religion. People who don't understand this essential point cover over their anxiety about meaning with beliefs that are naïve and extreme. Today, for example, caught up in the spirit of the times, people try to prove that prayer works by making scientific studies. Traditional religious societies don't need such proof. They pray no matter what. They believe not because of evidence but because of their reverence for tradition and their own spiritual insight.

Real faith is rooted in a basic ignorance about ultimate things, and religion helps us to be in relation to that mystery. This kind of ignorance can offer calm or create anxiety, depending on a person's faith. Often people fill in this emptiness by insisting that they possess the truth. The fragility of their faith is betrayed by their strident insistence on being right and by their efforts to force their views on others. They seem afraid of the very things that define religion: mystery and trust.

As I stood under the oculus of the Pantheon, for a moment I thought I could see lines extending from my eye, through the oculus of the building, and out into the sky. My own was the smallest and least significant of these eyes. I recalled the famous words of Meister Eckhart, "The eye with which I see God is the same eye with which God sees me," and Nicholas of Cusa's point that the name of God, *theos* in Greek, means to see, because God "looks on all things."[1]

To be is to be seen, and to be seen is to feel the weight of existence. We need to be seen by our friends and our communities. But we also need to be seen absolutely, to know that our lives are not lived in a vacuum of meaning. We have to know that the oculus of our temple and of the sky is real and that we live in relation to an absolute eye that regards us with interest and affection. It is not impossible for a sophisticated modern man or woman to look into the sky and, in a certain manner, behold angels and a trace of divinity.

The native people who live in the Great Lakes region, where I grew up, are taught by their shamans about this oculus, which they see represented in the Pleiades constellation and in the hole at the top of the shaman's lodge. The anthropologist Thor Conway says that these people believe there is a hole in the sky, to which they give a sacred name: Behgonay Ghizig. Through the hole in the lodge and the doorway of the Pleiades the soul can take flight and communicate with the heavens.[2] The tragedy of modern times is that we have closed off that opening with our facts and our measurements. We have no means of spiritual communication.

In their stories of emergence the Hopi pueblo people of the American Southwest tell of a similar doorway. At their first appearance, in the time of dark purple light, the people had moisture on their foreheads and a soft spot at the top of their heads. Eventually this soft spot hardened, but occasionally they can open it like a door and make themselves available to the influence of the spirit world. As they were drifting on the water looking for a livable fourth world, "not knowing what to do, the people stopped paddling, opened the doors on top of their heads, and let themselves be guided."[3]

This story tells how we can find direction in life by emptying ourselves of intention and goals. Anyone can—figuratively, of course—open the door of his head and be guided. This kind of emptiness is an aspect of faith, a calm ignorance coupled with trust, neither naïve nor simpleminded, in nature as it flows through us and has some regard for us.

Here we arrive at one of many definitions of religion I will propose: a constructive means for being open to the influence of mystery. We need a method for being poised to receive spiritual inspiration, and the combination of method and images is what we call religion. The oculus of the Pantheon is just such an image, a detail of architecture that shows what must also be a frame of mind. We need a gap in our thinking modeled on the hole in the temple. The ancient temple teaches us how to be.

A first step in spiritual progress is to find the empty place, the hole in the fabric of meaning and culture through which the infinite and mysterious can enter. That emptiness may be a lull in time, a moment of reflection, a day off, or an uninvited reverie. Spatially it may be represented in a broad expanse of land or in an empty chapel or meditation room. Emotionally it may be a painful loss or breakdown. Intellectually it could be an open question, a doubt, or a new way of thinking.

A theatrical stage, a movie screen, a dancer's floor, and a painter's canvas are also empty spaces where the imagination can make contact with the infinite. Insofar as it is empty, all art is religious. A canvas is an oculus if the painter treats it as such. The art of painting on an empty canvas is a meditation in the strict sense: it opens the artist to contact with all that is beyond.

This kind of ignorance and emptiness doesn't lead to negative despair or nihilism; it leads to emotional security and a deep comic sense of life. There is something ironic and absurd about living a serious life even though we don't know the origin, the end, or the meaning of it all. Spiritual teachers often laugh at this kind of ignorance, not a laugh of scorn but of appreciation for the willingness of human beings to go on even though they don't know what it's all about.

On that rainy day long ago I stared at the stone floor of the Pantheon, getting wet from the drizzle that sprinkled in from the hole in the roof. I had seen pictures of divine grace as drops of rain, and now for the first time I saw how grace pours into us—when we are foolish enough to leave a hole in our intelligence or smart enough to install a well-oiled door in the top of our heads.

Notes

1. Nicholas of Cusa, *Selected Spiritual Writings,* trans. Lawrence Bond (New York: Paulist Press, 1997), p. 237.
2. Thor Conway, "The Conjurer's Lodge: Celestial Narratives from Algonkian Shamans," in *Earth & Sky,* Ray A. Williamson and Claire R. Farrer, eds. (Albuquerque: University of New Mexico Press, 1992), pp. 236–59.
3. Frank Waters, *Book of the Hopi* (New York: Ballantine Books, 1969), p. 26.

Nothing to be done.

Samuel Beckett

2. The Empty Self

SPIRITUAL EMPTINESS is not only an open mind but also an open self. We have to get ourselves out of the way—our explanations, our goals, our habits, and our anxieties. We often try to avoid disaster and fill life with order and meaning, but just as often life unravels all our careful preparations. At that moment we can complain, but I have found it is best to go with the loss and be educated by it. The willingness to stand in our ignorance gives us character and keeps us honest.

I learned this painful lesson at the end of the crucial seventh year of my university teaching career. The chair of my department called me in to tell me the results of the closed faculty vote on my tenure. "We've decided not to give you tenure, Tom," he said. I was shocked. I had published and thought I showed promise as a writer. I had taken extra courses during my Ph.D. work so I could be a good teacher. But he said, "You've lost your zest for teaching, and you don't write in proper academic style." It probably shows in my words that I still feel the sting of that rejection.

The chairperson told me I could appeal the decision, but I heard his words as a sign to move on. I felt the hollowness of a career collapsing, and it was several years before I saw the gift of new life emerge from that failure. Today people say to me, "You must be happy that they made such a mistake, and they must be sorry for it now." The truth is, they were right, and I still feel the sense of failure. It doesn't seem right to claim ultimate victory or to distance myself from the pain. Celebrating victory can be a way of defending against the important and necessary loss. Deep emptiness lies in the vacant feeling you have when complaints and words of self-defense fall away.

When empty-headedness overtakes me, I find some relief in the religious doctrines of *sunyata* (Buddhism) and *kenosis* (Christianity). Long treatises have been written on these themes, but the ideas are fairly simple. In my own shorthand description, emptiness is the ignorance in our knowledge, the ineffectiveness in our actions, and the transparency in our beliefs. Kenosis is the process in which the self is sacrificed. Saint Paul used this word when he wrote that Jesus *emptied* himself to become human, taking the form of a slave (Philippians 2:7). I think we are all called to empty ourselves and become slaves to a greater design.

And so at moments when I feel forced to surrender to events and the feelings stirring inside me, I try not to complain but rather understand that my willfulness and egotism are being emptied. The process, so difficult to appreciate and so painful to endure, is profoundly religious. If we persist in it, we may discover that the self has no role in finding happiness and fulfillment and that we don't have to be somebody in order to feel content.

If any religious or spiritual act is lacking sacred emptiness, it becomes full of itself and turns into its opposite, a defensive edifice against the cleansing power of mystery. Spiritual teachings are of two kinds: those that are heavy and opaque, consisting in spiritual facts and required teachings, and those that are light and transparent, always pointing beyond themselves and never fully graspable. It's a rare pleasure to find a teacher or a teaching comfortable with this lightness and willing to be glass rather than stone.

For me Catholicism has always been more than adequate as a spiritual path. But over my lifetime my Catholicism has changed. I believe I have grown up spiritually. My relationship to the church now is more complex, and my interpretation of the teachings has become more poetic and mystical. As I have learned more and come of age, step by step my belief has been emptied. But this emptying has enriched it for me; indeed, the emptier it gets, the more valuable it is. Anyone, believer or skeptic, could go through the same kenotic or emptying process. As belief is emptied, vision expands and becomes sharper. The more we know, the more we may be humbled by our ignorance to the point of illumination.

The skeptic or the secularist may think that he is emptier than the believer, but in fact the opposite may be the case. A life of prayer and the achievement of genuine humility and compassion day by day empty the self, and many attain emptiness through the fullness of their practice. The writings of Mother Teresa suggest as much: she seems to have found compassionate emptiness through her ordinary pious devotions. Many people who look as though they are full of devotion and conviction are quite empty. The prayers and teachings that are so important to them allow them to let life pass through them unhindered, and that passage of another will defines their holiness.

But emptying can be threatening. When people feel the inadequacy of their knowledge, they may rush to fill in the gap with nervous belief and excessive information. Modern science and education are full of defensive, worried attempts to prove what can't be verified. Certainly facts can be tested, but in the long run human beings don't live by facts, they live by belief and imagination. To be comfortable with emptiness, which I believe is the same as having faith, is to tolerate free fall into a life made up of mysteries rather than facts.

Alan Watts warned against thinking of emptiness as a metaphysical idea. According to Watts, emptiness is a means of waking us up.[1] When people suddenly rise up from their unconsciousness, their first thought may be to get rid of something. They quit their jobs, abandon their marriages, or leave home. The emptying impulse liberates them and makes way for new ideas and a fresh start. The deep soul is forever giving us new possibilities, while the spirit performs the important task of thinning out and streamlining.

Spiritual emptiness doesn't lead to resignation or depression; on the contrary, it gives hope and frees us from the anxiety of having to be in control. Some people can't fly in an airplane because it asks for a degree of trust they can't muster. Similarly, some people can't be religious because they feel such a strong need to know and to be in control. The solution is to tread more lightly on the earth, to be more hollow than solid, to trust more and to believe less.

As an ideal or a spiritual theory, emptiness can become rigid. People say, "I have to live in the moment. I have to surrender my will." But emptiness doesn't work if it becomes a project. It is nothing in itself. It's a quality in everything we do and think. Once we resolve to be empty, it becomes an agenda, full of purpose. Not only do we have to give up our attachments and expectations, but we also have to give up our precious ideas on emptiness. Emptiness itself has to be empty.

The Prajna Paramita Sutra, the Buddhist creed of emptiness, ends with the mantra that expresses how empty emptiness should be: "*Gate gate para gate parasam gate bodhi svaha.* Gone, gone, totally gone, totally and completely gone, enlightened, so be it." How do you find such emptiness? It requires reflection on our failure to be empty and enough self-knowledge to recognize emptying when it happens. Emptying is both an art and a practice.

Psychoanalysis can help in the attainment of emptiness by teaching how to notice the slightest defensiveness. Psychologically, emptiness is the absence of neurosis, which is essentially an interfering with the unfolding of life and the desires of the deep soul. Various neuroses, such as jealousy, inferiority, and narcissism, are nothing more than anxious attempts to prevent life from happening, and when emptied, they transform into their opposites: Jealousy empty of ego is passion.

Inferiority empty of ego is humility. Narcissism empty of ego is love of one's soul. We could understand our struggles with these emotions as an invitation to emptiness. The point is not to get rid of them but to let them get rid of us.

Defensiveness shows what the soul wants by pointing indirectly to what we fear and therefore obstruct. When that defensiveness dissolves, we are taken directly to the soul's desire and feel that rare condition where nothing stands between what wants to be and what is. The sensation of life passing through us, as though we were clear conduits, is emptiness. It is pure pattern, pure flow. It is the mystical river mentioned by Heracleitus and echoed by James Joyce, who begins and ends his literary "bible," *Finnegans Wake*, with the Heraclitus word *riverrun*.

I remember a delicate moment in my own therapy. I was single and unattached when I became intrigued by a certain woman. My therapist clearly believed that it would be bad for me to pursue this attraction, and she began to foretell disaster and trouble. Quite suddenly, in the middle of a sentence, she shifted. She let go of her fears for me and once again became a disinterested guide. In those few seconds I learned much about emptiness in therapy and in general. It demands an intelligent surrender. It asks us to let life happen. My therapist had a brief but crucial struggle—whether to draw on her wisdom to warn me of the dangers she saw or to let me go on with my life. I learned the more valuable lesson about being empty.

Emptiness feels empty not because there is nothing present, but because whatever it is we're doing has no egotistic interference. The subtle arteries have no ego plaque in them, nothing to resist the smooth flow of the soul. Without our getting in the way, the life of the soul is rich and full, though unpredictable. But it isn't easy to trust strong desire and the life that keeps pouring into us. We always think we know better what should be and how it should all turn out. That is why the death principle—avoiding, worrying, being moralistic—is so popular. Often it seems easier to give up on life than to let it have its way.

In the practice of spirituality, emptiness may show itself in naturalness and an absence of effort and pride. When I was a child, it was the custom in our family as Catholics to abstain from meat on Friday. But this habit amounted to nothing more than a quite satisfying habit of eating fish. I don't recall any signs of superiority, exaggerated suffering, or ambition in the keeping of this rule. We simply didn't eat meat on that day. It was a way of life, unquestioned and quite natural. Insofar as it was nothing special, the rule was empty.

But when I don't eat fatty foods because I think they might be bad for my heart, my abstinence is not empty. I have a plan, and my choices stem from anxiety. The practice may be healthy and even correct, but it is not empty, and the anxiety in it betrays the failure of emptiness. The idea in emptiness is to trust life's own wisdom instead of ours.

The *Tao Te Ching*, an excellent manual in emptiness, says,

> *A truly good person is not aware of his goodness,*
> *And is therefore good.*
> *A foolish person tries to be good,*
> *And is therefore not good.*[2]

Emptiness is the very essence of religion and the spiritual life. It is the open window that allows divine grace to pour in. It is the gesture of standing out of the way and letting life proceed. It is the relaxed mind allowing mystery to enter more deeply into the heart and imagination. It is the pristine condition of the soul and the prerequisite for glimpsing the divine.

It is never found in pure form, but even a small measure of emptiness goes a long way toward quickening the spiritual life. It is a rare find in modern religious and spiritual practice, and when one comes across it, it is worth paying attention. I have seen it in Catholic priests and nuns, in Zen masters, and in a few good therapists. The actor Walter Matthau once said of his friend Jack Lemmon that he had no ego in him. An actor can be empty, too.

Of course, in itself emptiness is nothing, so it can't be explained, programmed, or taught. It is the most important and yet the least of all spiritual concerns. There is only one thing to do about it: heed Beckett's words and take them as a motto and a mantra: "nothing to be done."

Notes

1. Alan Watts, *The Way of Zen* (New York: Vintage Books, 1957), p. 64.
2. Lao Tsu, *The Tao Te Ching,* trans. Gia-Fu Feng and Jane English (New York: Vintage Books, 1972), n.p.

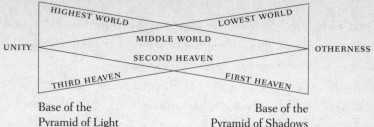

Nicholas of Cusa

3. *Holy Ignorance*

S PIRITUAL INTELLIGENCE requires a particular kind of emptiness, a sophisticated ignorance, an increasing ability to forget what you know and to give up the need to understand. Nicholas of Cusa, the brilliant fifteenth-century writer and ambassador for the Vatican, who wrote like James Joyce with made-up words and strong images, created a whole theology based on the idea of holy ignorance. He also sounds like Shunryu Suzuki, the Zen master who makes the remarkable observation that there is no need to have a deep understanding of Zen. Nicholas said we can never know as much as we want to know about the important things. What is crucial is not what we know but that we know we don't know.

Nicholas liked to use charts, stories, games, and images to express his ideas. The intersecting cones we see above show how opposites flood into each other. In his writings he often presents ignorance and knowledge as two extremes. Knowledge could be placed in the pyramid of light and precious ignorance in the dark, intersecting with each other. Knowledge always has a wedge of ignorance in it, because the only way to be wise is not to understand everything. Ignorance, too, should have a wedge of intelligence so that it isn't mere stupidity. Real understanding is a creative mixture of certainty and unknowing. The trick is to know even when you don't understand.

David Chadwick tells a story of Shunryu Suzuki that exemplifies holy ignorance. The Tassajara community was on a strict silent retreat, and Shunryu Suzuki and other members had been working all day trying to clear a heavy rock in a gully. Some people passed by on a bridge overhead and shouted down, "What are you doing down there?" Suzuki, breaking the sacred silence, cried out, "We don't know."

I like this story for many reasons, but especially because of the loud and irreverent admission that these monks, so devout in their silence, didn't know what they were doing. They were foolish in the eyes of the world, as is anyone who chooses to live from mystery rather than intelligence. The secret of Shunryu Suzuki's effectiveness as a spiritual teacher was his awareness that sometimes rules and teachings are best observed when they are ignored. Breaking the silence was emptiness, as was his statement, which I take quite seriously, that they didn't know what they were doing.

Nicholas noted that, rooted in holy uncertainty, we are left with approximations. He says that our language for God is like a polygon made of many tiny straight lines passing for a true circle. If we look closely at our reasonings, we find that for all their brilliance, in the end they come up short. We may be fooled by the illusion of knowledge, but we remain ignorant, and this failure of understanding allows us to be religious. The holy person is the one who has broken through self-deception and knows how much she doesn't know. The point in thinking is to reach the far edge of understanding and to stand there in wonder.

Since we are only approximately correct when we speak about spiritual matters, the part that remains unknown and unspoken gives our words and ideas the emptiness they require. If there is no respect for that edge of illusion, then we are left with literalism and fundamentalism, scourges of the spiritual life. This is one of those basic ideas on which religion stands or falls: Do we pretend to know more than we can know? Or do we admit to our ignorance and build an intelligent edifice on that lack of knowledge?

Sacred ignorance — that is Nicholas's exact phrase — is not nothingness. It can be the base of stories, images, and rituals that give us insight into the mysteries. Free of the pretense of knowledge, we can go deeper, asking better questions and being transformed as persons rather than merely teasing the mind. Emptiness frees the imagination to take us deep, where a certain kind of spirituality, closely tied to the soul, lies.

The sensation of knowing offers a certain kind of security, but it can easily be challenged. Religious and spiritual people are forever defending their beliefs, often with a belligerence that is unbecoming to them. But another kind of security is based on the sheer honesty of our opinions. This kind doesn't have to be defended or proven, and it is comforting precisely because it needs no propping up. It isn't arrogant and dominating but, rather, appreciates other sincere attempts.

With holy ignorance we don't have to berate ourselves for not knowing everything. There is no one to blame. We can even feel relief at not having to know everything. It is obvious, anyway, that we can't handle our most basic problems. Our emotions are often mystifying, and life has a way of working out in ways that are unpredictable and mysterious. As for society, in the long run none of our solutions work, as crime and warfare continue to plague us even as we develop technologically. To know that we don't know the ultimate secrets of human existence should give us hope, because this failure confirms that our efforts by themselves are incomplete. There is still room for that which is beyond comprehension and for a way of knowing that is profoundly satisfying instead of only superficially workable.

A secular society that desperately craves information and understanding operates from anxiety, while spiritual approaches to mystery offer calm and joy. I will never forget the few years when I lived in

Dallas and learned about the soul from my colleagues there, especially from James Hillman, Robert Sardello, and Patricia Berry. This was not specifically religious learning; it presented itself as psychology. There was excitement in every new twist of perspective and a thrill at every new insight. None of it could be proved, and the pragmatic and academic worlds had little interest in what we were doing. It was all based on imagination rather than fact. Yet this learning meant everything to me. It gave me my life work, and it also taught me how to live.

The pursuit of mystical participation in life goes further than the materialistic quest for knowledge. Although mysterious teachings and tales don't offer clear answers, they do take us to a solid place where we can live with considerable wisdom. Emotionally this is a far greater achievement than the modern trend toward quantitative studies. Religious ways of study go so deep that they touch that nerve center of anxiety that is existential and not just personal. They touch it and offer it peace.

I know from my years in the academic world that students are channeled into methods of study that put severe limits on their imaginations and intensify their egotism. They are taught to worry about the validity of their thoughts rather than to trust their intuitions and imaginations. All fields have succumbed to the lure of materialistic methods of learning. Even art students find security in machinery and numbers. All of this is aimed at saving the student from facing the limits of knowledge and talent. It is protective and therefore neurotic.

An alternative to worry about being right all the time would be to go for insight rather than provable fact. It is possible to reflect on our motives and the roots of our thinking without becoming insecure or foolish. All knowledge is rooted in a point of view and in a deep fantasy about how things are. In that sense it is all relative, all empty. But at the same time it is reliable and livable.

Notice how often in this discussion I use words like security and anxiety. Our problem with knowledge is largely an emotional one. Above all we don't want to be wrong. The secular form of scientific knowledge, in bracketing out mystery and mysticism, leaves us on shaky ground. Only part of our intelligence is engaged, the part that works with facts and measurement. Since that approach is incomplete, it leaves us worried, because intuitively we know that there is more to be considered. A sense of mystery, and even Nicholas's idea of sacred ignorance, would round out our intelligence. Not knowing would be part of intelligence — an idea many religions have taught for eons.

Nicholas's approach to spiritual intelligence had two parts: sacred ignorance and appeal to images. Once you glimpse that facts are rooted in deeper fantasies and images, you examine your world-picture in which the facts are set. As Joseph Campbell said so compellingly, we are always living a myth, not in the negative sense of that word, but a profound, life-shaping imagination of what the world is and how life works. This imagination may be supported by facts and experience, and can be consonant with other kinds of intelligence. But if we take our views literally and too seriously, we will be deluded.

The pyramid of darkness has a part to play in every expression of faith and belief, and it need not be negative. As a therapist I always worry when a client has a neat explanation for what is going on in his life. But when a person doesn't understand and yet trusts the processes at work, I sense a level of maturity. The anxiety level goes down significantly. Free of illusions of certainty, we can freely explore the mysteries that make up a life.

Imagery and poetic expression are especially effective in conveying the mixture of knowledge and ignorance that is faith. Stories give pleasure because they're free of the worry about being correct in every detail and provable. They allow us to consider insolvable issues and deepen rather than solidify our reflection. Images foster wonder rather than conclusions and make for people of wisdom rather than opinion.

Poetical expression always has a hollow at its center, which the critics try to fill by explaining as expertly as they can what the poem or the painting or the music is about. But of course they fail—we are always looking for a more discerning critic—because it is the nature of art to have an empty center. It has this in common with religion—its inherent emptiness—and for that reason is essential to the spiritual life.

Holy ignorance asks that we confess to our limitation. Thomas Aquinas said at the end of his career as a prolific and celebrated author that everything he wrote was straw, a good image for ignorance and emptiness. Toward the end of his life Emerson, unequalled for the beauty, aptness, and originality of his expression, lost his capacity for language. He knew what he wanted to say but couldn't find the words. A man of exquisite self-awareness, he became disconnected from his environment. His biographers tell the story of his going to Longfellow's funeral in Cambridge. Looking around he asked, "Where are we? What is the house? And who is the sleeper?" Emptiness came upon him in the form of an appropriate malady that gradually ended his career and prepared him for death. With grace and good humor he moved steadily from the pyramid of light to the pyramid of shadows. In his notebooks he had written, "All things have an accompaniment of magic. If the fact seem plain & thoroughly known to thee, tis plain thou knowest nothing about it."[1]

People often think that their emotional insecurity is due to a failure in their upbringing, and they interpret their anxiety in psychological terms. But insecurity can also derive from a failure of faith. Everyone needs a philosophy of life and a religious position that is worth the risk of one's life. A religious imagination that satisfies intelligence and inspires with honesty can give a person confidence and stability, but only if a degree of mystery is allowed.

Anxiety stems from a weakness in imagination. Instead of living courageously at the edge of understanding, knowing that they don't know everything, many latch onto a system of belief that answers any and all questions. These answers then become a protective fence around a nervous core. But this illusory edifice creates false certainty.

The failure to find a satisfying solution to mystery translates into extravagant claims and an attitude of righteousness.

Religion as I have been describing it, in many ways the opposite of religion practiced in the churches, offers many constructive and comforting ways to live in the presence of mystery. It teaches us how to perform rituals that connect us with nature and life without any need for explanations. It offers powerful, complex images as well as ancient techniques for contemplating the incomprehensible. It is at home with mystery and helps us live life deeply with full intelligence but without illusions.

The writings of Nicholas of Cusa, so old, so recondite, so convoluted, have been a primary support for me in my own religious explorations. He taught me to be comfortable with my uncertainty. As a result my wonder has increased. I am more interested in religious questions than ever before. I would still like to know how things work. I'd like to know just who Jesus was and is. I'd like to know the Buddha's role in the nature of things and what Mohammed was inspired to create. I certainly would like to know what happens after death and if all the tragedies and conflicts in the world ultimately make some sense.

But I feel little attachment to these questions. I feel free to ignore some of the issues that worry many people. I don't have to know how everything works. I don't have to have an opinion about the afterlife. I can even be ambivalent about certain moral questions that are too complex for my small mind to solve. My ignorance is a ticket to a kind of wonder and experience that would not be accessible otherwise. Yes, it makes me feel inferior at times, but that feeling, too, is comforting. It relaxes the urgency, felt all around me, to know everything and to be in control.

Acknowledging basic ignorance offers a measure of security. I can be at ease in my honesty, admitting that I don't know much about the most important things. Pretending that I know more may make me feel superior, but the price is deep anxiety. Owning my uncertainty, I can laugh in my ignorance and enjoy the comic nature of my puny efforts. An ironic trust in life comes into existence at that liminal point between knowing and not knowing. Take away the ignorance and there would be no room for the faith that keeps us going and the humor that keeps us sane.

The central paradox, of course, is that it takes considerable knowledge and thoughtfulness to arrive at what Nicholas calls *educated* ignorance. We have to school ourselves to the point where we are at ease with our unknowing. And the education never ends, for there is always that remnant of illusion, the sensation of knowing who we are and what we're talking about, that needs to be burned away.

Note

1.   Ralph Waldo Emerson, *Topical Notebooks,* vol. 1, ed. Susan Sutton Smith (Columbia: University of Missouri Press, 1990), p. 246.

II

Mystery

If we have learned the lessons of emptiness, we are ready to move closer to the mysteries, the real substance of the spiritual and religious life. Mystery is not just a great blob of the unknown. Particular mysteries, full of fantasy and meaning, surround us: death, love, illness, sex, aggression, beauty, failure, and desire. Over time the religions of the world have created rituals and told stories focused on these and other mysteries. They show us how to enter them and be initiated by them without ever figuring them out.

It makes no sense to try to prove or disprove a mystery, and certainly to banish its mysteriousness. An alternative is to discover how the mysteries lie at the very center of our lives and make us who we are. We can contemplate them, see how they affect our everyday life, and in ritual and story weave them into our imagination of life. Our devotion to these mysteries becomes our belief—not a purely intellectual assent to a body of propositions but a totally engaging way of giving our lives direction and value.

We are born with the seed of belief buried deep inside us. Over the years it may go through many different external forms, but it is profoundly personal and not consciously chosen. It is inseparable from our angel, the guiding presence that Heraclitus said is our character and Wordsworth pictures as a star. Each person among a thousand gathered in worship has a particular belief that can't be fully expressed by the creed or philosophy of the group.

To believe is to be attentive to that seed that is part of our makeup. It will grow us into who we are called to be. It will give us the security we need to make a contribution to the world, the trust to be a confident member of society, and the bottomless depth to be a person with soul. Our initial naïve belief, its development into a basic trust in life, our adult struggles with doubt and questioning—they are all part of the spiritual life, to be faced steadfastly and lived wholeheartedly. Eventually we may discover that this kind of belief is the meaning of life and that it has been with us, guiding and shaping, from the very beginning.

He who Loves feels love descend into him and if he
has wisdom may perceive it is from the Poetic Genius
which is the Lord.

William Blake, "Annotations to Swedenborg's
Divine Love and Divine Wisdom"

4. *To Believe Is to Love*

BELIEF IS A WORD of love, not thought. It comes from a Germanic root meaning to hold dear. Belief is an endearment. We are drawn to a certain way of imagining experience by its beauty. We become familiar with it and then feel loyal to it. People may try to show us how our belief is wrong or deluded, but we may be profoundly attached to it. We love life as we see it and don't want others to take that precious vision away from us.

All human love is complicated, even religious belief. Infatuation and needy dependence usually play a role in it. Love is always a risk. A spiritual leader comes along and presents a persuasive and appealing worldview. The heart may respond first even if the mind is wary. For all the talk of dogma and teaching, attachment to a religion or a spiritual system is almost always a matter of the heart rather than the head.

When I reflect on my own belief, I realize that emotionally I would love to keep my childlike attachment to Catholicism. But those primal emotions, perhaps the eternal child's wish for the comfort of Mother Church, don't satisfy my adult desires. I want both belonging and adventure. I want to have a spiritual home, but at the same time I need to explore.

At first I was an unconscious Catholic, born into the religion and raised in the atmosphere created by nuns and priests. I was loyal to the church for many years and considered devoting my entire life to it. When I left the religious order in the mid-1960s, I expected the church to change radically for the better. I thought that the second Vatican council marked a major shift and offered the promise of a new and more intelligent spirituality. I left that life, not because I thought the religion was irrelevant or reactionary, but because I was going through a profound spiritual change. I had been reading brilliant theologians like Teilhard de Chardin and Paul Tillich, who gave me fresh ways of looking at my traditional beliefs. I was also learning how to read the Scriptures less literally and naïvely. It was a time when change and hope were in the air. In spite of everything I have written about the importance of ignorance, study and learning have been my major route to spirit.

Then I went through a period of disillusionment. I saw politics and the church reacting against change. I found myself, with my own brand of radicalism, being left behind by a world generally trying to restore a golden past. I could imagine Christianity, and Catholicism in particular, radically changed and profoundly relevant in a so-called postmodern world, but now I don't expect such a change to happen during my lifetime. As the years have gone by, I have felt the need to know my tradition well and adapt it to my own vision.

A few years after leaving the order I discovered the broader realms of depth psychology and world religions, which had a powerful impact on my spirituality. I came to see how each addresses the great questions of human existence, and each in its own way sustains the mystery. Today my belief is profoundly Catholic at its base, but it has been colored by many other influences. I feel a brotherhood with people of all traditions, and I see that art, when it is carried out with an imagination absolutely open to inspiration, also serves the purpose of keeping us in touch with the mysteries. And so in the same sentence I may call upon a theologian and a novelist to explore a point of ultimate meaning.

Personal belief comes first, but it is always in process. A church may expect us to be constant and unwavering, but that is a perfection not accorded those who are living at the edge of belief. When people ask me, as they often do, if I am a practicing Catholic, I hedge. I'd like to be part of the community and contribute to it from within, but I know that my own guiding angel has taken me far from its center. I feel that I have been loyal to the soul of Catholicism but not to its structures and rules. The church has made considerable changes, but I have changed even more radically, and it's difficult to put the two together.

I put all my energy into the constant reimagination of my religious heritage, while at the same time serving the principle of diversity. The most significant change is that my belief is directed toward living well and compassionately, and toward making a contribution in a context of diversity on matters of meaning. I no longer funnel my belief toward maintaining Catholicism. I am a Zen Catholic, a Taoist Catholic, a Jain Catholic, and even an agnostic Catholic. The Catholicism I love is a way into the great mysteries rather than the tightly defended citadel in which they are imprisoned.

I have little patience for the kind of belief that doesn't allow me my own. It seems jealous, like a lover who is not sure of himself. It is demanding, insecure, and often mean-spirited. Belief can generate feelings of superiority and arrogance, which force the believer out of the mainstream and into small groups of like-minded, self-protective people. For all its value, belief has a huge shadow, a capacity for evil as great as its potential for good.

Sometimes the fence placed around belief isn't belligerent but just cozily defensive. Once, during a radio program at election time, the interviewer, a kind and sympathetic man, assumed that I would be voting for the conservative candidate. Like many people, he linked religion with political conservatism. While I have a strong attachment to old, even ancient ideas, politically I tend to be liberal. I want to preserve deep and ancient values, but I find most conservative positions self-centered and paranoid. You could call me a preservative rather than a conservative. At the same time, typical liberal politics is too tied to eighteenth-century deism — natural religion without the mystery. What I really want to do politically is find a way out of the dualism of factions and parties.

It should be no surprise that people are often uneasy about their religious convictions. Belief not only points to the mysterious, but arises from the depths and therefore can't be fully understood and controlled. It has its roots in the heart, where thought is not entirely at home. It arises out of desire and is shrouded in anxiety. Our beliefs form the fundamental imagination by which we live. Our very lives depend on them, and yet, because they lie so deep, it may be difficult to articulate them. For all these reasons people are touchy about their beliefs.

It is a serious mistake on the part of religious and spiritual people to divide the world into believers and unbelievers. We are all believers. The real question has to do with the object of our belief. Is it sufficiently great, infinite, worthy of our absolute endearment? Anything can become a god and idol. The substitutes for divinity are innumerable. They betray the fact that we haven't yet found deep religion, and they are the raw material to be transformed into the mysteries by which we can live.

The object of belief is never pure. We all worship a golden calf, but day by day we can always purify our way of imagining divinity. Religion is a process, not an attainment. It is not a body of beliefs but an exploration that in the best of circumstances is always being refined. Belief is like human love. It shifts from time to time, and any resistance to that shifting, any effort to keep it rigid, weakens it.

Who then are the unbelievers? Certainly not the skeptics and atheists who battle with religion all their lives from the side of unbelief. The spiritual imagination that shapes their lives is vivid and strong. Their struggle with eternal issues puts many churchgoers to shame. And can the churchgoer who defends his fixed notions of God and morality with belligerence and intolerance truly be a believer? Aren't fixity and defensiveness in the spiritual life signs of failure in belief? Can we trust that people are believers just because they say they are?

If belief is rooted in love, one might expect believers to be good at loving themselves and others. Yet those who publicly proclaim themselves to be believers are often the least tolerant and the least loving. Sometimes it is more difficult for someone complacent in his spirituality to be a loving believer than it is for someone who questions and experiments and doubts.

Many people complain that they don't believe in anything and that they feel aimless and empty. They may be stuck in their honest and maybe necessary rejection of the rote creed they had been taught. They may think that belief by nature is naïve and simplistic. They may not know where to turn next or may never have discovered a fresh approach to the question. Maybe if belief were presented with more subtlety and sophistication, they would have a way back. To offer an alternative, of course, is the purpose of this book.

Belief provides an anchor and even makes life feel meaningful. I have never been far from belief and haven't felt fundamentally aimless. My problem has been the opposite: I believe so strongly that I can't enter the secular life as fully as I would like. I am more aimful than aimless. But my beliefs are always forming, and each day offers a new twist in my theology. I have my fundamentalisms and my doubts, and between them lies a sliver of living belief.

Some people don't seem to have the kind of imagination that would allow them to believe in something worthy of them. They are attached to immediate gratifications and to idols that only make them crazy and shallow in their thoughts and values. Instead of belief, which is a joyous involvement in a worthy vision, many people merely survive, finding relief from that task in one entertainment after another. Belief can be symptomatic, taking the form of strong surrender to something that is dangerous and numbing.

Alcoholism, for example, like all addictions, is a skewed belief system. There is plenty of belief in it, but the real object lies deep in the fluid. Maybe what is sought in alcohol is fluidity itself. Because it is a fetish, a substance that both satisfies and frustrates desire, alcohol takes away more than it gives. The desire never changes because drinking doesn't incorporate the beloved. The same is true of drugs, food, and other substitutes. They represent an object of devotion, but at the same time they obscure it. In this sense they are inadequate, secular satisfactions of a deep religious need.

Perhaps because of a certain spiritual inattentiveness or confusion, people often choose the wrong things in which to believe. They fail to see the finiteness of what they take to be an ultimate concern. Today especially it seems that otherwise intelligent people, often highly trained and skilled, go after money this way—religiously. They think that money is a worthy lover, and they give their all to it. They may not recognize the signs of their misjudgment—obsession, alcoholism, depression, marital strife, drugs, and the hollowness of life. It isn't that money is evil, but making it into an idol makes us crazy.

Therefore, the primary task in belief is to educate the imagination to a point where it can conceive of the infinite, so it can transcend the many limited objects that appeal to our belief. In the best of circumstances the religious institution should provide sure guidance in that task, but the church is easily corrupted. Belief is so subtle and mysterious that we can't always count on ministers, rabbis, priests, and other spiritual counselors to get it right. Even a professional may confuse faith with allegiance to an organization.

Belief is close to faith and requires sophisticated love and trust. A believer is one who can remain loyal to life no matter what happens. When writer Bernie Glassman's wife died unexpectedly, friends asked him how he was getting along. "I'm raw, I tell them. . . . Raw is letting whatever happens happen, what arises, arise. Feelings, too: grief, pain, loss, a desire to disappear, even the desire to die. One feeling follows another, one sensation after the next. I just listen deeply, bear witness."[1] This, in my book, is belief.

I began my life as a believer by agreeing to a certain vision and understanding of life that I received from my church. Now, after going through many phases of belief, I believe in many things—art, religion, cultural diversity, peace, nature, honest work, real community, passion. These are secular things, but as the objects of my belief they become part of my religion. My belief has expanded, and yet it is still rooted in the vision I received the very moment I was born. And as long as I still believe, I know that I can love.

Note

1.   Bernie Glassman, quoted in *A Light in the Mist* 5, no. 1 (2000), n.p.

Sermons of unbelief did ever attract me.

Emily Dickinson, *Letters*

5. Unbelief Is as Important as Belief

As important as it is to believe, it is even more important not to believe. Pure belief is too thick. There is no room for movement and no motive for reflection. When belief is rigid, it is infinitely more dangerous than unbelief. And belief becomes thick and rigid so frequently that it is often difficult for a thoughtful person to want to believe or admit to being a believer.

Some people believe too strongly. Of course religious leaders will say the opposite, that faith can never be too strong. But a person can be so full of belief that he is blinded to the unorganized, raw, and chaotic life all around him. He spits out his belief, but it is irrelevant in a world infinitely more complex than his beliefs. Even a small amount of unbelief gives life a chance to proceed.

On the other hand, a person of no belief lives an unconscious existence as though he were in a river that he has never observed from the banks. Belief gives daily life the hesitancy of reflection and a little air. Maybe just a dot of belief would save the secularist from absorption in his culture, and a dot of unbelief might save the devotee from drowning in his faith.

I remember the day I had an interview with the prior in my monastery just six months before I would have been ordained a priest. I had stuck it out for almost thirteen years, living a life of many rewards but just as many sacrifices. He said to me with simple logic, "If you have any doubt about going ahead with your ordination, you will have to either withdraw or postpone it." I thought for just a moment. I had come to him with some misgivings but without a decision. Faced with the situation as he presented it, I had no choice.

It has never made sense to me to postpone something so big. I have been a procrastinator all my life, but I have been willing to make decisions in the crunch. "Of course I have some doubt," I said. Nothing ever seemed — nothing even now ever seems — pure and completely certain. So I decided then and there to leave the life to which I had been dedicated for many years.

People often ask me why I left the religious community and gave up the opportunity, so close and so hard-won, to be a priest. I don't know the answer, but I do know that the reason had nothing to do directly with my external life. I could have gone on pursuing my ideals. But something else was being born in me. I could feel it, though I couldn't name it. It was an embryo. I hadn't chosen it; it had come to me. I couldn't refuse it because it didn't exist on a plane where you accept or deny. It was like my hair turning gray or a mole appearing on my skin. It was only a spot of doubt, but that tiny particle was a life form I couldn't ignore. It generated all the life that followed.

I had been a true believer in my vocation for many years, and the new life that began to flow in the minute I left my prior's office found entry only through the tiniest speck of self-questioning. I had not spent my life as a monk struggling with the decision to stay or leave. I had considered it seriously maybe twice. My doubt at the end was minuscule but life-changing.

But what about belief in God or in your spiritual path? Is there room for doubt there? W. B. Yeats spoke of gyres that intersect, where opposites are reconciled as one passes into the other. He quotes William Blake: "There is a place at the bottom of the graves where contraries are equally true." I'm reminded of Dietrich Bonhoeffer's last thoughts about religion and secular life. He said that we should enter this secular life and at its strongest point find God there, but perhaps not mention him. If we don't doubt God and our spiritual path, we are out of the gyre. There is no more hum, no music, no movement. We may enjoy the peace of not having to struggle with belief, but that silence may signal the end of spiritual vitality.

Maybe doubt is not the word. Today people don't seem to struggle with belief as much as they ask what's in it for them. Doubt may be too much an expectation in an age of unconsciousness. The real threat to belief may not be doubt but sheer lack of interest in anything beyond the immediate gratification of the moment. This is not so much unbelief as nonbelief. Today people look for meaning in success and money, and experience both belief and unbelief from the underside, as they are clobbered by all the symptoms of faith ignored. Only then, in the midst of suffering and confusion, in a life falling apart, do people begin to wonder.

Wonder is a sign that we are intellectually and emotionally alive. But we can't wonder if we don't ask questions. Only the most nervous belief would criticize spiritual wonder. I find every reason to live as though God were a personal presence in my life and world, but every day I wonder if I am deceiving myself. I live as though the human soul were immortal in some way, but I feel challenged by friends and colleagues who declare themselves materialists on this point. I wonder about Jung's enigmatic yet considered statement, when asked about life after death, that he doesn't believe, he knows. Is Jung the deluded Gnostic, alchemical Fascist, self-important guru as many characterize him today, or is he the gifted, intelligent, open-minded magus I take him to be?

Can I trust that Jung knew something about the soul more directly than I have ever experienced? Can I place some credence in the story a friend tells of a classic near-death experience? Are they genuine forays into wonder about the greatest of mysteries? Or are these merely instances of spiritual materialism — giving empirical evidence for what is essentially a matter of faith.

These questions and this wonder about the mysteries of God and immortality at the very least deepen my thoughts and have a strong impact on my values and way of life. I don't expect ever to find answers or to feel that I have come to an end of my questions. But this gyre of wonder paradoxically leads me over to the gyre of tranquil faith. It allows for a vibrant peace that would be impossible with simple belief. Maybe the secularist today would benefit from a little doubt about his belief in capitalism and self-realization.

And so I enjoy reading about Emily Dickinson's penchant for unbelief — this in a person who deeply trusted and loved the life and world in which she found herself. Her questioning was a scandal to some, but out of it she created a kind of scripture of the soul — her poems — that is trustworthy for its strong questioning confidence in life. To me she is a prime example of the holy fool, a woman who followed her muse toward a lifestyle that many still find highly eccentric, and toward a poetic style that her contemporaries felt compelled to correct.

It is important not to believe: to criticize, be skeptical, and enter life so fully that belief is put off until later — but only if belief has its day and is implicated subtly and mysteriously in our unbelief. I don't trust unadulterated belief. Where is its humanity? Where is its weakness? Where is the voice that argues against God and in that puny expression of individuality and humanity makes the dialogue that is the essence of the religious spirit? Nor do I trust pure unbelief or nonbelief. What's the point in living a wonderless life?

You've been told, and it was a mistake, that I am an
intelligent man. . . . But, first of all, I am not intelligent. . . .
Secondly, I never try to make up my mind about a case
until it is finished.

Inspector Maigret in Georges Simenon's *Maigret in New York*

6. *Keeping the Mysteries*

I T TAKES CONSIDERABLE skill to enter deeply into mystery without
violating it or even destroying it. With the hope of learning more
about mysteries and how to live with them, a few years ago I began to
read detective novels. The ones I found at first were crude. Their language lacked art, and they had few real characters and fewer ideas.
Many popular writers today bore me with their blood-and-guts realism.
But then I stumbled across stories that were both entertaining and
beautifully written, like the tales of Inspector Alleyn by Ngaio Marsh
and the sophisticated adventures of Lord Peter Wimsey by Dorothy L.
Sayers. I was also drawn to the appealingly imperfect Inspector Morse
of Colin Dexter and Georges Simenon's Inspector Maigret.

Looking for clues and noticing what is invisible to others, the detective shares much in common with the spiritual guide. Like the best of
teachers, the thoughtful sleuth confesses that he is not so smart and
must reserve all judgments until the matter has been resolved. Around
him are lesser police and a few civilians who try to be intelligent, but
they always come to the wrong conclusions and bungle the case. This

is not a bad lesson in living with our own mysteries. The detective knows all about the virtues of unbelief as he trusts his intuitions.

The detective surrenders himself to a mystery until in his imagination facts gather together and reveal connections and motives that had been invisible up to then. In one of Ngaio Marsh's stories, two of the characters express their suspicions about foul play and a policeman takes out his notebook to fix their opinions. But Inspector Alleyn warns, "There are unexplained discrepancies. They may add up to accident, suicide or homicide and I know no better than any one of you what the answer will be. And now, if you please, we will try to arrive at a few possibly unimportant facts."[1] Colin Dexter's Inspector Morse says, "This morning I thought I had a fair idea about what we were dealing with. But now that I'm perfectly sure that I've none . . ."[2] The inspector seems to know about Keats's negative capability, the capacity to sustain doubt and ignorance.

It's a good way to deal with all mysteries: concentrate on being keenly observant and patient, watching for near-invisible clues, and holding off final judgment about the nature of things until the last possible moment. That's why in spiritual matters contemplation is more advisable than action, and waiting is a special virtue and an art.

The detective knows something about the imagination. He knows that it works well on its own without being forced, hurried, or prodded. He knows that he has to be actively engaged with it but receptive. He has to allow elements to enter, mix, and form patterns. He has to be careful not to draw hasty conclusions and arrive at a solution before all the pieces have sorted themselves out.

Many times as a therapist I have felt like a detective. I listen to many stories, many memories, and many emotions. I hear conclusions and resolutions based on these materials, but I am much slower to draw a plan of action. I always need more material, and I'm interested in seeing how it all moves slowly in life as the result of consideration rather than plan. I never know the complete answer or solution. People make life decisions: They get married or divorced. They move off to a new locale. They get a different job. They vent their anger and confess their love. And all the while I sense a prematurity about it all, and I know that the decisions and actions don't solve the mystery.

I am patient in these matters to a fault. Friends think it is my neurosis rather than my skill or style. Certainly it doesn't look like a virtue. I'm sure much of this resistance to action is temperamental, but I wonder if it was nurtured by my years in a religious community where the really important events of the day were carried out while sitting quietly or singing or reading. Most therapists think they should be skilled and intelligent, but I learned that it is equally important to value your ignorance and foolishness.

Therapy also taught me that the mysteries are revealed in the slightest nuances and innuendos. Superintendent Alleyn builds his case on a slight twitch that he senses in the fingers of a suspect with whom he is dancing. Inspector Maigret notices the way a longshoreman cocks his hat, and then confident but hesitant he steps further into the mystery. As a therapist I pay attention to the way a woman looks at the room in which we hold our conversations and how she sits down. This is not just reading body language, it is looking for the faint epiphanies in which mysteries betray themselves.

What are these mysteries that are revealed with such subtlety? Where to be, how to live, who to love, how to be sick, how to die. In a psychological era these issues are often presented as problems to solve, but they are our mysteries. In a secular context we usually advise weighing the pros and cons and making a timely and firm decision about them, but in a spiritual context these are mysteries to ponder and enter with circumspection.

What we are looking for lies far in the mist of the unknown. The farther we go, the closer we get, but the closer we get, the more we realize that we have farther to go. We become more sophisticated about mysteries, but that means we are more reluctant than ever to solve them. Therefore—and I saw this often in therapy—the goal we have on entering the material and the processes is changed as we progress. Our need to understand metamorphoses gradually into the pleasure of being affected and changed by the search. We are different just for having the patience to remain within the mystery for an extended time, and though we didn't know it at the beginning, this change in perspective was the point of entering in the first place.

I have seen many different kinds of people make the discovery that their original questions were only tickets to enter the theater. Once inside, the tickets were no longer necessary or interesting. Everything had changed more quickly than expected even though the experience of change seemed slower than what was originally desired.

In these odd and paradoxical excursions into mystery I believe we are getting to know the reality of the soul and in particular its eternal qualities; these aspects are less dependent on time than usual life is, and this taste of eternity is an essential first step into spirituality. When the two are in harmony, the spirit is contained within the soul. Diving into that misty realm we begin to sense the peculiar atmospheres and ways of the spirit. You see these changes sometimes in the eyes and faces of people of spirit. They are living on the cusp between life and eternity, and it shows.

People hungry for spirit but misled and caught by its external forms are often preoccupied with morality. Often they are afraid of the very things that would enhance their spirituality, such as sex and a more open relationship to truth. Seasoned spiritual people have a refined morality, but in some areas they may appear immoral. David Chadwick tells a story about Shunryu Suzuki that touched me at a tender spot when I first read it. The celebrated writer and teacher of Zen, Alan Watts, was visiting the Zen monastery. Frequently he excused himself for a glass of water, which everyone knew was alcohol of some variety. He behaved badly, and the next day someone apologized on his behalf to the Zen master. But Shunryu Suzuki answered, "You completely miss the point about Alan Watts! . . . He is a great bodhisattva."[3] Chadwick describes Shunryu Suzuki himself as having had a mild form of kleptomania.

The person who has discovered deep spirituality by entering through the mysteries of the soul is slow to judge another by conventional standards and can see precious individuality shining behind the screen of foibles. Here we run into another paradox in the spiritual life. The person who is comfortably and intelligently moral, neither egotistic about it nor perfectionistic, is the very one who is slow to judge another and stands up forcefully for his values.

The way into mystery is not by knowledge or purity of life but by initiation. It isn't easy to find the way, the point of entry, the stamina to remain, or an attitude for remaining in life, and yet once the initial step is made with courage and abandon, the rest, though arduous in some ways, is easy. It is indeed like a birth into a new way of perceiving and living, at once more demanding and surprisingly relaxed.

Notes

1. Ngaio Marsh, *False Scent* (New York: St. Martin's Press, 1960), pp. 119–20.
2. Colin Dexter, *The Remorseful Day* (London: Macmillan, 1999), p. 185.
3. David Chadwick, *Crooked Cucumber*, p. 381.

Try to forget yourself and rely on your true voice,
your voiceless voice, your nonverbal voice.

Shunryu Suzuki, *Zen Mind, Beginner's Mind*

7. *Faith Begins in Ordinary Trust*

SPIRITUAL FAITH is grounded in ordinary human faith, in emotional trust in life, and in self. A list of beliefs that can be written down and memorized provides a shorthand for this faith and a kind of guiding poetry that satisfies the intellect, but not the heart and soul. The fullness of faith is revealed in the attitudes and decisions that shape life from minute to minute.

Early in my practice I discovered that people coming to me for therapy had little faith in themselves. They were so overwhelmed by troubles which were begging for attention that they couldn't see their own worth. But in every case I could see their strengths, and I did my best to make clear and explicit my faith in them and in the processes going on in their lives.

My faith in these people wasn't a naïve belief that they could handle their situations. Some of them couldn't. Rather, I trusted the processes of the soul, which is always in motion, going backward and forward, up and down, in and out, and sometimes stuck and frozen—all of them valid conditions. These people learned from my loyalty to them to trust the deeper stuff of their personalities and experiences. It was important for me to be honest and yet not to waver. Faith is not sentimental self-assurance that everything will turn out in the end but is instead, trust that the mysteries which shroud us have meaning.

Nor is faith endurance, the assumption that eventually you'll get what you want. Faith doesn't have a specific object. I never got exactly what I wanted, and the good stuff I did get came rather late in life and was entirely different from what I expected. I saw a similar pattern in others. People came to me in despair that life would never work out, but it did, and often in the most unusual ways.

I remember a chain-smoking young woman, pale and gaunt, her hands shaking as she expressed her despair of never having an identity. Within a few years she had become a competent and successful judge. Another, a man who could hardly walk down the street, addicted to everything in sight, eventually became a community leader and counselor, loved by many. The faith these people had was not obvious, but it was there. It allowed them to move ahead when circumstances gave them no reason for hope.

Faith need not be based on any talent or achievement. Sometimes I wondered if I had sufficient training to be a good therapist, but I always had strong confidence in my ability to be honest and imaginative with my clients. I trusted my vision and believed in the unconventional education I did have. I was surprised to meet colleagues who had all the standard credentials but lacked confidence. They often betrayed their doubts, with a worried look on their faces, by insisting on their degrees and certifications, and by parading their theories.

Faith is trust in a way of thinking and living that may not be universally accepted or intellectually verifiable. There may be no reasonableness involved at all, no obvious intelligence, no criteria of reliability, and no clear signs of prudence. Faith is always a kind of folly, and so it may entail a feeling of inferiority. Maybe that is why some religious people take excessive pride in their faith, to obscure the foolishness involved.

But even Saint Paul could write: "If any one of you imagines that he is wiser than the rest of you, in what this world calls wisdom, he had better become a fool, so as to become really wise." (1 Corinthians 3:18) And according to the *I Ching*:

> *Youthful folly has success,*
> *It is not I who seek the young fool,*
> *The young fool seeks me.*

In faith one leaps; one doesn't study the options. Faith is not the result of willpower mixed with information. Faith arises out of a concoction of desires, intuitions, habits, influences, and a generosity of spirit. All of these are qualified by intelligence and skepticism, but the heart of faith is a leap. There are no sequential steps, no secure path to a well-prepared goal. And therefore it may look like folly.

I often hear religious faith described as a kind of certainty, and indeed many religious people who believe themselves to be full of faith sound too certain. What they call faith looks like its opposite. Like those who whistle in the dark, some seem to parade their beliefs precisely so they don't have to face the anxiety of not knowing the answers to the basic issues in life. Being brutally honest with ourselves we go through the core of existential anxiety and find faith on the other side. Faith is not hiding from reality but rather confronting it so boldly and cleanly that the anxiety bursts into a calming surrender.

We find ourselves in a life that doesn't have an owner's manual, with people who believe all kinds of things, in a dangerous world that threatens at every turn. It makes sense to be anxious to a degree, and yet people who flaunt their faith appear either not to experience this anxiety or camouflage it with an overlay of bravado. I think churches would transform overnight if they gave up false assurance and faced the difficult questions of meaning and values with absolute honesty.

As a parent I find that I need yet another dimension of faith. I have to trust that the children will make it through life without my overprotective interference. I have to trust that my own neuroses will not cripple them for life. I have to trust my judgments day after day as the family inches its way forward. I have to be a person full of faith because I don't know how best to be a parent.

I think of this faith, which keeps me up some nights, as inseparable from religious faith. Family life has its own inherent spirituality, irrespective of any tradition or belief system. It has its traditions, its rituals, and its mysteries. In a real sense parents are the priest and priestess of a family spirituality. If I can be faithful as a parent, I have added a piece to my religious faith. If parents have no faith in their children and in the family process, their religious faith is to that extent weakened, and children don't learn to trust. People are always wondering how to nurture the spiritual life of a child. I think a good way to start is by instilling trust. This deep confidence in life will serve as a spiritual foundation much more effectively than religious teachings learned by rote and meaningless to a child.

When parents and teachers have faith in children, young people pick up that faith like a contagion. They learn to deal with obstacles and face their lives with confidence. Giving this kind of faith to others is a key form of service and a major element in any spiritual life. Yes, it is a psychological kind of trust, but one of my premises in this book is that psychology intertwines with spirituality, sometimes as a foundation and starting point. Emotional trust leads seamlessly into spiritual faith.

Faith in a teaching or way of life not grounded in personal trust unsettles the soul. With hollow faith people insist on their beliefs too strongly and force them on others. They are rigid in their beliefs and eventually become belligerent. The most difficult clients I had in psychotherapy were those who believed so strongly in some spiritual system that they weren't able to explore ideas or themselves. Their faith was rigid and brittle, and they seemed to want only further confirmation that they were right. If I didn't kowtow to that plan, we either argued or they quickly sized up the situation and left.

Trust in life is essential — not naïve or blind trust, but basic faith that has been hammered out through experience. When that kind of faith is lacking, specific problems appear, such as paranoia and cynicism; they are found within spiritual groups and in the secularistic culture. The absence of faith is not just a gap; it takes the form of neurotic and psychotic behavior that is threatening to the faithless one and to all in the vicinity.

PARANOIA APPEARS when there is no religious insight into good and evil. We can't sort out the complexities of personality and so assume that certain people are simply evil. We may have no insight into ourselves and believe that we are incapable of ignorance or doing anything bad, and so we externalize evil and identify with pure, victimized goodness. It's obvious how this pattern might dovetail with spiritual teachings, which urge people toward virtue.

As a therapist I know that paranoia can be a deep-seated, dangerous, and impenetrable condition, a full-fledged thick screen of self-protection that is often militant and fierce. People consumed by their paranoia have lost their judgment and capacity to reflect. They see through one lens only, and that one is focused unerringly on evil. No matter what facts you bring to this paranoia, it persists, immovable and ugly. The paranoid person sees himself as the complete victim of evil intentions. In some ways paranoia is even more self-centered than narcissism, but here the emphasis is on the self as victim.

Working with paranoid people I discovered how their perception of evil in the world had the effect of making them appear threatening, and I felt that threat directed against me. I would occasionally wake up at night in terror, perhaps from a nightmare in which I saw my client trying to kill me, sometimes afraid that one of them would actually attack me. Many years later I still feel uneasy when thinking about certain people I liked very much but whose paranoia was chilling.

These people couldn't begin to imagine that I had good intentions for them. They took pleasure in various bizarre thoughts about how I was trying to hurt them, and if I tried to deny that I was up to no good, they simply twisted my statements to increase the evidence of my ill will. Yet, in spite of all this suspicion, beneath and beyond it we could connect with each other.

A version of this extreme paranoia can be found in society, where it is also dangerous. People entertain all kinds of ideas about the evil in other races, nationalities, and religions. They mistrust anyone who hasn't proven himself innocent. This seething paranoia can spread easily and create a climate of fear. Reason doesn't penetrate it because its roots are deep, and it is camouflaged with good intentions or with the illusion that it is accurate.

James Hillman has analyzed the religious problem in paranoia. The paranoid person, he says, doesn't have the imagination for the spirits that fill the air and affect us every day—fear, jealousy, competition, and many others. Not having an appreciation for the reality of these things, he imagines them only as personified in others. Other people are ignorant, unworthy, and capable of evil.

It is a general problem in Western societies that we have lost interest in giving image to evil. We show it somewhat stylized in countless movies of evil characters and outrageous destruction, but these movies merely present us with our situation. We sit mesmerized by the evil in front of us but are not led to imagine evil as a presence in our world. These films don't take us deeper into reflection, nor do they present images we can relate to directly, such as a goddess in India who embodies the destructive power of life. They are almost always part of the symptom rather than its cure.

I also think that the loss of faith in ourselves adds to our paranoia. If we weren't so suspicious and judgmental about ourselves, we might be less paranoid about others. Today it seems difficult for ordinary people to feel good about themselves and to enjoy a sense of innocence. The moralism in America is especially strong, and we're judged for the way we look, the way we eat, and the way we play. Many people play at sports only after many expensive lessons—they have to do it right. I took tennis lessons for two years and then played a game with an old friend. "Why don't you forget how to do it and have some fun?" he said to me.

Deep faith is paranoia turned inside out. It is open instead of closed. It creates religion instead of secularism. It allows us to trust ourselves and others even if we and they have proven untrustworthy in the past. Religion is always telling us to forgive because without forgiveness we can't have faith. If we're paranoid, we can't forgive, and if we can't find forgiveness, chances are we're paranoid.

Like all genuine religious elements, faith is empty. It is not full of itself or full of ideology, which might better be called ideolotry—the blind worship of a set of ideas. There is no room in ideology for questioning and for difference of opinion. This kind of "faith" has to be constant and simplistic. But faith that has any soul in it will have familiar qualities of soul: change, failure, developments, and regressions.

Faith is strong trust in self and life even in the face of evidence to the contrary. Like belief, it consists more in love than knowledge, or perhaps it is just that love takes precedence. It is intuitive. It is a power of the soul, not of the mind alone, and therefore it is exercised more like religion than psychology. It is based on the most subtle of perceptions. It is born and nurtured in the area of the third eye, the open heart, and the sensitivity of an ear tuned to mystery.

III | *Alchemy*

An appreciation for emptiness and mystery allows further movement into spirit, a movement that is inward, downward, and deep. Spiritual literature often portrays the way to spirit as an ascent. The shaman carries a ladder, the guru is on the mountaintop, steeples point heavenward, and a pulpit looms high over a gathering of worshipers. The emotional tone of spirituality is also often high—full of inspiration, ideals, expectation, and even superiority. The alternative, which I want to emphasize here, is not to give up on all those lofty goals but to give equal time to the lower aspects. In reaction to the accent on enlightenment and progress I prefer to focus on spiritual depth.

Some people find this depth in a painful fall from their loftiness, while others struggle through the muck of an ordinary life and discover vision and transcendence there. If spiritual teachers and communities seriously considered this point, spirituality might lose its sentimental idealism and appeal to the intelligent person whose life is already weighty with the challenges of making a living and making sense of it all.

At this point in our reflections we have left behind the prerequisites and are coming to a crossroads that many people face. Do we escape into self-enlightenment and the feeling that we are chosen or special? Or do we bring our spiritual sensitivities to the ordinary struggles of survival and meaning? If I do anything in this book, I want to show the way of spiritual depth, to take the way Wallace Stevens describes — the way through the world rather than around it.

In this section I use the word alchemy, *by which I mean a natural process of transformation, usually starting with the most mundane and difficult of experiences that eventually reveal the gold lying hidden in them. Alchemy begins with a descent into the stuff of everyday life, but it ends, as many old alchemical images show, with the release of the winged spirit. At first the descent may not look like a spiritual process at all, but in the end it proves to be an effective way, if somewhat paradoxical, toward a fullness of spirit.*

Alchemy is one way of imagining the release of spirit from the thick of matter. It has the advantage of depicting the whole process as a natural one, asking us to observe carefully and tend the subtle transformations instead of becoming strutting heroes full of ego and our own agendas. Again we're challenged to be wise but not smart, to cultivate the subtle virtue of foolishness without becoming plain fools.

You say he flew too far?
He flew just far enough. He flew precisely
to the point of wisdom.

Stephen Dobyns, Icarus's Flight

8. Flying Lessons

*I*T IS QUITE NATURAL to expect spirituality to make you enlightened and perfect. This attitude is not personal but comes with the territory. No one imagines spirituality as the means to be an ordinary person, struggling with the ordinary issues and resulting in an ordinary life. Spirituality is more like a rocket aimed at the moon, the planets, and the unknown universe. The extravagance of the vision it creates is both its strength and its danger.

The Icarus myth, which lies deep within many a spiritual person, offers an important lesson: be careful not to fly too high in your moral and intellectual ambitions. Icarus, the young boy who represents the youthful idealism of much spirituality, makes wings of wax and flies too close to the sun. He spurns the warning of his father against flying too high and comes crashing down. The spiritual realm can have a strong attraction that may lift you out of the doldrums of everyday struggles, but it can also destroy you by taking you too far from reality.

In a small town in Massachusetts, not far from where I live, in front of a modern church stands a tall bell tower so thin that from a certain angle it almost disappears from view. There is a wing on its end, an evaporating steeple. It joins many other images of the spirit as soaring, lofty, and ascendant. Wings, mountains, birds, stupas, thrones, prayer flags, obelisks, pyramids — they all picture the spirit as at home in the air and on the rise. Even Marc Chagall's fiddler on the roof and his floating lovers take some spiritual innocence from their unearthedness. Whenever I pass that tower in Massachusetts, I think of Icarus and both the appeal and the dangers in spirituality.

Many spirited people, including myself, often dream of flying. I see these dreams as strong reflections of a basic attitude toward life, which sometimes seems to resemble Icarus's ambition. The soul is largely embedded deep in the ordinary struggles and feelings of frustration and survival, but the spirit usually soars in ideals of liberation and salvation. It wants to be free of the limitations of family and place and the complications of relationship. Spiritual people sometimes are happy to be free and on their own as they pursue the spirit without the encumbrances of work, marriage, and children.

Jung names this aspect of the spirit *puer aeternus,* the eternal boy, a pattern found in both men and women. It announces fragile beginnings and may appear at any time in the course of a life. But there are those of us who by nature are like those airborne boys of myth. We are almost always lofty in our ambitions and our way of life, and this preference for the undiluted air naturally attracts us to spiritual things. Often we try to break loose from gravity in utopian fantasies of perfect worlds and ideal situations. When a spiritual teacher promises a desirable way of life, it is difficult for us to turn away. We are like moths who can't resist the bright lamp.

I have worked in therapy with people whose intense spirituality was offset by sexual preoccupations and problems, which forced them to keep in touch with their bodies and the people around them and their so-called lower natures. In some cases the spiritual loftiness appeared as moral superiority, an attitude they learned from church leaders who convinced them their sexuality had to be under strict control. Their sexual purity set them up for some disastrous experiences. I've known men and women who ended their lives in bitterness over misguided sexual repressions. For others the problem was their enthusiasm for a less traditional spiritual practice within a community run by an idealistic yet equally challenging leader. A disproportionate emphasis on the spiritual often creates confusion about sexuality, relationships, and daily survival.

I know this problem well because I am a flyer, too, and all my life I have had dreams of piloting single-engine airplanes and flying self-powered. In one recurring dream, which must go back thirty years but has eased since I've become a parent, I wave my arms and easily float like an angel up to the ceiling. I hover there and feel blissful from the height and weightlessness. On waking I feel exhilarated but also disappointed at knowing that in life I have to stay on the ground.

Recently I asked a large audience of psychiatrists and social workers how many of them had dreams in which they were flying on their own power. Dozens of hands went up, and a few flapped their elbows to signal the way in which they flew. I was surprised to find so many flyers in this particular group of professionals, but then I remembered that they were largely self-selected. They had freely come to me, a flyer, and were probably quite different from their colleagues who preferred more solid, weighty stuff.

A related dream I have often had, even very recently, is of an airplane landing on a city street. In the last version I am a passenger. The pilot is having a pleasant conversation with me when suddenly I notice that the plane is coming close to the main street of a small town. We land on the street and taxi along the thoroughfare. A group of people are waiting for a bus. One of them jokingly jabs his thumb out as though looking for a ride. Everyone is happy, but I'm afraid the wings will clip the buildings along the street.

From the viewpoint of the dream there is something natural and good about a plane traveling a roadway in the middle of town, but I'm anxious. I wake up to thoughts of keeping my flyer's imagination down to earth and in the middle of the village. Many people attracted to spirit find it difficult being an ordinary human being. Often they expect so much of themselves and others that they do everything possible to avoid being one of the crowd. I suspect this is why Shunryu Suzuki was so eloquent about having an attitude of "nothing special" about every aspect of the spiritual life.

This last dream figures in this book as I try to show how we might keep our spirituality grounded, deep, and in the thick of life. The dream reveals my struggle to stay grounded with my flyer's temperament. Maybe this book is a working through of the dream, not only for myself but for my fellow idealists. I make much of deepening spirituality because I, too, have trouble keeping it down to earth.

People who are fired up about spirituality need to resolve the tension between ordinary life and their spiritual ambitions. Sometimes they soar high to escape the drone of life. High in their clouds they come up with ideas that are inspiring and beautiful but unrealistic and naïve. People with few resources may spend all their money on some exciting but unworkable idea for saving humanity. They surrender their practical intelligence to their idealistic visions.

Usually the flyer has immense appeal. He or she may be gentle and soft-spoken and speak easily of great ideas and stunning projects. But in all this zeal you may detect some craziness. The idealism may have a hole in it, a small neurotic gap that makes the whole thing suspicious. I see this unease often, especially among people recently fired up about a new source of spirituality. When I travel, people beg me to read a book, go to a workshop, or visit a place that has saved them. When I tell them I have my own enthusiasms, they look at me with pity. I'll be one of the lost ones who missed the boat to bliss.

This inflation, for that is what it is, can get hold of people and send them into a stupor. They may have struggled for a long time just to survive when suddenly they stumble on a new spiritual movement or teacher, a new religion, a community, a great idea, a book, and feel that life has finally opened up. In their excitement they may want to share their discovery with the rest of the world. But this enthusiasm, so full of fire and emotional oxygen, may soon deflate and turn defensive and brittle.

It is rare to find the flyer inspired by a good idea who can be self-critical without losing the enthusiasm that has brought him to life. But this more complex bundle of emotions—feeling inspired and rejuvenated yet still questioning—is generally more trustworthy and workable. There need be no loss of enthusiasm for allowing several voices of caution into the mix, and the complexity can preserve a person's humanity. Spirituality tends to simplify the personality around a teaching or a movement, and the soul, chronically deep and subtle, disappears from view.

As a teacher I have seen many young students full of passion and ideas that are too simple and untested. I always saw myself reflected in them because I, too, have been slow to grow up out of that kind of zeal. But then, years later, I saw those same students ripen and become complex. They are still enthusiastic and full of ideas, but the many sides of their thoughts and personalities shine through. Now they seem more trustworthy, and I feel secure about those who follow their leadership.

Recently I received a book by a teacher of mine whom I revere and admire, Huston Smith. On the title page he scribbled a note that sent me into reverie about my Icarus complex and its developments: "To celebrate your transition from student to mentor." Reading the inscription I realized how important it is to acknowledge the settling we may enjoy as we age. In years past, full of certainties and causes, I battled with Huston over ideas. Now I can't find the limits of my appreciation for his mentorship.

If the tendency in the spirit toward inflation is so prevalent, what can we do about it? The most effective tool is simple intelligence. In matters of the spirit we need to be critical at all times without becoming cynical and dispirited. We could benefit from friends who are willing to tell us exactly what they think. We could be reflective and try to notice when our enthusiasms are getting out of hand. We could watch for signs of intolerance, superiority, and a tendency to go emotionally from high to low.

The voice of caution is often so quiet that it goes unnoticed, and so it is especially important for a spiritual explorer to amplify that voice when it appears. Tell someone about it. Do something in response then and there, even if only slight and tentative. It often happens that I realize the importance of such an intuition after the fact when it is too late. Small sensations of inhibition are always worth noticing. We have to distinguish them from fear, but then give them serious consideration.

I sometimes wonder about my own timing in life. I came late to my serious work. For a long while it seemed I'd be a perpetual student, shifting from one interest to another. But I know that in my youth I was a zealot about many things. In my late forties I began to ease up, learn about compromise and subtlety, and temper the passion to convert others to my thinking. Only then was I ready to be married, to become a parent, and to write about the soul.

The ultimate goal is an examined life, a habit of reflection that leads to a measured philosophy of life. Spiritual ardor can be woven into a thoughtful life, a combination that represents a reconciliation of spirit and soul. Deep and reflective psychotherapy can be useful, too—first as a way of slowing down and reflecting, and then as a way of sorting through passions and attractions.

The tendency to fly high, the Icarus syndrome, can easily infect our spirituality, but it is also valuable. It accounts for fresh vision, the willingness to experiment, the questioning of old and established ideas, and the energy to move into a new future. It is a welcome counter to the dry, deathly, controlling attitudes usually found among institutional leaders. Spiritual ideas coagulate quickly, and we need imaginations ready for reform and questioning. The ability to contain both rich old ideas and fresh new ones keeps spirituality grounded and alive, but unfortunately this mixture is relatively rare.

Jesus, Buddha, and even Moses had fire in them, but they were equally sanguine and thoughtful. You sense the moderation in each of them, the willingness to break out on their own against the establishment without unrealistic expectations or a rebellious attitude. In this way they were liminal leaders, always on the edge, difficult to pin down.

In an ancient alchemical picture, birds of spirit fly out of the tree of life. The son of Aeneas hands his father a branch from this tree as the father is about to make his journey into the underworld. This is a beautiful image of spirituality rooted, compassionate, full of life and relatedness where the soaring birds of spirit have an essential role to play in the larger scheme of things. They are part of the picture in which the human being bravely enters the underworld of the soul holding the branch of life. The birds, representatives of spirit, are part of a larger and more complicated scenario where life has both roots and branches.

Spirituality finds depth in the descent into the soul rather than in flights of inspiration and enthusiasm. In this way it serves life, and the birds offer encouraging moments of bliss. In recent centuries it seems that we have generally forgotten this lesson in the spiritual life. We admire the flight and try to avoid the descent or judge it to be pathological. But if spirituality is not in and of this world, chances are it is neurotic.

I looked up when Icarus came down —
but who would notice?
People are always crashing.

Dashka Slater, "Orpheus and Company"

9. *The Fortunate Fall*

*I*N MANY PLACES TODAY, religion is rotting. Priests and other leaders are losing their prestige and in some cases being exposed as pedophiles and sexual manipulators. The churches are trying to keep up with the attitudes of the times, sometimes successfully and sometimes without effect. Science wants to explain all the mysteries, taking over for religion, and many people now follow the new creeds of secularism. But in all this corruption of traditional values we might keep in mind the alchemical point of view: rot is a necessary and fruitful stage, provided it is handled carefully.

At first blush it may appear that religion falling from grace marks a decline in spirituality, but a closer look reveals that religion is in dire need of renewal. Generally it hasn't done its job of speaking for the timeless and the mysterious but instead has colluded with the progress of a secular society. My own church — and this is a shock to me — has glimpsed a secularized future and has often retreated into a more rigid insistence on the old ways and a glorified past. The wish literally to restore a golden age of the past is self-protective. It is rooted in the death principle, not life.

Depth psychology says that we should enter the negative place, feel the emotions of decay, and allow life to proceed from there. The alternative, trying cleverly to avoid the fall, is defensive and full of ego. In the long run it gets us nowhere. Church leaders have responded to signs of corruption in many ways. They've denied it, tried to hide it, and excused it. They've promised it will never happen again, and they use modern methods of therapy and testing to assure the public. But these are all defensive or shallow responses.

The more fruitful way might be simply to acknowledge that religious professionals are human after all and are at least as neurotic as the rest of us, and maybe more so because of their calling. These leaders could reflect honestly and painfully, if necessary, on their failures, and out of that self-confrontation let arise a less arrogant form of spiritual guidance. They might let go of their imperialism and superiority and be as members of the community rather than princes.

To be honest, I've known many grounded spiritual guides who have worked selflessly for others. But I also regularly come across those who feel special, chosen, and gifted. They don't seem to recognize their arrogance as they tell me what I should think and how I should live. They seem to believe in their altruism even as they engage in a one-sided conversation, telling me how life works and not listening to an alternative viewpoint.

Over the years I've heard many Icarian dreams from people in therapy. The dreamer flies high over the countryside, sometimes seemingly condemned to flight. For these flyers a crash, though initially painful, might eventually bring peace. Their zeal and idealism prove exhausting. I feel the same about formal religion. Its current travails and confusion could represent a creative descent from questionable glory. If it landed on the ground, listened to people's desires, and responded without hubris, we might have a renaissance of religion in our time.

In my own story, leaving the monastery and falling far from my initial dreams left me lonely and aimless. I really didn't get back on a high road until I found a lost part of myself at Syracuse University in the study of religion, a passion I seem to have been born with. Until then I tried to make sense of life with fragments of agnosticism and visionary humanism. I felt disconnected from the strong ties I had had and not yet secure in a new and grounded place.

Gradually I came to understand religion as something far deeper than I had experienced before. And the deeper I ventured into it, the more subtle it became. Slowly I realized I could no longer count on religion to make me feel like a good person — I'd have to confront my own moral complexity — and I gave up naïve beliefs. I discovered the poetics of religion, the importance of imagery in the expression of sacred mysteries. Gradually I found religion's soul.

I've met people, though, who crashed in disillusionment and failed to see the possibilities there. They felt deeply betrayed by a church or spiritual leader. Many are still angry because a teacher didn't live up to their ideals or because they didn't get what they expected. I'm writing much of this book in Ireland, where I have met many men and women who want nothing to do with any kind of spiritual life, so wounded were they by a once arrogant and dominating clergy. They feel liberated by the new secularism that has become available to them and see no point in risking another encounter with religion.

Enthusiasm for spirit can be so strong that the fall is particularly devastating. During the years of my practice I heard many stories of spiritual adventure. A quiet, nervous woman told me she was moving her family to the West Coast because of a brilliant priest there. A kind and humorous man told me he was going to resettle in Utah because of the spiritual atmosphere of the landscape. A single woman who had raised her family said she was going to India, the very source of holiness. Sometimes the spiritual adventurer was moving geographically, sometimes only intellectually and emotionally, but always with the zeal of a hero stunned by the vision of a new world.

In each case I saw the dangers of spiritual intoxication, people in love with an idea and an ideal, not to be held back from acting on their excitement. In most cases I was witness to the aftermath as well — disillusionment, anger, betrayal, feeling foolish, trying to restore a former lifestyle. Icarus is alive and well in spiritual communities. Following this pattern people try, as Dashka Slater says in her poem, "Orpheus and Company," to look God in the eye. But it is God's eye, she says, that burns the waxen wings. The very thing we want so badly brings us down.

The Icarus pattern includes both the flight and the fall: the crash is not the undoing of the archetype but its resolution. The innocent virgin says yes to an angel and sets in motion a lovely sequence of events from an angelic birth to a life of healing, but then she becomes the Mother of Sorrows. Oscar Wilde says that he wouldn't take back a minute of his life of blissful pleasuring, and yet he understands its fulfillment in the pain of imprisonment.

The question is not will I crash as a result of my spiritual ambitions and explorations but how and when I will fall. As a young monk I watched many friends suddenly begin to question their vocation and eventually decide to leave. But for years I felt secure in my choice. The change came late and unexpectedly, and ever since the day I stepped out of the protective atmosphere of the cloister I have been falling. Writing this book is yet another attempt to put back together all the pieces of that Humpty Dumpty who left home prematurely, like an unbroken egg, and fell to pieces when the dream didn't materialize.

I stand in a Boston subway listening to a tall young man play his guitar and sing familiar songs. I appreciate how he transforms the dreary place with his music, how in his own way he plays a tune on his blue guitar, and things are changed, even a subway station. But it is also sad to see that this Icarus can't make a living with his music but has to hold out his hat. He seems to be in descent, the underground railway a perfect symbol of his wings turned soft. Watching him I see both the promise and the reality.

For me the fall from staring in God's eye has taken many forms. One was the emotional dismemberment in a series of collapsed romances, which I see as part of the life of both spirit and soul. These failures in relationships that began with the highest expectations drove me to low levels of despair, and yet they also gave me my life and work. Trying to live through my own chaos of emotions I fell in love with the process and decided to be with others in their struggles.

I began practicing therapy full of ideals and an exaggerated view of my own skills. I ended with fewer illusions, having gone through many hundreds of hours in hellish confusion and turmoil. My clients gave me my initiation as they placed their complicated and intense lives in the space I had created in my little consulting room. One might have thought that what was going on all those years was the healing of broken lives, but now it is clear to me that those were hours of my own deepening as well. One hopes that one thing was connected to the other. Perhaps some healing took place through the very same process that gave me my initiation.

It is curious to me that my most challenging years were the very ones in which I was most active as a therapist. Adolf Guggenbühl-Craig's excellent manual for psychoanalysts, *Power in the Helping Professions*, describes some of the shadow facets of the work and the position,[1] warning against the inescapable fantasy of charlatan that always plays a role. My version of that pattern was to be in as much need of therapy as my clients and to be going through as much confusion and struggle as they were.

At its imperfect best the crash of our idealizing spirit presses our visionary hopes deep into ordinary life like seeds into a moist earth. We find our grounding and inspirations within the complexities of our ordinary lives. This is incarnation, the greatest of the Christian mysteries applied to our individual situations. It is nirvana and samsara as two sides of a coin. It is the secular and the sacred together.

The crash is usually bitter and painful, and yet necessary. Again and again I have seen friends who were unswervingly Icarian, full of ideas of changing the world and achieving great things, spend years filled with wishes and hopes but accomplishing almost nothing. Then one day, clutching their ideals, they experienced personal or professional failure or endured a series of setbacks. In many cases these crashes gave them the lessons they needed, and out of failure and tragedy they found more earthbound ways to live out their vision.

One man, a spiritual leader, had a compulsion to expose himself. Another was brilliant in his teaching of religion but kept sinking deeper into alcoholism. Several made special contributions to the study of religion but watched their lives fall apart because of their sexual obsessions. An intense spirituality, it seems, may create a corresponding fascination for the emotional underworld.

The fall I am describing is not news to most people. Everyone talks about the necessity of going through what they perhaps too easily call their dark night of the soul. I think what happens is that some of us are too smart about crashes and falls. Too easily we weave them into our progress and actually celebrate them as steps toward our goal. But the dark night is not a phase; it is a part of experience that is always hovering close by, ready to do its job of sullying the untarnished innocence that usually arrives with spiritual awakening.

To complicate the picture, only a certain kind of fall takes us deep enough or deep in the right direction so that we find ourselves in the land of the soul. People sometimes proclaim the misfortunes that have come their way, but their story and their language suggest that they have not yet really fallen. Their treasured tragedies fit too neatly into their plan, and now that they've had their anticipated fall, they expect their lives to be glorious.

The role of a spiritual teacher is to help us distinguish the real from the illusory. Simple failure is not a sure sign that you have fallen deep into the soul. Maybe the fall was real but not enough or not the precise kind to initiate a significant shift in imagination. People fail and yet persist in their inadequate spiritual outlook. A perceptive spiritual guide quickly sizes up the situation and helps keep open the path toward significant deepening.

When the crash comes, how should we react? Do we restore ourselves and go ahead with our plans feeling even more justified because we have survived a collapse? Do we think that just because we've felt some sadness that the depths have been reached? Or are we taken out of our illusions and ferried into new territory? Do we stand out of the way and allow a resurrection of belief in its own time?

In the ancient story of Icarus his father tries to teach him how to fly. The soaring of the spirit can be done artfully, with technique rather than thoughtlessly. There is an art to falling. We may take on the mood and tone of the fall, allowing this perhaps unwanted development to leave its mark on the way we act, feel, and even appear. As I grow older, I speak more freely from the fallen place. I allow myself to express my ignorance and my uncertainties. I decline to participate in the spiritual adventures and ideals of those who are still full of ambition. I carry the weight of one who has been spiritually motivated all my life but who has also suffered, an angel who has been wounded and disillusioned. At this point in my life I feel that more often I am free-falling limply into the deep spirit rather than soaring high on wings of power.

Note

1.   Adolf Guggenbühl-Craig, *Power in the Helping Professions* (New York: Spring Publications, 1971), pp. 20–35.

The modern world is desacrilized, that is why it is in a crisis.
The modern person must rediscover *a deeper source of his
own spiritual life*.

C. G. Jung, interview with Mircea Eliade (1952)

10. *Down and Within*

WHILE SPIRITUAL INFLATION is always a danger and a temptation, it isn't inevitable. Spirituality can be grounded in the
awareness that everything reveals its spiritual depth if you go far enough
into it. Spirit is not an added level and not a veneer but is to be found
deep in emotional struggles and painful life situations, and in simple
pleasures as well. All that is needed is an imagination for the holy.

A Sufi master once set himself up at a crossroads. He lit a very bright
lamp and, a distance away, a candle. Then he sat by the candle and read
his book. People watching him were confused. Why didn't he read by
the bright light? The bright lamp, he explained, attracted all the moths,
leaving him to read in peace.[1] Similarly, he said, people go into a frenzy
when they find something attractive that they then can't get away from.

This important teaching highlights a special problem in the pursuit
of spirit. It is often tempting to behave like a moth and go after the
bright thing—enlightenment, truth, the revered teacher or the great
teaching. Sufi masters seem to have a special calling to warn us about
this kind of spiritual extravagance. It is better to keep the much touted
light small and modest, and rather than get lost in the crowd trying to

reach the high place of wisdom, it might be wiser to go deep where the way is not so bright.

One day many years ago, before we were married, my wife and I visited Saint Peter's Basilica in Rome for the first time. We explored the lustrous marble main church but then found our way down to the musty, chalky crypt where the popes are entombed. We felt more at home in the lower level where the aesthetic was entirely different from the upper — more austere, less triumphant. Down there we were immersed in mystery, while upstairs we were overwhelmed by glory. The upper church is wondrous, like a vision, but the lower crypt is like a dream and represents the religion of the soul in contrast with that of the high spirit.

According to some philosophies, the ones I favor, the soul is at home in the lower levels of everyday existence while the spirit pursues the cosmic heights. The soul proceeds by a process of deepening, getting nowhere, yet all the time rooting and ripening. The spirit has a motoring quality. It wants badly to transcend and progress. It keeps a goal in mind and carefully marks the stages of its progress. In this sense modern culture is more spiritual than soulful.

Without the deep soul the spirit risks cutting itself off from humanity. Swept away by the spirit, we'd like to become angels, but steeped in the soul we'd like a good meal with friends. The soul tames ambition, which can be one of the great dangers of the spirit. Without depth, spirit can be dangerously volatile, like spirits in chemistry that can blow up. Without the ballast of the soul, the spirit drifts, floats, and zooms away from the earth.

Jung's warning is full of insight. The crisis of modern life is due to a loss of an appreciation for the sacred and the holy. This is easily said, but we often don't take it seriously enough. In the personal sphere, in the face of violence and conflict we look to personal history, family, and experiences for signs of disturbance. Internationally we examine historical and economic developments, constructing theories and laying out strategies. We don't consider the deep factors or take soundings of what is going on in the rumbling depths of the soul.

Because religion is so deep, as profound as it is transcendent, it touches upon those issues that motivate us and yet remain hidden from awareness. Not paying attention to the soul, we carry on disconnected from the roots of our thoughts, feelings, and behavior. When we imagine religion to be only of the spirit and not of the soul, high but not deep, the whole world of feeling and imagination is left ignored and chaotic. The spiritual person is tempted, like Saint George and the dragon or Saint Patrick and the Druids, to battle these ordinary emotions and fantasies, which only makes them more of a problem.

The struggle for a meaningful life may not be an intellectual quest alone or primarily a hunt for consciousness and values. It may entail a working through of relationships, experiences, memories, and unaccountable desires and fears. Often the deeper narratives and feelings that compel a person in a certain spiritual direction go unnoticed and unreflected even though they play a major role. Enlightenment can take the form of emotional liberation as well as sudden understanding.

While it may seem obvious that deep feelings have a significant part in our spiritual wanderings, often they don't get the attention they deserve or are dealt with superficially. Once, when I was in my teens and just before a major step in my monastic life, I went to confession and told the priest I felt confused about some mysterious erotic events among children in the neighborhood when I was growing up. The memories still lingered and were disturbing many years later. They were pressing directly on my spiritual development.

"How long have you had the habit?" he asked.

I didn't have the slightest idea what he was talking about. I fumbled for a response of my own, but I felt terribly vulnerable at the moment.

"Ask God to help you not to do it," he said.

"Not do what?" I thought.

"Now for your penance . . . ," he said, obviously eager to get out of a situation that made him uncomfortable. And this was not a crusty old man who might be expected to be out of touch with youth. His job was to travel around from school to school talking to young people and helping them with their spirituality.

During the twelve years I lived in a monastery, I don't recall being given any real counseling for my emotions. The priests were all authority figures, and you couldn't have much confidence in their impartiality. The only outlet was confession, which only added a layer of guilt and complexity to ordinary emotional issues. As often happens in spiritual communities, the spirit was given plenty of care and tending, but the deep soul was left to its rumblings and everyone hoped it would not raise its complicating head.

For many of us the deep life of soul shows itself in our sexuality and in our difficulties finding love. But in our highly categorized culture we have a habit of separating life into walled compartments so that while pursuing spirituality we may overlook the importance of sex, friends, lovers, work, and home. Spiritual people are sometimes embarrassed by these other issues that seem trifling in comparison to their ideals.

Maybe the best way to get the high and low together in our spiritual lives is to refuse to compartmentalize life. I recently found myself talking with someone who was having trouble in a marriage, and I asked how his work was going. "What does my work have to do with my marriage?" he asked. With very spiritual people I will often ask about their children, and they look puzzled, as though one area of life has nothing to do with the other. Yet I have often seen how the narcissism in people's pursuit of the spirit causes them to overlook the needs of their children and in the worst cases to use their children as pawns in their own anxious spiritual strategies.

It also works the other way around: a solid spiritual life plays a key role in working out the deeper issues. Some people have no philosophy of life, no vision for themselves and their world. They just take things one step at a time or, more often, go from one crisis to another, improvising all the way. It takes considerable effort to establish a vision that embraces the whole of life and satisfies one's temperament and past experiences. Some people spend a lifetime of travel and reading, experiment and exploration to find a worthy purpose and way of life.

Educators, generally in line with the secular viewpoint, are often reluctant to help young people focus on their spiritual quest. Understandably they don't want to impose values or religious dogma, but leaving young people without guidance and inspiration in this important area abandons them to spiritual hucksterism, even to the lure of subtle philosophies that can sweep them up. Instead of leaving the spirit to chance, teachers could present the wisdom of the religious traditions without violating the separation of church and state, and they could explore the existential questions of their students through literature and art.

Rich, distilled ideas help clarify an otherwise swampy, humid morass of emotions and impressions. A transcendent vision or a religious point of view can help immeasurably in getting through tough times, such as a divorce or the death of a loved one, and is necessary for an ethical way of life; without it a person chooses self-interest by default. Spirit serves the damp, earthy soul by giving it air and fire.

Religious traditions take mystery and complexity into account and are less reductionistic than psychology. In the best of circumstances they dispense their wisdom in highly complex and poetic expressions. I prefer a parable of Jesus or an Old Testament story over the Ten Commandments, and I would rather read a tale about a Zen master than a Buddhist theological commentary. The stories penetrate to the depths, while the progressive steps and stages in spiritual programs, though popular, tend to oversimplify. Transcendence by depth is as sacred and as religious as the upward path of enlightenment, and the voice of God can be heard from the holy well, the sacred cavern, and the profound emotion as certainly as from a mountain top or an elevated altar.

The deep voices may not sound as pure and sparkling as the high ones. The path of depth passes through depression, anger, failure, and doubt, but still it can lead to a visionary place. It can clear a way through the emotional clouds that obscure spiritual vision. Avoiding and escaping troublesome emotions in effect cuts us off from an important part of ourselves. Suppress one emotion, and the whole of the psyche is affected. But when we dare to enter those difficult places, we discover that life is more intense, more complex, and more interesting than we might have previously imagined. This greater view of what it means to be a person prepares us for the even greater mysteries that are the concern of religion.

I am advocating an alchemy of the spirit, an honest and imaginative refining of the emotions and life's complexities to the point of vision. The spirit is squeezed like wine from grapes out of the ugly habits that cause so much pain. By going down into the depths of the soul we find the raw material for a grounded spiritual life, and we discover a different quality of vision, deep forms of prayer and meditation, and a highly individual call to ethics. The spirit that vaporizes from the depths is in tune with the body and in league with desire.

Notes

1. Idries Shah, *A Perfumed Scorpion* (London: The Octagon Press, 1978), pp. 121–22.

A score of words and deeds issue from me daily, of which
I am not the master. They are begotten of weakness and
born of shame. I cannot assume the elevation I ought . . .
for want of sufficient bottom in my nature.

Ralph Waldo Emerson, Journals

11. The Spirit of the Bottoms

THE IMAGE OF SPIRITUALITY as pure and remote is only one fantasy among many. My spiritual heroes have been stronger personalities, such as Thomas More of England, whose humor and language were coarse and who thrived in the thick of politics and the law. Thomas Merton, too, was a person of flesh and blood, a powerful personality whose earthiness seeped through the persona of the monk. In these pages I also celebrate the spirituality of the American poet Anne Sexton, whose life and writing showed none of the neat and high-minded qualities of the pure spirit. Yet she was a person of considerable spiritual intensity and the unlikely creator of an earthy theology.

Picasso said that if he connected the dots of his life they would take the shape of a minotaur. His minotaur drawings evoke brute power and thick animality, and yet they depict the spiritual force of life. The dots of my life would be a labyrinth. I wish I could have taken a straighter path to the point where I am now, such as it is, but then it wouldn't be my path. Life doesn't often move in a straight line, and that's all right.

Religions around the world have striking images for spiritual depth. The Pueblo Indians center their religion around the kiva, which is sometimes a cave within a cave and illustrated with images of the maze. Irish funeral processions sometimes intentionally wander, taking the longest route from church to cemetery. Cretan religion made much of the dance of the labyrinth. And certain Freudians see the emergence from the mother's body as the archetype of this tortuous way of emerging into life.

At one time people looked deep into and beneath the earth for images of spirituality. The crypt, the cave, the cairn, the well, and the kiva are among the few sacred earth sites that still remain as testimonies to this deep spirituality, sometimes called chthonic. But they also represent our personal experience of the spirit, which may be in the caves and crypts of memory and in powerful bodily emotions. The human soul has been compared to a cave — hidden, dark, mysterious. Its beauty often lies shrouded in emotional haze and mist.

When religion is well grounded, it not only has a solid base in ordinary life and is natural like the holy green grains of mother earth, but it also reaches deep into tortuous patterns of personality and life. This underworld quality of spirit completes the vertical perspective that religion favors. Spiritual organizations today think of their mission as focusing on the high spirit and are forced to deal with social problems and personal conflicts by default. Today many clergy play two separate roles as they go back and forth between rituals at the high altar and counseling in the small private room. The consulting room is the underworld to the church's upperworld.

Young Emerson's confession that he lacked a certain bottom in his nature is fascinating, not only for our notion of who Emerson was — some would say he never found an opening to depth but remained only transcendental — but also for our very idea of what religion and spirituality are and could be. Emerson is faulted for his supposed moralism and his emphasis on self-reliance. But to me he represents the best in the spiritual explorer. I can't read enough by him or about him. He was a complicated man who over 150 years ago made a radical decision to reject the life of the typical minister to follow his own daimonic calling into an original life that was invented anew each day.

The deep spirit worried Emerson. He admitted that he didn't have complete control over his words and actions and that he was overwhelmed by a feeling of shame. He couldn't have the "elevation" he wanted because he didn't have sufficient bottom. He had made this discovery when he was young, and like most of us, it took tragedies and criticism to give him a more grounded sense as he grew older. He lost his young wife and went mad in grief. It is thought that in desperation he actually opened her grave—a profound chthonic act. He lost his beloved young son and could hardly handle the pain. He lost his friends, including one who challenged his life and thought, Margaret Fuller. She died in a shipwreck in the shallows off Long Island. Emerson was active in the underground railway for runaway slaves, and he was criticized regularly for his ideas and his art.

It is an elusive law of spirit: you can't safely go high unless you also visit the depths. Without attention and cultivation, deep thoughts and emotions remain raw and wild. Spiritual people often ignore them, thinking them irrelevant. Yet no one is more plagued by freewheeling bigotries, sexual confusion, and aggression than the religious or spiritual zealot. The underworld of the saint echoes Dante's inferno and Sade's cellars.

Spiritual people may be anxious to avoid shame, the emotional realization that we are of earth and have a close and mysterious relationship to the animals. Shame is not guilt for having done something wrong; it is the sensation of not being the light and airy person we might aspire to. Shame connects us to our earthy nature, and though it is not entirely a comfortable feeling, it can initiate us into much needed depth. Shame corrects the hubris of the spiritual ascent.

The deepening of religion—making it earthy and chthonic—is one of the greatest challenges facing religion in the West today. Without depth, religion can become too sweetly spiritual and top-heavy with its focus on higher consciousness and the idealized moral life. In fact, morality is more secure and effective when it is grounded in an appreciation for the human passions, which can only come from close acquaintance with the fullness of pain and pleasure. Encounters with these passions may take place entirely or for the most part internally, as seems to have been the case with Emily Dickinson; others, of course, work them through in the dramas of everyday existence.

Without the blood and guts of the lower self, religion appears otherworldly, anachronistic, and often disconnected from day-to-day living. It becomes too precious. But when we feel our shame and recognize the limits of our capacity, we are forced to seek wisdom and support outside ourselves, not just in other people but in methods that are religious rather than secular. In these moments our existential questions are hammered out so that when we are exposed to the great spiritual teachings, we know where they come from and the issues they are addressing.

People who are encased in the collective unconsciousness of the time may not feel the struggle for meaning. They may be numbed by the questions and answers provided by a superficial media and an over-technical educational system. Religion comes alive in people as they ask certain tough questions for the first time in their lives. Their questioning and doubt move them toward deepening. The questions may be painful and their answers elusive—all the better to scoop out room for mystery and to make the great hollow space of wonder that is the beginning of spiritual wisdom.

A steady line runs between honest self-inquiry and spiritual awareness, and it is this biting self-examination that keeps our higher spiritual reflections honest. The unsettled self and the yearning spirit constitute two sides of the movement into genuine religion. The person who has never questioned and never searched may practice a spirituality that is incomplete. The emotions of uncertainty and the fever of wonder are essential components of the spiritual life.

Recently I heard the sad story of a man whose brother was seriously ill from adolescence on. The tale was full of pathos and tragedy but empty of reflection. The most the man could muster in the way of spiritual insight was to stand under the stars one night and wonder why his brother had to suffer so. But his wonder seemed to be simple curiosity. The stars were his backdrop, but he didn't penetrate the mysteries they usually evoke. He worried about himself: Did he do the right thing? Would he get sick as well? Could he get on with his life and not worry about his brother? It seemed to me that his questions took him to the doorway where he might find a deeper self, but he refused to enter, satisfied that he had gone that far.

Dealing with tragedy is not an automatic invitation to deepen one's thoughts, and I'm afraid that this man's story, told with naïveté and narcissism, reflects the state of our culture: we don't know how to perform the alchemy on our lives that would transform our experience from plain emotion into a deepening of self, and from self-awareness to a sense of community. And we don't see this important process as having anything to do with religion.

As a therapist I know too well how the average person deals with strong feeling by trying to get rid of it. In its origins the word *pathology* means to be affected. But today we have reversed the meaning of that word. We see pathology as dis-ease that should not affect us, and as soon as we feel it, we look for a way out. In much of psychology this attitude reigns, but the religious point of view is different. There the idea is to be affected emotionally and intellectually to the point where our vision deepens and character comes into view. The moral and the psychological blend in a moment of transformation.

Often we go about with naïve expectations of life and then treat tragedy as a meaningless interference. Rather than change under the influence of pain and confusion, we resolve not to get into difficult situations again. We long for the day when suffering will have been banished by a smart science. All the while we are becoming less rooted in the mysteries that make us people of substance. Indeed, spirituality itself has become yet another way to avoid the alchemy by which we enter the vertical life, where the sublime and the tragic give us wide range.

It seems hardly necessary to say it, but religion could make us more human, not less. Yet there is a kind of spirituality that distracts from the bottoms of human life, and that kind is dangerous because it divides us into a hopeful transcendent self and a miserable actual self. The transcendent spirituality tends to glorify certain teachers, methods, and traditions. The techniques of practice often take precedence over the deep questioning and wisdom out of which the techniques have arisen. Followers and devotees are shocked when a revered teacher is revealed to have a bottom—to be interested in money or sex. Apparently they imagine these leaders as disembodied entities free of the weight of their humanity.

Of the many spiritual teachers I have met over the years, I could give myself as a student to only a precious few precisely because so many lack depth. They may have technical skills and knowledge of tradition, and they certainly don't lack enthusiasm and vision, but they seem to have decided somewhere along the way to separate the ordinary challenges from their visionary activities. In this to me they are untrustworthy.

To put it simply, many spiritual leaders lack character. The Greek philosopher Heraclitus said that character is daimon. That means we develop into interesting, complex, and compelling persons because we have struggled with the daimon, that inner driving force W. B. Yeats referred to as the antithetical self. We have battled our way into personhood, forging all the raw emotions and experiences into a strong and idiosyncratic complexity we call a person. Some of the best priests I know are homosexual; they have struggled with themselves in a fearful, phobic, and unaccepting culture. Some of the holiest people I have met are alcoholics; their daimon has a face, and they dare to wrestle with him.

The goals of spiritual practice are often uniform. Everyone is expected to become a certain kind of person. Yet eccentricity and character usually emerge from the transgression of social expectation and from the failure of ideals, an alchemy that few spiritual systems seem to understand and allow. Almost none foster it. As Emerson says, so much rises from weakness and shame. Fired by the spirit, people usually want to grow out of their backward tendencies, but these regressive elements are fertile conditions of the soul, out of which, as ancient philosophy taught, our humanity comes into being.

Yet another dimension of the earthy spirit is humor. Spiritual people are generally too serious. With excessive earnestness they pursue perfection and are hard on themselves and others. The saving factor would be a sense of irony supported by the ability to laugh. When spirit shows itself at the bottom of our emotions and our struggles, it causes deep and trustworthy humor. The divine perspective on our human efforts at meaning is sheer comedy. There is a kind of laughter that comes from the gods, saving us from our depressive seriousness and opening the way toward the only happiness that counts: a forgiving, far-seeing perspective on our efforts to know what can't be known and to become what we can never be.

IV | *Ordeal*

Even the person well grounded and earthy may go through a long series of ordeals and over a lifetime undergo severe tests of character. Life is usually rich in the variety of sufferings and torments it concocts. The important question is not why we suffer but how do we respond to it. Ordinary suffering can be transformed into an ordeal, in the old and classical sense of the word: suffering that initiates and serves the soul. It is interesting that many images for spirit are pointed, not only directing the gaze skyward but also taking the form of a weapon. Spirit can be comforting, but just as often it wounds. One of the great mysteries is why we suffer and how we should respond to tragedy.

It is one thing to be a person of depth and substance, but quite another to be faced with devastating loss, failure, and illness. It seems that people respond in one of two ways to such challenges: either they collapse and never recover, or they find unknown strength and acquire remarkable vision. Many find meaning in everyday struggles of illness, misfortune, relationship, depression, and addiction. These, too, are routes to spirit, and it may be quite enlightening to see them not only as psychological issues in need of care but also as spiritual conditions with the promise of transformation and initiation.

The alchemists said that spirit can be extracted from the raw material, and they showed this process as one of hard work and toil. This kind of spirit is *not to be found in the church, temple, Zendo, or yoga room, but at home and at work, in marriage and with children. It is a spirituality that never loses its connection with life and is therefore trustworthy and solid. It is the spirituality of the ordinary.*

The Eagle which aloft doth fly
See that thou bring to ground;
And give unto the Snake some wings,
Which in the earth is found.

Alchemical text

12. *The Way of Disintegration*

ALTHOUGH WE TEND to think of emotional turmoil as an aberration and a sickness, every life is composed of an emotional ebb and flow. Things go right, things go wrong. A therapist soon discovers that the painful situations people get into cause them to reflect. People are often moved to consider their lives seriously in the midst of confusion, and this enforced reflection may be the beginning of spiritual insight.

The spirit is not always discovered in a positive and blissful quest for meaning. Sometimes it is found only after we have been broken and torn apart by failure and sadness. There is a path to spirituality that is painful and challenging. That is how I see the achievement of Jackson Pollock, Sylvia Plath, and Anne Sexton. Sexton committed suicide in the end, after years of painful disintegration, but her poetry shows that she had her dark glimpse of the divine and found a way to share it with her fellow sufferers. You couldn't ask more from anyone.

Sometimes the fall from grace is not only a fact but also a symbol.

One summer my daughter, then six years old, was doing flips while diving into a swimming pool when she came tumbling down too close to the side of the pool and hurt her head badly. I worried about her brain while a friend said that the fall marked her exit from the deepest innocence of childhood. I know several parents who lost young children and immediately found their imagination breaking out in unexpected directions. Through their unbearable grief they discovered a concrete spirituality of a kind they had never considered.

Religious literature is full of debililtating falls and disasters, all signifying a low entry into the mysterious and the infinite. The ascent usually gets the process going, but the fall is also necessary, and it may take a variety of forms. Maybe it is true that our clumsy and literal tumblings mark a deeper descent into life.

Black Elk tells how his visions began right after a serious illness when his legs especially were weak. John of the Cross wrote some of his poetry while imprisoned for eight months in a tiny room. He escaped by tying blankets together and falling to the ground. The religion scholar Mircea Eliade says that some communities spot a potential shaman in a young person falling out of a tree.

The necessity of failing seems foreign to modern sensitivities. We expect to increase steadily in knowledge and awareness. There is no room for backsliding. When we do go through a setback, we do everything possible to recover quickly and get back on track. It goes against the heroism of our age to tolerate regression and incapacity. But how can we pray if we never falter? How can we turn to a larger source of meaning if we can go it alone smoothly and uninterruptedly?

The spiritual life is incomplete if it is imagined only as a wondrous world of miracles and healings. As religious imagery shows in its terrifying deities, it also has its terrors and challenges. It demands that we let go finally of all supports and make our own fated descent into the mysteries that underlie all our surface activities. Illness can be eye-opening, and failure can remove blockages to life. Merton's power struggle with his abbot and his temptation to leave his chosen life for a woman were both part of his spiritual practice, not aberrations or literal obstacles.

Frida Kahlo is one of many artists whose suffering translated often and immediately into transcendent images. After her miscarriage she painted *Henry Ford Hospital,* a painting that shows her lying in her bed, surrounded by objects that represent her pain, but on a wide expanse of dark green earth which she said offered her comfort. I would see this important patch of earth as the divine support of a life full of suffering. Later she painted herself as a deer in a green forest. She has a rack of nine-pointed antlers on her head and nine bloody arrows piercing her body. The image echoes paintings of Jesus as a deer in the visions of Saint Hubert; the Greek story of Iphegenia, who is a human deer; and paintings of Piero di Cosimo, who gave faces to animals just as Frida Kahlo does. All these paintings suggest the mystery by which our suffering is inseparably linked to our spirituality.

I turn to painters and poets as models of spirituality's depth because we can see the transcendent not in their lives and personalities but in their creative expression. Their art demonstrates how deeply spirituality may place itself and how it may never produce a healthy, whole life. Jackson Pollock is another example—a man whose life never came together but whose art continues to inspire with its special lively mysticism. It is a mistake, in other words—and perhaps a fall into sentimentality—to expect spiritual depth to result in a placid life.

In 1932, Jung wrote a fascinating essay on Picasso in which he connects the artist's blue paintings with the Tuat-blue of the Egyptian Underworld. He uses the word *nekyia* (underworld journey) for the artist's interest in broken and fragmented images as well as his frequent portrayal of the Harlequin, which he says derives from an ancient earth deity.

The Egyptians believed in an underworld parallel to our upperworld, where everyone and everything is upside down and the sky has a special underworld tint. This is a good image for where we go when our spiritual brilliance dims and we are faced with living our spirituality down within the thick textures of ordinary living. Not just an interior but a deeper world sets the stage for our spiritual progress and regress, a world that mirrors the ordinary one but is dimmer. It lies within the earth, within the earthy crust in which our daily lives are lived out. On the surface it may not be visible, but to the person living in both dimensions it is seen, felt, and appreciated.

Commenting on this passage in Jung, James Hillman describes the anima or soul as a bridge between the known and unknown. "The deeper we descend into her ontology," he writes approvingly, "the more opaque consciousness becomes."[1] Opaque is the opposite, of course, of what most people want from their spirituality. They seek clarity and awareness. Spiritual people like crystals, not mud. But if we sought a life thick with vitality, we might not esteem clarity quite so much. We might realize that to live from fullness is to be down close to the earth where clarity is not an option, where the sky is blue but shaded. This is spirituality, too, a necessary complement to the brilliant and clarifying spirit we seek in the other direction.

In therapy I always thought it was more important to go deeper into an issue than to stand back and try to find a clear analysis. People often believe that they have fully entered an emotion or a turning point in life, while to an observer it is clear that they have gone only halfway in. A person tells me, "It's too painful to remember what happened." I reply, "Let's try anyway to enter that memory and find out what it has for us." Rather than analyze I prefer to find some way to break through the skin of protection and feel the thing more acutely.

A man once came to me and said that he felt tired and exhausted being in therapy once again. I suggested that we both go to sleep for a while then and there. And we did, both of us, fall asleep immediately. We woke up about fifteen minutes later and found ourselves deeper into the tension of the material at hand—yet another version of nekyia, a visit to the Tuat-blue. Spiritual teachers often respect the sacred sleep of the devotee.

One of the most striking instances for me happened while teaching a summer class to therapists in training. At the end of the course a woman asked to perform a ritual. She put a black veil over her face and asked everyone to stand in a circle. Then she proceeded to say the most vile things to each of us. When she had completed the circle, she turned to me as the teacher as if to say, "What next?" I didn't know what to do. Everyone felt shocked and devastated. From somewhere in me I said, "Do it again." This time her tone was entirely different, more reflective and halting, and midway around the circle she broke down. Later she burned the black veil. As I was leaving for the day, I saw the flames outside, behind the school building, marking a simple modern sacrifice.

The Egyptian underworld Jung mentions is a good image for deep spirituality. When the sun has set in the day world, it rises in the land of the dead, giving the underworld a blue sky and a blue blush of reality. Whatever is happening in life, even in the spiritual life, has its underworld counterpart, and if we don't cultivate that bluer life, we have no way of knowing what we're doing in the light of the sun. The activities of a day may seem to be full of facts and external events, but from another point of view, one in tune with Tuat hues and tones, it may become clear that the facts and the events register as well in an underworld of meaning.

I stand in a pulpit to give a talk at a church. The people in the audience see me as a visiting speaker, perhaps with a message to give. But I stand there aware of confusing memories of my adolescence when I was preparing to be a priest and to address people from pulpits. I sense the irony of my position and the pain of all the initiations that led me to this point. I feel the underworld of that situation, but the audience may not be aware of this hidden dimension to the evening. Often the underworld counterpart to a life event is invisible to those who know only the ordinary landscape.

The tone of going down differs from the feeling of ascent. As we move toward consciousness and enlightenment, we expect wholeness, integration, inspiration, and healing. Hillman uses very different words for the way of descent: dissolving, decomposing, detaching, and disintegrating. These words are not in the bright vocabulary of the new spirituality, or in much of modern psychology for that matter, and yet they offer a sometimes bitter path that completes the otherwise sentimental and partial view of the spiritual process.

As I talk to men and women sincerely trying to find meaning and an end to a confusing and sputtering life, often I hear the jargon of popular psychology and the glowing, bloated terms of the new spirituality. Emotionally it is always tempting to go from one extreme to another, from the bottoms to the heights, from feelings of deflation to inflation. This bounce from earthy despair to airy hope is a particular problem in the spiritual life.

The downward way toward spirit is unflinchingly disintegrative. In an early book of mine I made much of the alchemical saying "*Solve et coagula* — dissolve and congeal." Apparently we need to be dissolving all the time, even as we get ourselves back together. But saying it doesn't accomplish it. We may have to give up the words that cheer us on and discover, simply by being open to the life unfolding in front of us, the particular way of disintegrating that turns us inside out and shows us our spiritual potential. For this mystery Renaissance thinkers, so sophisticated in these matters, used Plato's image of a Silenus, an ugly and grotesque statue that opened up to reveal the gods.

Dis-integrate means not to feel whole. The word has an interesting and, to me, unexpected origin. It comes from the Latin *tangere,* to touch, and eventually came to mean untouched or complete in itself. *Dis-in-tegrate* is a double negative, leaving us with touched, messed with, not original. We may have two different fantasies about our spiritual condition: one is to be pure and whole as we are from the beginning; the other, common in alchemy, is to be in process, to be making soul rather than just being. Spiritual people often speak glowingly of wholeness and pursue it as an ideal. But the soul is present in disintegration as well when we have entered life generously and have been affected, having lost our original innocence and ideals.

To be spiritual is to be taken over by a mysterious, divine compulsion to manifest some aspect of life's deepest force. We become most who we are when we allow the spirit to dismember us, unsettling our plans and understandings, remaking us from the very foundations of our existence. Nothing is more challenging, nothing less sentimental, than the invitation of spirit to become who we are and not who we think we ought to be.

When we disintegrate, going down into life and into our potential for vitality, we may have to give up the fantasy of ourselves as sentimentally whole. We may have to risk experience instead of keeping it at bay; for it is the impact of life and soul that makes us into persons of depth and character. I suspect that the common glorification of wholeness and unity is a defense against the alchemical dismembering of our emotions and thoughts into a mature, tempered soul. We are always becoming whole, and that means we are never whole but always disintegrating as we go. We find our wholeness as we are peeled away, like an onion, with the process finished when there is nothing left to peel. Perhaps only then will we be moved to give up the idea of wholeness altogether, having disintegrated sufficiently to be touched by life, and are therefore empty.

Note

1.   James Hillman, *Anima: Anatomy of a Personified Notion* (Dallas: Spring Publications, 1985), p. 133.

It is only by living completely in this world that one learns to have faith. One must completely abandon any attempt to make something of oneself. . . . In so doing we throw ourselves completely into the arms of God, taking seriously, not our own suffering, but those of God in the world.

Dietrich Bonhoeffer

13. *Sweet Suffering*

A CONSTANT AND SERIOUS concern of all spiritual traditions is the role of suffering in human life. Buddhism is based on the Four Noble Truths, all centered around suffering. One, there is suffering in the world. Two, it is caused by desire. Three, it can be dealt with. Four, the way to deal with suffering is to follow the eightfold path. Christianity contemplates the image of Jesus tortured and crucified, and teaches that suffering redeems humanity's sins. The Greeks had many images of suffering, such as Prometheus bound to a rock so that an eagle could come regularly and feed on his liver. Even the great Aphrodite bends over in pain as she mourns the loss of her lover Adonis.

I grew up making the Stations of the Cross, walking along while contemplating the series of fourteen images of Jesus' torments. At an early age I read books describing the medical aspects of his torture and the specific pain he would have felt. I was taught that my own suffering could be modeled on his and could make up for my faults and the bad things I had done. I was often told that it is good to suffer, that it would make me a better person.

This absorption in suffering is not only part of traditional religion but occupies new forms of spirituality as well. Recently I heard of a spiritual group whose members train themselves by seeing how long they can hold their arms in the air and endure the pain. I once attended a workshop in which we were asked to stand in a circle, similarly holding our arms in the air, and go through stages of pain. The idea was that our endurance would strengthen the will and therefore make for better living. At the time I did my best with the exercise, but today I'd decline the test. Willpower is not the answer to our problems, and I no longer believe in pursuing suffering.

The point where spirit and soul meet is a thin one, and it takes little to cross the line into pure spirit, where suffering may be treated at a distance. People move easily from making sense of suffering to rationalizing it or, worse, seeking it as a way toward virtue. Spirituality can draw out the native masochism in everyone and make suffering look desirable.

Many people find joy in suffering. I've worked with many married couples who wanted desperately to have a happy marriage, but it was apparent that they enjoyed their pain and struggle, too. If the torment were to disappear, I wasn't sure there would be anything to keep the marriage together. I know from my own experience of jealousy that there is satisfaction in finding new reasons to feel the pain of betrayal.

In the practice of spirituality this tendency toward the love of pain reaches a level of sophistication. I've known priests and nuns who regularly sought opportunities for humiliation and physical discomfort. Thomas More wore a hair shirt under his fine robes as a way of subduing his flesh. In my monastic days I had to keep my hair short in order to avoid vanity and personal pleasure, and I was told not to use shampoo, which was too much of an indulgence. I know many well-intentioned people who have taken to heart the lessons they learned at church on self-denial.

Julian of Norwich, the fourteenth-century English Christian mystic, describes an illness from which she almost died. When the sickness reversed its course, her first thought was "I ought to wish for a second wound as a gift and a grace from our Lord." The thirteenth-century Egyptian Sufi sage Ibn'Ata'Illah said, "States of need are gift-laden carpets." And Moses Maimonides, the influential twelfth-century Jewish philosopher, offered many suggestions for daily self-denial, especially in the area of sex.

In my book *Dark Eros* I examine the emotions and fantasies of masochism and come up with a formula that applies to this spiritual tendency to overvalue suffering. I suggest that masochism, like all isms, is a defense against the pain that comes naturally when we give ourselves to life. When we defend ourselves against the natural challenges of life, the ordinary embrace of pain turns into masochism, a flirtation with suffering and a chronic disposition toward pain. The pleasure in this suffering lies, at least in part, with the satisfaction of having avoided the more threatening demands of really living.

One has to be careful when blending spiritual ideals and an appreciation of suffering. Do the teachings offer some guidance and insight into the role of suffering? Or are they, at least unconsciously, a means of avoiding the pain of living by retreating into measured and highly stylized forms of pain? It is difficult to imagine programmed pain that is not full of ego.

People take real risks for their principles and values, and their generosity takes them deep into community. I have a friend who is a nun. She is a very sensitive woman, educated as a professor of English. At one point she decided to work in a tough neighborhood at a shelter for abused women. It was a dangerous job, and she often went to work in the evening so frightened that she would get sick on her way. This was not a glorified form of spiritual suffering but, rather, the natural pain that accompanies a compassionate way of life.

I'm not saying that all self-conscious and formal methods of deprivation are neurotic. The spiritual life benefits from such things as fasting, simplicity of lifestyle, withdrawal, and sexual abstinence. But it takes considerable awareness to keep these practices focused so that they don't devolve into mere masochism. In their extreme forms they are only for the chosen few who can live lives of self-denial cleanly and effectively. Even then I would expect to find in such a person a sense of humor (a sign of a comfortable ego) and enjoyment of life's simple pleasures.

The secular society approaches suffering from an entirely different angle. It sees its job as one of eliminating suffering altogether. Medical institutions, especially recently, dedicate themselves to relieving pain at all costs. They are engaged in a "war on pain," which they see as the enemy. Other social institutions take the same approach. Government professes to remove the social conditions that result in poverty and distress. What is fascinating about this anti-suffering philosophy is that it doesn't work. Millions of people suffer from hunger, war, crime, and inadequate housing. Social responses to suffering, though often expensive and of a large scale, may be lacking in real compassion and insight. When pain is only a problem, our response may be only heroic.

But medicine is changing. Teaching institutions now often address the human aspects of suffering and treatment. The hospice movement is a model of compassion and intelligent management of pain and spiritual preparation for death. I have sat in on medical classes in which students took a break from their technical training to hear patients and former patients describe the human dimension of their treatment. Teaching hospitals are developing programs in medicine and spirituality. But even with all this progress, reflection on the nature of illness and suffering could be taken far deeper.

We could ask ourselves tough questions about suffering in the world. How is it that we continue to make a poisonous environment even though we know we are being self-destructive? What is it about our way of life that allows so many to be deprived of its advantages? Why do we still resolve conflicts through violence? What do our prisons say about suffering in society as a whole? Today we ascribe much of our pain to "stress," a broad, inarticulate term that hides a wealth of particular pressures we place on ourselves and our children. But our solution to stress is to find palliative retreats so that ultimately our stressful way of life won't be lost.

In a simple statement frequently cited, Jung said that the gods now appear in our diseases. In a secular culture we don't grasp the mystery in all the various aspects of life. Instead we see problems to be solved, as though one day we would have it all explained and under control. Therefore, the gods appear in our lives as illness and disease — physical, emotional, and social. Our suffering shows us something of the nature of the divine, and dealing intimately and sensitively with our suffering could bring us in touch with divinity.

Bonhoeffer's observation makes greater sense in this light. We throw ourselves into life, addressing not our own pain and our ego concerns but, he says, the suffering of God in the world. This is yet a further way to press beyond self-absorption to the deep mysteries of life. Instead of merely trying to solve the problem of pain, we are challenged to appreciate the role of suffering, at least to keep asking the question and wondering about its meaning.

The heroism in attempts to overcome suffering gets nowhere, but reflection on suffering sensitizes. The result of reflection is a change in consciousness and values, while the product of heroism is an increase in drugs, machines, and methods but no meaningful decrease in the world's suffering. Of course modern medicine has made amazing progress in extending life and reducing physical pain, but suffering is not just physical and can't be reduced to material terms. In the imagery of Jung and Bonhoeffer we might see how illness is intimately connected to the way we live and has an ultimate significance.

Many stories tell how people have dealt with suffering by looking for a scapegoat. For example, people on board a ship are in trouble, and so they select the individual who they suspect has offended the gods and throw him overboard. Jonah in the Bible and Tristan in literature are scapegoats of this kind. Finding a scapegoat is not the same as making a sacrifice. The scapegoat is an object of blame, and frequently in our modern world, maybe as an aspect of modernism itself, we look for many kinds of scapegoat — smoke, fat, lack of exercise, bad parenting. We make ourselves into scapegoats by tracing our emotional problems back to our families and our physical problems to our pleasures. But problems and illnesses, having their roots in the world in which we live and in the culture we are making, are more mysterious than that. Our reflections have to go further and deeper, beyond scapegoating to sacrifice, beyond personal blame to an appreciation for the wonders of this world we inhabit.

A spiritual approach to suffering asks us to sacrifice our hubris and adopt a genuine attitude of humility, to sacrifice our fantasies of a glorious future and become reacquainted with the world in front of us, to sacrifice our ego anxieties and live with greater regard for community, animals, and the natural world. These would be deeply spiritual responses to suffering, free of ego; masochism could be defined as egotistic suffering.

Suffering also teaches that we are dependent on each other. When we are sick, we go to the doctor. When we are emotionally distraught, we visit a therapist. When life presses, we call a friend. Suffering opens a channel through which we can speak honestly to another person, maybe for the first time. We may feel some relief knowing that we are in tune with others who are suffering as well or who can at least offer support.

In traditional religious language, suffering brings us to the heart of the Christ-nature and the Buddha-nature. We are beyond ourselves and yet most ourselves as we join great vision with depth of soul. When we suffer, we are invited to join with the suffering of the entirety of existence and in that way expand and discover the full range of experience. Suffering can school the imagination to rise up out of self-absorption into an infinitely greater connection with the world.

To see suffering as a mystery, as God's torment, is to understand that it lies deep in the nature of things. Buddha taught that suffering is caused by a certain kind of desire, perhaps self-will or narrow appetites. Certainly we imagine that suffering can end—a valid goal in medicine and social action. The great physician Paracelsus said that if we were not so ignorant, we could cure every disease, without exception. To see the divine mystery in suffering is not to give up out of discouragement but to realize that suffering has to be addressed from the deepest place possible.

Jesus dying on the cross, Thomas More in fear and trembling in the Tower of London, Thomas Merton always questioning his vocation, Dietrich Bonhoeffer in prison about to be hanged, Anne Sexton always on the verge of suicide, Socrates executed for his bold teachings, the Marquis de Sade ever reviled for the audacity of his insights, Oscar Wilde prosecuted and imprisoned for his sexuality, Samuel Beckett alone and resigned, Emily Dickinson hiding in the security of her home—the list is long of those who have suffered greatly and have created beauty from their pain. It is no accident that these writers have all explored the spiritual life in unique and imaginative ways.

I can't explain suffering, but I can suggest new and ancient ways of reflecting on it. It is a great theological mystery how suffering redeems, how one person's pain helps another, and how some are called to suffering and others to tranquillity. In the end we are asked to acknowledge the mystery and embrace as our own exactly what life offers. This is divinity suffering redemptively in and through us.

Love and power are not opponents.

James Hillman, *Kinds of Power*

14. *Spiritual Anger*

LIKE AN ALCHEMIST of old, I'm asking you, the reader, to look closely at the many subtle variations in spirituality's shadow. We all need inspiration, but we also need a realistic view of this area that is so easily sentimentalized. If you don't know the depths of the spiritual territory, you might well succumb to its dangers. Noble beliefs, purified values, and openhearted devotion can all turn into their opposites, and spirituality can become the most dangerous thing on earth.

On the bright side, spirit is a creative, seminal, and driving force. People sometimes ask if we can have too much soul. Certainly we can get caught in the swamps of relationship and emotion. We need spirit to keep us afloat and awake. At its best, spirit gives us the energy and vision to make a life and world. But that same force can cause problems, as when it turns into displays of anger and power. There is nothing wrong with these forces in themselves, but in the spiritual life where there is a tendency to be only positive, they can become unusually destructive.

The contemporary trend to view spirituality as something sweet disguises its power and persuades people to take it too lightly. They may present themselves to a church or community with an innocence that sets them up for betrayal or control. They may easily excuse or not even perceive the anger in their leaders because they've never considered this emotion in relation to spirit. Then they may "catch" the arrogance and the rage, and battle those who believe differently or who seem merely "unenlightened."

I'm not talking about what believers call "the Holy Spirit" but, rather, spirit as a factor in all of life. We see it in the energy of a great prophet, ancient or modern, who is driven to shake society out of its lethargy and blindness. But we also see it on a city street corner in a demented man shouting at passersby to change their ways because the end of the world is coming. We see it in people gathered to protest the execution of a criminal and also in the people gathered to celebrate the execution. We see it in a community inspired to become models of an ethical life, and we see it in a political party bent on controlling society.

It isn't always easy to tell the difference between a spirituality based on profound inspiration and a spirituality rooted in paranoia or unrestrained enthusiasm. Even subtle movements for change can become soulless in their zeal. The twentieth century knew many spiritual leaders, in churches and on street corners, who breathed fire and preached militancy. Some, like Martin Luther King, Jr., inspired us toward much needed change, while others, like Timothy McVeigh, turned our belief in devotion into tragic violence. It is a short step from spiritual vision to aggression, and I believe a case can be made for a spiritual base, albeit twisted and sometimes psychotic, to all warfare and political conflict.

The sharp edge of spirit appears when well-intentioned people try to convert others to their beliefs or when a community attempts to control its members. It is especially sharp in spiritual moralism when one person tells another how to live. People seized by spirit have a strong tendency to become judgmental, authoritarian, and punishing. The farther spirit moves away from the humanizing soul, the more dangerous this inclination toward anger and assertion.

Because in modern times we tend to personalize everything, we may assume that menacing leaders are simply angry by nature, that some quirk of personality or personal history accounts for their rage. We may not realize that spirit itself has this potential. Most of us have been brought up to believe that everything spiritual is good. In my family I was taught to respect the priests and nuns and be very slow to criticize them. My elders weren't completely naïve about this, but they gave so much respect to the clergy that they closed their eyes to the aggression coming from the church. Catholics joke about the toughness of the nuns, but beneath that humor lies deep resentment at being humiliated and frightened. I have known men and women in therapy who felt confused all their lives about the abuse they received from leaders they felt they should respect.

As one who speaks publicly about the soul, I am occasionally confronted by spiritual anger. I remember a woman standing up one evening at a lecture and shouting, "You've spoken all evening about sexuality and never once mentioned love. What's wrong with you?" A man insisted on interrupting a talk by saying, "I'm a Buddhist. Nothing you say has any relevance to me. I don't believe in God." I sometimes hear this criticism even when I haven't used the word *God*. At a conference of psychotherapists, to my astonishment, a woman said to all present, "Nothing this man says matters because he's a man, and men have ruined the world." These are mild examples, but they represent the anger that can accompany strong belief, especially when that belief is rooted in insecurity and emotional confusion.

The archetype of the spirit also adds a tinge of righteousness, which easily increases and justifies the anger. People who feel that God is on their side may pick up some of the anger associated with divinity. Sacred stories from around the world tell of the gods' fury — a hint that spirituality itself is aggressive by nature. These stories teach that nature can be destructive and that a certain degree of aggression is necessary in human life, but they also hint that belief can be dangerously sharp, that spirit needs some containment and watchfulness to soften its force.

I don't think my critics' anger is entirely personal. The spirit has an inherent sharpness reflected in steeples, pyramid hierarchies, and harsh rules. It is often prone to a moralistic, pure, and punishing impatience with human weakness. The God of the Old Testament is sometimes an angry God who teaches by fear. In Deuteronomy 9:8 Moses says to his people, "You provoked the Lord to wrath, and the Lord was so angry with you that he was ready to destroy you." How many preachers and priests identify with this kind of divinity! Today I find it more challenging to address a new spiritual community than a traditional church because the zeal of the newly converted quickly turns angry and moralistic even though the morals are new and countertraditional.

Many of the gods and goddesses of the Greeks were capable of phenomenal anger, such as Artemis who flashed out punishment whenever she was slightly offended; Hera whose jealousy and vengeance were fierce; and Zeus who had to be placated regularly. The gods and goddesses of India, like Kali with her dagger eyes, threatening tongue, and sharp fangs, can be terrifying in their rage. These deities represent the natural violence of life itself, and yet they are also honored as being loving and gracious. The Homeric *Hymn to Ares*, the war god, asks for help not only against cowardice but also in restraining the fury that can seize the human heart. The god who brings anger is also a god of peace.

Religious images of angry gods and fierce goddesses suggest that aggression is natural and compatible with grace and kindness. But like anything else it comes unrefined, in need of reflection and maturing. Harsh spiritual leaders, which we never seem to lack, are simply immature. They are overtaken by their righteousness and don't have the presence of mind to see what is happening in them. It takes an unusual degree of sophistication to be a good spiritual leader, to see past good intentions to the shadow potential of what appears to be a spotless vocation.

The stereotype of the hellfire and brimstone preacher says something about all forms of spirituality. I spent fifteen years in Catholic schools under certain nuns and priests whose righteous and well-intentioned rage was always bubbling just beneath the surface of their sweet smiles. Sometimes they would explode with a ferocity that was shocking. At other times their anger would take the form of harsh rules and sanctions. As a therapist I have heard countless tales of ministers and nuns, and leaders of new spiritual communities as well, leaving deep scars, physical and emotional, on people who have never forgotten the violence done to them by representatives of the spirit.

Contemporary Ireland has only recently discovered that many of its children suffered beatings and sexual abuse at the hands of religious teachers and priests and nuns. People have been shocked at the revelations, and their naïve respect for the church has changed into wariness and bitterness. But I haven't seen any serious reflection on the roots of that abuse and especially its connection with spirituality. We assume the perpetrators were personally disturbed, but we fail to notice how spirituality itself can lose touch with compassion and other qualities that keep it benign.

Spiritual anger may be hidden in kind words and leak out in passive-aggressive forms. For centuries in the Catholic Church, bishops and laity around the world have been trying to share authority with the Roman leaders and dampen their despotism. Yet I've never come across an analysis of the rage that bleeds through benign-sounding church edicts, through it takes only a minute of close attention to see it. People are taught to be sheep, but they don't realize how often that image justifies spiritual tyranny. In this very year, women have been warned by the Vatican not even to discuss the possibility of women priests.

To analyze this anger, to own it and reflect on it, doesn't entail a wholesale criticism of the church or the clergy. Every individual has to reflect on his own prejudices and emotional reactions, and the same is true of institutions. Honest self-analysis might be embarrassing initially, but in the long run it would almost certainly strengthen the emotional base of the leadership and the organization.

Yet if we personalize all this anger, we will waste our time analyzing ourselves, hoping that an explanation will soften the rage. It might be better to depsychologize and deepen our very notion of anger. As James Hillman says, anger lets us know when something is wrong. It also strengthens our resolve and lets others know when we are serious and feel strongly about something. Anger serves the soul, but not when it is camouflaged as goodwill. There are many solutions to the problem of institutional rage, but I think a sober appreciation of spirit's shadow is a good start.

ANGER CAN HELP US make important decisions and find our way in a life filled with obstacles. A solid spiritual existence requires tough choices and judgments. Saint George attacks the dragon of thickhead-edness and church spires pierce the heavens in an attempt at transcendence. Even the haunting mysteries of the Tarot deck, a relatively recent version of ancient images, has an entire suit of swords, which can be seen as a useful weapon for discerning arguments and setting out positions. But one of the cards shows a man lying prone, his body pierced by those same swords. The deep soul tends to be soft and receptive, while the transcending spirit has a sometimes wounding point.

In ancient writings Mars is a militant spirit who needs fencing in, but he also offers courage, strength, acumen, assurance, and deep personal power. The task is not to get rid of spirituality's sharpness but to acknowledge it and then find concrete ways to cultivate it so that it doesn't do us in. The image of a placid, harmonious world, a notion favored by spiritual people, overlooks and therefore suppresses necessary anger, and the repressed returns to spoil the illusion. I believe that the Irish are now in a position to develop a mature Christianity. Their unrealistic ideals have been exposed, and the new, more complex image of spirituality might allow for a better life.

I still wince when I remember my teachers in the early grades whacking the hands of my classmates, who stoically presented themselves for corporal punishment. I was shocked by what I saw and heard. My own tortures were emotional, not physical. Now when I see how my children can learn joyfully without any of that cruelty, I feel sad about my own childhood and frustrated about the continuing arrogance of cruel authorities still forcing their subjects into submission and still creating wounded and fearful souls.

As we practice it today, education is rich in spirit but not always full of soul, and anger colors every aspect. In my high school days we had a headmaster who was far too strict. We called him "Iron John." In retrospect he was a fine man in a job that wasn't right for him. It might have helped if someone could have sat down with him and discussed his anger, which translated into his style of authority. As a teacher myself I saw my colleagues showing their anger constantly in the way they treated students, and occasionally I felt anger rising in me at inappropriate times. The role of teacher lent itself to such feelings.

When spiritual anger is not dealt with creatively, it can also turn self-destructive. People beat themselves emotionally because they have failed to live up to their ideals or the prescripts of their church or teacher. They judge themselves harshly and then lack the basic joy needed to make a spiritual life for themselves and for others. Leadership in all areas of life tries, explicitly or unconsciously, to garner power by nurturing masochism in its followers. Those spiritual communities that have committed mass suicide are only extreme examples of a pattern repeated over and over among well-intentioned but duped men and women who sadly bring their children into their desperate but misguided longings for transcendence.

A start toward dealing with spiritual anger would be to realize that spirituality has a shadow, and since it focuses on the highest things—enlightenment, morality, truth—it has the deepest shadow of all. Anyone attending a church, a community meeting, or even a lecture might be aware always of the potential for sadomasochism — the unconscious splitting of power in which one person dominates another. It may look as though the leaders embody the epitome of selflessness, but we should always know that no one, especially a person in authority, is ever free of the power syndrome.

For their part, spiritual leaders require an exceptional degree of awareness and self-reflection. Like psychotherapists they have a special duty to consider their attitudes and be as aware as possible of their own emotional instabilities as they deal with people. Neither perpetrator nor victim may be conscious of the emotions at work. And so it is of great importance in the training of spiritual guides to have at least a rudimentary method of continuing self-analysis and a subtle understanding of spiritual anger.

Anger that is abusive is power, strength, and, indeed, spirit gone awry. In itself anger has its truth, its role, and even its beauty. As the Renaissance philosophers said, anger can be transformed into necessary and valuable qualities: personal power, creativity, effectiveness, and individuality. It should not be repressed but rather refined into these qualities, giving definition to life and personality. In spiritual and religious contexts, anger transformed gives us the drive and courage needed to live out our ideals and become people of vision.

But anger calls for discernment. Am I angry because I'm repressing my creativity and individuality? Am I angry because I see injustice around me? Or am I angry because I have lost touch with my compassionate soul and have been taken up too much into the spirit? I find it difficult to sort out all the elements that go into a moment's anger or rage. It never seems to be pure and clean. I have to trust my anger even as I reflect on its background and meaning.

In the sometimes wild emotionalism of therapy I had to distinguish frustration pouring out of an emotional complex from creative and well-founded anger. I had to discover the hard way, through experience and mistakes, not to get caught in the former kind. I developed many different strategies for not participating in it while at the same time over-coming my tendencies to quash my own anger when it appeared. My conclusion is that it is a struggle for most of us to sort out various forms of anger and even to see it when it is present. It can be hidden beneath layers of indoctrination about being peaceful and harmonious, and can be forced into passive-aggressive and self-denying forms where it is hardly recognizable.

A woman once consulted with me about her marriage. After many years of an ostensibly peaceful life together, her husband had "gone crazy" and talked about seeing a prostitute. The mere suggestion threw my client into a frenzy. She went to a psychiatrist who told her to begin expressing her pent-up anger. She told me it was ludicrous for her to begin acting angry after years of silence. I felt it would be more useful for her to begin living her own life within the marriage. In all areas, not only in relation to her husband, she had a habit of surrendering her will to that of others. Her anger could be woven into a new life based on her own wishes and inspirations, and would sustain her in this new way.

For this woman anger could be a means for finding her life, which had been hidden under her belief in self-sacrifice. Venting her anger would only show her the strength of her emotion. Instead she could stay close to it and let it give her the strength to live her own life, and in that way get out of the neurotic pattern with her husband. For the moment, her anger would be her spiritual path, giving wings to her trapped soul.

There is a long tradition in painting and literature focused on the connection between Venus and Mars. I keep it in mind and use it prac-tically for my own dealings with anger. I think back frequently on the image in Botticelli's famous painting that captures the relation of the soul and the spirit in anger. In the painting Mars lies asleep, vanquished by love. Baby satyrs are playing with his weapons, but around his head fly a few threatening wasps. This small circle of wasps says a great deal about love and anger. The soul brings a temperate influence to the spirit of anger, but it doesn't do away with it altogether. Here it transforms swords not into ploughshares but into wasps. The art historian Edgar Wind refers to the outcome as a discordant harmony, a paradox and oxymoron, which is what anger must always be — a powerful Mars expression of spirit tamed and made beautiful by the Venus soul.

God won't be in life like a bright morning.
We have to go down into the shaft
And through the hard work of mining
bring up the earth's abundance.
We have to stand hunched over
And in tunnels dig him out.

Rainer Maria Rilke

15. Unearthing the Gold

*T*HE WAYS TO SPIRIT are many: emptying, deepening, going high and going low, believing and disbelieving, and falling apart. Our world may have to crack open for spirit to reveal itself, or we may have to engage in the demanding process of taking what is objectionable and seemingly worthless and finding the gold hiding there. We have yet to understand a secret that Jung discovered but that today still lies buried in esoteric and generally inaccessible studies: an important and perhaps necessary way to spirit is through alchemy, a subtle transformation of the ordinary stuff of experience into a new style of thinking and living that is exquisitely moral and poetic.

During the years of my therapy practice I got to know many men and women who wanted more than anything to live happier and more creative lives. Often they imagined that they needed a complete overhaul, that they had to become other than what they were. But what I saw were people who had all that was needed. The problem was that all the material of their soul was tightly compacted, and the object of their search was so hidden behind a rigid persona and habits of living that it never showed itself. What was this "it" but the very spirit that would offer meaning and vitality. Jung called it animus, and others refer to it as the daimon, not to be confused with demon. Both words are used for spirit.

Fairy tales often tell of the release of spirit. An unusually direct story recorded by the Brothers Grimm, "The Spirit in the Bottle," offers several hints about the process of extracting spirit. In the story a father and son are very poor. The boy goes to school for two years, but then the family money runs out. He goes into the forest with his father to cut trees, but the boy, foolishly in his father's opinion, wanders in search of birds' nests. He hears a voice coming from the earth at the bottom of an ancient oak tree. The voice is saying, "Let me out, let me out." The boy digs deep among the roots and finds a glass bottle holding a froglike creature. He uncorks the bottle, and the tiny frog becomes a huge giant, who says that his name is Mercurius and that as a reward for his release he'll strangle the boy.

Cleverly the boy tricks the spirit back into the bottle and corks it. But the spirit begs him to release him, offering him riches. Once again acting foolishly, the boy uncorks the bottle and the spirit is liberated. This time he gives the boy a rag, which he says will heal wounds and turn steel and iron into silver.

The boy goes back to his father and picks up an ax; it turns to silver when he strikes it against a tree. But silver is soft, so it bends. He goes to town and sells it for a considerable sum. Now he has money and the precious rag. In the end the boy becomes the most famous doctor in the world.

Jung refers to this story in his alchemical papers with reference to the development of the personality, but I'd like to take it in a slightly different direction. I'm interested in noting how the spirit has to be dug up, how it is trapped among the roots of the tree of life. It is an ancient tree, this oak, and the story suggests that spirit, too, is to be found, not in the ways of one's own time and era or even in the themes of one's lifetime, but in the ancient past, in the very nature of things. The word *secular* means age, implying that the secular world sees itself within the framework of its own interests and experiences. But *religion* means connected back, and it is by being in a relationship to the absolute past and the ancient, archetypal roots that we find the spirit.

The boy has to have an ear for the faint voice of this buried spirit. He has to be foolish enough to wander away from the task at hand to find it, and then foolish enough to release it even after he discovers how dangerous it can be. He starts out like many of us, looking up into the branches where the birds nest, but he finds the spirit down among the roots of the same tree.

The story is full of references to alchemy — the name Mercurius, the glass vessel, the rag that changes iron to silver. In a sense the boy becomes an alchemist, equipped with the elixir rag that is the catalyst for transmutation. When we do finally discover the spirit that has been buried, we can then set out on the work that will transform everything from the usual pragmatic, literal worries about survival and success into a much deeper appreciation for the poetic and symbolic level of experience. There the spiritual is revealed.

This spirit that is extracted from deep in the life of the forest, which can be an image of the thickness of the lives we lead, not only offers riches but also the capacity to heal. Healing is of the essence of spirituality, and all real healing is spiritual. As Paracelsus and other great physicians of the past have shown, we need a spiritual point of view in order to heal and be healed. He says, "a person becomes a physician only when he knows that which is unnamed, invisible, and immaterial, yet efficacious."[1] Without taking anything away from the professions of medicine and various therapies, we are all called to heal as part of our spirituality. We heal from our compassion and in our daily relationships to others and to society. A spiritual point of view allows us to appreciate the source of our illnesses and the means of their healing, both of which arise, says Paracelsus, from the same place.

Paracelsus was, among other things, an alchemical physician. His spirituality was tightly woven in with his honoring nature, and in the story we see that the boy becomes a great doctor, not through his schooling but from his foray into nature, by listening to nature's voice. A healer—or for that matter anyone trying to accomplish anything with spiritual force—must find and use a silver axe, a tool and method that has been raised to a new level by the elixir of imagination.

The churches and spiritual leaders don't automatically have possession of the all-important elixir. They may get stuck in authoritarianism, moralism, and the crass concerns of membership and their own success. In that case the spirit can prove to be a threatening monster. On the other hand, they may direct their vision downward, away from the birds' nests of a too exalted spirituality, and discover the holiness of nature and culture, the kind preserved in a glass bottle and covered with dirt.

For myself I have found what I think is the elixir in certain writers of theology and secular prose and poetry; in the mystics of many traditions; in the art and stories of the religions; in psychoanalysis and in conversations and reflections on meaningful experiences. All of these things have helped me glimpse the invisible and find a healing point of view toward ordinary daily life. The key is to be liberated from the dirt that hides spirit: prejudices, defensiveness, egotism, literalism, laziness of thought, and literal ignorance. These are all closely related and keep the spirit locked away and hidden. Any spirituality that is in league with these attitudes is a false one that does indeed strangle all those who believe in it.

The alternative to this alchemical extraction of spirit is to find a highminded philosophy and apply it to daily life. This is not an ongoing process but a once-and-for-all act of belief that attempts to spiritualize everything from the outside. It runs the risk of being nothing more than ideology, a point of view that dominates one's own thinking and attempts to dominate others. Alchemy, by which I mean a way of life rather than a historical practice, is always an ongoing, unending process. The alchemists always taught that the material at hand should be returned again and again to the glass vessel for further processing. All bits of life should be "iterated," sent through the complicated journey of refinement. This difference is crucial in the spiritual life: Do we land on a belief system and enforce it all our lives, or do we enter a lifelong process, a spiritual adventure that continually transforms our perspective and therefore our lives? Are our spiritual resources and practice ends in themselves or means to a constant spiritual iteration—a journey that never ends?

In the story, the boy is given a silver cutting tool, not a vulgar (a word of condemnation favored by the alchemists) and undistinguished instrument. Without such a tool we are left with the thick unconsciousness of pragmatism and anxiety about the less important things. Wallace Stevens's famous poem "The Man with the Blue Guitar" makes a similar point: there is a way in which we have to play experience like music—sense its rhythms and hear its themes so that literal events are shown to be significant in relation to the soul's progress.

This is what I mean when I say that Catholicism has now become a means by which I can make sense of life rather than a doctrine that I have to honor for its own sake. I see the religious authorities trying to force people to focus on rules and dogmas rather than using those teachings as a source of spiritual insight. The result is that many Catholics practice their religion by rote and don't see the point of the teachings in relation to their daily lives except moralistically. Of course, in spite of all the obstacles, people do find a spiritual life in the churches, but generally the religious climate falls far short of what it could be. From that kind of religion we have made a secular society, which can't last long because of the shallowness of its roots.

Finding spirit in a dense and demanding world may involve long hours of self-analysis and years of exploration. Alchemical textbooks picture this labor in images not unrelated to the Grimm Brothers' story. In the first, from the book *Splendor Solis*, two miners dig away at a small rocky mountain. The sun is shining on the opposite side so that they don't see it. Near them the moon lies underwater in what looks like a river running through the uninhabited terrain. This is a way to spirit for some — digging away at layers of habit and enculturation — and for the rest of us perhaps at different times in our lives. Because we are submerged in some passing lunacy, we don't see the sunshine.

Another image, from *Aurora Consurgens,* shows a bird-demon with an arrow in his hand standing near a cauldron in which a winged monster biting its tail lies encircled as flames lick high up on the vessel. The dragon may be the tormented soul of an average person tortured by the endless cycles of bitter experiences. He feels caught in them and wonders if there is any escape. The alchemists taught that the beast within the vessel had to be burned to ashes and brought back to life through twelve distillations. In other words we have to go through the burning heat of transformation and the waters of renewal that cleanse us in a long series of baths and submersions. You don't get rid of the beast, you transform it through a long emotional process.

The dragon also suggests that we have to discover how to stop feeding off ourselves — our outmoded ideas and styles, our familiar desires and fears, our old moralisms and expectations. We can't kill this beast directly but have to contain it in some way. People who write me from prison tell me that their situation has its good side. Now they are faced with themselves and have the time to do this internal work. But even then it is tempting to turn to spiritualities of escape rather than spiritualities of transformation. It may seem better to get rid of the habits that got us into trouble rather than stew in them.

People sometimes turn to escapist spirituality because they can't imagine themselves as normal, upright citizens. They have the mistaken idea that the process should result in a shining personality, completely rehabilitated. But spirituality is not so one-dimensional. It may become firm and rich and yet remain hidden behind a rough persona. Just as Shunryu Suzuki could see the bodhisattva in Alan Watts, who was deep in his alcoholism, we might glimpse the holiness in a person trying to make something of a disadvantaged life.

The Greeks had a fascinating religious image for the one who mines in a spiritual way—Hephaestus. He was small and ugly, but he was the husband of Aphrodite, the very goddess of beauty and sexuality. There is a Hephaestus quality to the spiritual life, one that is not so beautiful and inspiring. Here we have to work hard finding spirit in a dense world of practical concerns and materialistic explanations. We may well feel, like Hephaestus, small and imperfect. But our hard work away from the light and warmth of the sun will be rewarded at the end of the day in the company of our soul-spouse Aphrodite. The work of extraction draws out the spirituality we crave and also leads to the pleasures of soul.

The image of Hephaestus also invites us to think about technique in these matters, for he was a master craftsperson. Today we have reduced the ancient idea of technique to machinery—technology, we call it inaccurately. There is a technique for spirituality just as there is for music and the other arts. We have to learn not only physical craft but soul craft, the art of extracting spirituality from a busy, perhaps troubled or at least preoccupied life. We have to learn how to house the spirit in our homes and work and in objects. The life of a monk, male or female, which is a model for anyone serious about spirituality, is full of technical details for tending the spirit from morning until night, and the modern man and woman can find specific techniques that craft a personal spirituality.

There are two sides to the spiritual life: transcending and crafting. Spirituality is incomplete without either of them. As I have tried to show, transcendence may be no more than finding the faintest hint of meaning and value in a life full of misadventures. Crafting, which may be no more than learning how to chant or sit or paint a piece of wood, is equal in value to transcendence and merits our attention and esteem. But more about craft later.

Honest struggle with past traumas and troubling emotions is an essential part of the spiritual process. The deep work is not just preparation because it is always an issue. The constant initiations of the soul form a necessary aspect of the spiritual life. The work of processing soul and releasing spirit is one, and if either is omitted, the work is incomplete.

From another point of view, any therapeutic effort, formal or otherwise, can liberate the spirit from its imprisonment in the dense details of life.

The alchemy of spirit reestablishes the center from which we view experience, shifting it away from the anxious ego to a more distant, many-sided perspective. From there we can be more tolerant of ourselves and others, and allow life to pass through us, shaping us as it does so, taking us to places we didn't have the wisdom to wish for.

Note

1. Jolande Jacobi, ed. *Paracelsus: Selected Writings,* transl. Norbert Guterman, Bollingen Series XXVIII (Princeton: Princeton University Press, 1979), p. 64.

He who would lead a Christlike life is he who is perfectly
and absolutely himself.

Oscar Wilde, *The Soul of Man Under Socialism*

16. *The Beauty of Imperfection*

FANTASIES OF PERFECTION grow like weeds in a mind focused on
the spirit. The very thought of becoming perfect or healthy or
enlightened is riddled with ego. Why worry about the level of your
progress when there is a world of people in need of whatever sensitivity
you have? The spiritual traditions focus on a loss of self-consciousness,
but fantasies of perfection magnify the self and make it the object of
spiritual practice.

During my monastic years, retreat masters frequently admonished
me to live a perfect life, and what they meant was a life without fault.
But etymologically the word *perfect* means to do something all the way
through. A perfect person would be someone without blemish, but the
perfected person is someone who has really lived. You can usually tell if
a person has lived life fully, just as you can glimpse the hollowness in
someone trying to be perfect.

In Oscar Wilde's romantic theology, presented most precisely in his
letter from prison, *De Profundis,* perfection plays a central role, but it is

radically redefined. For Wilde perfection is the unfolding and unveiling of one's own genius, however ordinary or outstanding it may be. We are perfected when we live out our own natures as faithfully as possible, and the life that emerges, as in Wilde's own case, may be far from flawless. As he says, "There are as many perfections as there are imperfect persons."

The romantic idea of perfection that Wilde espouses could change our notion of spirituality at its foundations. We would not strive to be other than we are but would take the risk to be ourselves. Our perfection would include living our imperfections until they reveal the secret of our nature. Suffering and confusion are an integral part of this process, but so is joy and a certain comfort with knowing that life has not been avoided.

Another romantic writer, the American Margaret Fuller, writing to William Channing in the summer of 1842, made the case that parents need not be perfect in order to raise their children well. "God is patient for us; why should not we be for them? Aspiration teaches always, and God leads, by inches. A perfect being would hurt a child no less than an imperfect." A person who risks life may be a better guide than one who is always trying to be virtuous. Yet many spiritual people pursue perfection. They may not use the term, but their desperate search for health and enlightenment often amounts to the same thing.

I find a counterpoint in my life between what I imagine I should be and what destiny makes of me. I have always liked to write, but I never had any desire to be a writer. My long and strenuous education was aimed at being something else — a musician, a priest, a teacher. I never wanted to have a family and imagined perfection as living in blissful solitude. Now I am a gray-haired father of two children, and I'm painfully aware of my imperfection in that role.

I wish I could play and write music much better than I can. I would love to know many languages, but I don't have an aptitude for them. My work demands that I travel to many places, but I don't enjoy traveling.

I would love to be a psychic and a good astrologer, but I don't have the mind for either. People have many glowing fantasies about me because of the themes of my books, and I seem to disappoint them time after time, as I often disappoint myself. I have made many mistakes and done a lot of foolish things, but when I look back on the person I was, I feel affection for him and laugh at him.

The religious institution has a tendency to disregard the ordinary individual and focus instead on a perfect ideal. It expects everyone to believe and live alike. It often presents morality as negative conformity to standard values: don't do this, don't do that. In fifty years of church-going I don't recall ever hearing from any church pulpit about creating and discovering my own individual spirituality. I was never encouraged to follow my intuitions and passions. I was never inspired to assume my own kind of responsibility in a needy world but only to adopt minimal standards. I was told to be a saint, but later in life I discovered that the real saints are people who go against the current of culture and often against church rules and expectations.

I am always suspicious when people tell me they want to change. I assume that someone has given them the impression that they are not all right as they are. So I often say, "You're all right. No need for change." But we all know that we could be better in some ways, some of us more than others. My concern is that the fantasy of change can get us into trouble. Yes, we can all be better, but if we try to be better according to any idea we have or someone else has given us, we will only get caught in a maelstrom of self-improvement. And all that chaos is full of ego. Any change that takes place from that center is bound to make us worse, not better. I meet people everywhere who brag to me about their newly discovered spiritual path, and they do so with so much anxiety in their manner that I can't help wondering what monster this new spiritual movement could be.

Spirituality generates a host of emotional complexes — ideas that get hold of us and make us crazed. One of these is the perfection complex.

I call it that to distinguish it from the simple idea that it might be good to change and live a better life. The perfection complex maddens a person. Perfectionists are never satisfied with who they or others are but are always reaching for a goal and never enjoying the imperfect moment they're in.

This annoying preoccupation with perfection may be a corruption of the proper spiritual calling to be a prophet. Certainly we can all stand up at times and complain about the state of things and try to inspire toward improvement. This is the calling to justice, which is a profound way to fulfill your spirituality. But the corruption of it is a mundane, misplaced expectation of personal perfection. It makes the spiritual life a burden to those who practice it and to anyone in the vicinity. It is unnecessary and can be transformed into the more convivial task of being exactly who you are — completely and imperfectly.

I try, I try, I try to gravitate toward the positive emotions,
and there are many God-given experiences and people. Yet
there is a motor in me that keeps vibrating, sucking up the room,
and at the same time embracing the people who are in it.

Anne Sexton, A Self-Portrait in Letters

17. *Spirituality by Ordeal*

THE UNPLEASANT SENSATION of falling apart need not be literally negative. It can open us up to receive the creative impulses of the spirit and take another step toward what fate has in store for us. Let's look even more closely now at ordeals, at the initiatory aspect of falling apart. This is one way spirit and soul come together. The emotional struggle, engaged but not necessarily "won," affects the soul profoundly and allows us to have a larger view of life and its mysteries. Initiations —it seems we're always in one or another—pulverize those parts of us that are rigid and break up self-protective explanations and understandings. The suffering involved allows something infinitely large to penetrate, and simple pain turns into ordeal, trial, and initiation. The passages of the soul give birth to the spirit.

During twenty-five years of practicing therapy I sat with men and women making difficult, life-changing reconciliations with their parents and painful separations from their spouses. I was with them in their depressions and their jealousies, and tried to help them find some insight into their obsessions and hallucinations. It is rather too easy to sum up these struggles as initiations, but that, I'm sure, is what they were. We might remember that initiations in older societies involved blood, burials, blindfolds, and separations, and each of these, if only symbolically, plays a role in emotional transitions today. A real initiation is an ordeal, not a ceremony, and all emotional ordeals are potential initiations.

At first I considered my clients' struggles as psychological problems, but then I saw that they had to do with meaning and the discovery of important values. People sufficiently confused to seek therapy were finding their way spiritually and getting past the limited idea of a self. Learning to connect — the gist of their relational problems — is a form of transcendence. The emotional turmoil was taking them from ego to soul, from a limited notion of personality to a greater vision that could be called religious.

Sometimes the spirit lies buried beneath a pile of bad influences and experiences. With courage and persistence it has to be excavated and retrieved. Some of us have quite ordinary blockages — excess narcissism, inherited guilt and self-judgment, and bad experiences of love. For others the spirit is lodged deep under heavier debris: serious illness, family violence, sexual abuse, and crime. In all these instances the spirit has to be freed with persistence and imagination, usually over a long period of time.

People with an extreme load of bad fortune may be drawn to spirituality initially as a balm or even as an escape from the burden of life, but eventually, with luck, they may deepen their quest and uncover their spirituality. Troubled men and women sometimes proclaim that they have found Jesus or have discovered a new approach to spirit that has saved them from their habits of self-destruction. One worries that this first discovery will not be followed by the equally important deepening of spirit. Liberation from old habits and traumas is only a first step.

A spiritual life is not necessarily a successful life. Anne Sexton expresses it perfectly when she confesses that she wants to be positive but is overwhelmed by the struggle of just staying alive and being with her family. In her case, moments of clarity were just that — mere breaks in an otherwise tormenting series of emotional crashes. But in my view they were sufficient. Spirituality doesn't have to end in the perfect personality or a healthy way of life.

Often the effort to deal with pressing life situations becomes the meaning of life. There simply isn't room for anything more positive. Recently, after a lecture, a woman whispered to me, "My husband is a wonderful man, but he can't deal with his alcoholism." It was clear that she couldn't deal with his alcoholism either, but because of her love and loyalty she was in it nevertheless. His alcoholism was her spiritual path.

A woman says that she had to leave her marriage because of her husband's insane jealousy. A man says he's been suffering for years because his wife can't stop herself from being with other men. A man says he's depressed because he let his life pass by without doing what he wanted to do. There are as many impossible entanglements as there are people, and the working through of these ordeals can be religion.

In situations like these some people look to spiritual teachings for relief, to get beyond the stuckness and discouragement they feel. It can be helpful to find a slim reason for hope or a glimpse of a larger world. But there is another, more complicated way that spirit and ordeal can get together. Working out life's conundrums can be a way of wandering through the labyrinth and ultimately finding a spirituality that is tough and grounded. Each step of the way can reveal otherwise undiscoverable truths about human nature and about our own individuality — our calling and destiny, the importance of love, the need for community. Gradually, pieces of insight may appear, indicating a breakthrough of awareness and the establishment of a deeper, more visionary self. Spirituality is then a tough achievement rather than an easy revelation.

An example from my own life is jealousy. At certain times in the past I have been susceptible to this powerful emotion to the extent that it obliterated all other concerns. It took the joy out of life, and I became preoccupied with the effort to resolve it. Its dark and poisonous mood colored everything I did. As I look back on these periods of turmoil, I realize that the jealousy made me assess the whole of my life and all my convictions.

I hated being a jealous person. Jealousy didn't fit in with my philosophy or my image of myself. It taught me that my passions could throw me and that my self-confidence was not as strong as I thought it was. It also occurs to me now that I never fully resolved the jealousy. I'm sure I could fall into it at any time. Fortunately, it doesn't visit often. But I believe that I became more grounded by wrestling with all the contradictions that jealousy presented. In connection with our theme I also found some of the deep spirituality, so essential for a full life, in those battering emotional struggles.

I notice in myself that jealousy gives rise to many thoughts about freedom, dependence, justice, and individuality. I sort through all these issues trying to find relief from the emotions. The turmoil of my feelings generates philosophical questions, questions that ultimately have to do with my beliefs. I keep reflecting on all the various facets of my convictions as they shift and change until at least a temporary resolution falls into place. The resolution may feel like a simple calming of emotions, but that calm is due to a sophistication of vision and a more subtle view of how things work.

In an interview with Mircea Eliade in 1952, Jung described this kind of process in the imagery of alchemy: "The alchemists believed in the truth of 'matter,' because 'matter' was actually their own psychic life. But it was a question of freeing this 'matter,' of saving it — in a word, of finding the philosophers' stone."[1] Feelings of jealousy, insecurity, fear — these are the material of the soul. My appreciation for Jung's work lies mostly in his ability, at a time when he felt great pressure to keep psychology cool and scientific, to deal with psychological and spiritual issues seamlessly. The philosopher's stone is a mystical elixir of life. Jung is suggesting that precisely out of the rotten material of an ordinary life something as precious as the philosopher's stone emerges. Out of our struggles the key to our life's meaning may appear.

The many ordeals that press on us can be redeemed by becoming an essential part of us. We might find in all their depressing weight a heavy condensation, the stone that is the tough, hard, substantive core of a self. But this stone is not only personal, it is our humanity. It is made up, too, of the grace we receive to get on with life even at its most difficult. The stone is an image for spirit — not the winged kind and not the empty ether, but the weighty, deep, and central burden of a life — the awesome and heavy truth about what it means to be a human being.

In my own life, as I have wrestled with the deep soul through being a therapist and working through my own struggles, I have found all the concerns of spirit located there as well — faith, moral values, and possibilities for transcendence. The psychological and the spiritual are completely intertwined. Religion is a passion, and it is built up of many efforts at weaving the other passions into a loving and creative way of life.

Ordinary conflicts teach another important spiritual lesson: we can't go it alone. In a fundamental way to be human is to be dependent on each other. We expect the religious organizations to be available to people, to offer help when all else fails. We also expect the institution to remind us that our dependence is even more basic, that we owe our lives to a divine source. Our severe problems drive us out of ourselves to resources beyond reason. We turn to prayer and wonder, connecting our desperate lives to life itself and to the divinity we glimpse there.

Note

1.   *C. G. Jung Speaking*, ed. Willliam McGuire and R. F. C. Hull, Bollingen Series XCVII (Princeton: Princeton University Press, 1977), p.228.

Then all of them together, crying loudly,
moved to the malevolent shore that awaits anyone
who has no fear of God.

Dante, *Inferno*, Canto III

18. All Human
Problems Are Spiritual

WHEN I FIRST SET UP shop as a psychotherapist, having academic degrees in religious studies and a strong background in Jungian psychology, I expected to spend the hours sitting in soft chairs, sagely sifting through dreams and memories, ferrying my clients toward the tranquility offered by self-understanding. I couldn't have been more mistaken. Instead, ordinary people, many of them my neighbors and students, came to me with extraordinary and unique torments. Each story was strong and unsettling, each a challenge.

Early on I found that I was drawing more on my studies in religion than on my training in counseling. Now I look back and realize that although at the time I used the word *psychology* for what I was doing, defining it as carefully as I could, what was really at the root of those unsettled lives was religion. And although I used the phrase "care of the soul" for what I was doing, I didn't always realize the extent to which spiritual issues were playing a central role.

The obvious spiritual problems had to do with disturbing experiences surrounding religion in childhood. Many of the men and women I counseled told stories of trauma associated with religion. Many felt that their lives had been inhibited by early moral pressures and later efforts to control their beliefs and their way of life. Some told stories of sexual abuse at the hands of religious leaders and pious family members. Some had followed the lead of their parents and grandparents and had become spiritual leaders of one kind or another, and they came to therapy to sort out their strong emotional symptoms and blockages. In these ordinary, troubled lives, spirit and psyche were closely connected.

In other cases the spiritual issues were more subtle and required a broadening of the very idea of spirituality. Several women came to me stuck in a pattern of being a mother to everyone in sight. We explored the usual psychological issues, but it was clear to me, especially from the ritual nature of many of their dreams, that this mother myth was deep-seated and beyond psychology. I believed it had to do with our failure as a society to include maternal spirituality throughout the culture.

Unconsciously our society, to the extent that it is religious at all, sees itself in relation to an image of a gentleman God, the grandfather and patriarch. This has pushed the goddess, the Woman Nature, into hiding. But she doesn't disappear. She rules from beneath the surface of understanding and life structures. In her neglected condition she impacts lives as an oppressive and mysterious force that makes life impossible.

In therapy we saw this noble and strong goddess in dreams and caught glimpses of her reality in life situations. These women were trying to avoid anything that looked motherly and were therefore blind to the extravagant but hidden ways they mothered everyone around them. Three of them I recall eventually entered professions that gave expression to their motherhood in more complex ways — teaching, medicine, and social service. Of course merely doing this kind of work doesn't solve the spiritual problem of the neglected Mother. We all know teachers, nurses, and dentists who mother us to death. Nevertheless, the extension of the mother figure, from mere personal psychology to a spiritual role in the community, is an effective way to heal the spiritual problem that is a mother complex.

I have also worked with several women who call themselves feminists and are well known in their communities for their efforts on behalf of women. In the privacy of the dream work and tales of the past we discovered together that they, too, in a deep corner of their soul, rejected women and didn't really appreciate the value of feminine qualities. It is almost trite to say that outward behavior, when it is unusually strong and focused, often represents its opposite: "She protests too much." I thought the women with whom I discussed this reversal of values had unusual courage as they explored this contradiction that was embarrassing to them.

I sat with several men, too, who were caught up in a dishonoring of the mother goddess and were therefore excessive in their adoration of women. Every woman they came to love they adored and worshiped to the point that the women became afraid or at least put off. These men had dreams of goddess worship, and they showed as well many signs of anger and even violence toward women in general. They both loved and hated too much—the result, I believe, of not surrendering to the particular religion of the goddess. They saw their loved one as the goddess instead of an avatar of the goddess. In matters of the soul and spirit, things are not always what they seem to be. I came to understand sexism and violence against women as a spiritual issue, as a failure to appreciate the feminine mysteries.

Today many spiritual passions are often disguised in warfare, politics, sex, money, and even athletics. The hierarchies, rituals, uniforms, sermons, and life-and-death concerns of armies and navies taken together make a religion. The hysterical rallies and conventions of political parties, the adoration of celebrities, the social ideologies and creeds—they all point to a secular kind of religion. Sex and money, too, are still numinous—charged with emotion and meaning that easily become the ultimate concern of a life. And the rituals and passions of spectator sports can come to dominate lives that are otherwise surrendered to the secular machine of commerce and labor. Some people go to church on their respective holy day and then come home to watch a "big game" on television — two devotional rituals.

But most secular outlets for spiritual passion are inadequate because they address various levels of meaning only indirectly. We don't admit that they are religious. We no longer have a priest present at the games and the theater. We no longer worship at the altar of a sexual god or goddess. We no longer seek out a diviner or give prayer a central place in the selection of a government leader. Our indirect forms siphon off some spiritual steam, but they don't satisfy or fulfill religious needs.

As far as I know, we are the first people on the planet not to have a religious and spiritual perspective on all of experience. Publicly we offer sincere but nevertheless token prayers in our civil ceremonies. Many bring their moral obsessions to political causes, but then they fail to serve as true visionaries and exemplars of the deep moral life. Public expressions of moral outrage seem more ideological than rooted in deep holiness.

This loss of religion as a way of life — a constant attitude, a source of morals, an education in character, and a form of worship — leaves a blank space certainly, but worse, it accounts for much of our suffering. I think that our marriages and families are failing because we now treat them as sociological constructions or psychological arrangements rather than as holy mysteries. We talk about them in terms of what we can get from them rather than as sacred ways of being. Steeped in this vacant secularism, of course they fall apart.

Our addictions are also inverted forms of worship. People seek liberating loss of self in drugs and become stuck on them because these substitutes for religious ecstasy can only create a semblance of bliss. Whatever gives the illusion of religion, whether it be alcohol, ill-placed love, or defensive churchgoing, can make us crazy. We crave religion of the deepest kind, and so we try out all kinds of inadequate forms, which only increase the craving and the emptiness. Our response to emotional problems must be spiritual to be effective. Religious issues, matters of profound belief and meaning, work themselves out in our struggles. It is no accident that recovery programs entail a heavy dose of nondenominational spirituality. Our addictions are spiritual in nature and must be handled accordingly.

Why is it so difficult to find the right practice and a suitable community? Simply because spirituality has the aspect of quest and search. Usually it doesn't happen immediately and full-blown. We have to look around or experiment in some way even within a single tradition. We mature in spirituality just as we mature in all other ways, as we expose ourselves to wisdom and go through regular initiations that deepen our perceptions. Spiritual developments in the culture at large also have a profound impact on individuals.

For many the spiritual life never feels settled. We may continue to reflect on our beliefs and experiences. I am constantly wondering about my unusual desire for the monk's life in my late childhood. I still benefit, I believe, from periods of doubt and skepticism. After sixty years my questions have been refined, and yet from minute to minute, even as I write these pages, I feel that I always slide back to an original ignorance, to a beginner's mind.

There is, therefore, a paradox at work. We advance in holiness as much by losing religion as by gaining it. The two impulses become the breathing in and the breathing out of belief. Not defending against loss, we find the gift of new life. Going deep in our emotions and relationships, standing in our confusion and our wonder, eventually we discover the deep abyss that is the counterpart to the sublime heaven. Both ends of this vast spiritual spectrum are necessary for the establishment of a spiritual existence, the most important task of all.

V | *God*

The presence of God is more real to me now than it ever was, and yet it is also emptier of ideas and certainties. I feel that my notion of God has matured year by year, and yet I now know less about God, not more. The old paradoxes express God's nature better than any plain statements. God is greater than great, smaller than small. God is the most transcendent being and yet the most intimate. God is beyond any image I might have and yet requires the best of images. Anything I say about God I must undo at the very moment I say it, and yet I don't need to stop talking.

The name of God can be used to freeze our wonder, to make a comforting and useful idol, or it can be the opposite: a name that opens into continuing mystery. I learn from Islam to use the name carefully, from Judaism to use it rarely, and from my own experience to use it almost not at all. It makes sense to light a candle every time I call on God, just to remember that the name is holy and never means what I think it means. For these reasons I use it much more in the privacy of my thoughts and devotions than in public.

My reluctance to speak of God apparently leads some people to question my religiousness and my faith. Maybe that is a good thing because when people see your piety, it has probably already passed too far into form. It is better to be on the cusp between religion and secularity than to fall into either category. For there is another paradox at work: the appearance of religiosity is often in inverse proportion to the quality of religious practice.

There are those who for many different reasons don't use the word God. *I can't presume to know what anyone believes or disbelieves, but my guess is that emphasizing the ancient theological "negative way," or the way of emptiness, at least brings my approach to God close to that of Buddhism and other religions. I am not suggesting that everyone means the same thing when using different languages but that we can all explore these difficult matters of spirit with some commonality of understanding. Even within particular communities, understanding and belief will differ from person to person.*

So I speak of God in order to stop speaking of God. Usually I avoid the name in order to evoke the reality or, better, the mystery. As long as these contradictions and paradoxes are in place, I don't worry. But if some truth or some firm position sneaks in, I have to go back and read the mystics once again to cleanse my thoughts and restore the emptiness that gives God reality.

The World is charged with the grandeur of God.
It will flame out, like shining from shook foil.

Gerard Manley Hopkins, "God's Grandeur"

19. *The Unnameable*

*T*HE GOD I WANT to honor is the hidden one, *deus absconditus,* or the withdrawn one, *deus otiosus.* I don't mind talking about God in the proper context and in moderation, but the first commandment—Do not honor false gods—always gives me pause. Unless I say the minimum and use the name cautiously, I fear I will fall into the worst kind of idolatry—the illusion that in these mysterious matters I know exactly what I'm talking about or that I have pinned it down to my comfort.

People sometimes tell me that they are surprised and disappointed to find that I write about the soul, a religious topic, but rarely refer to God. This remark startles me because to me everything I write is theology and therefore about God. In my own mind I am a theologian—admittedly a new brand, but a theologian nevertheless. God is a quiet presence on every page of my writing. But maybe that is the problem: I have a preference for those theologies that go out of their way to safeguard the infinitude, the ineffability, and the mysteriousness of God.

Dietrich Bonhoeffer says something similar in one of his letters from prison. "I'm often reluctant to mention God by name to religious people —because that name somehow seems to me here not to ring true, and

I feel myself to be slightly dishonest."[1] Yet at the same time Bonhoeffer devoted his life to theology and to the Christian ministry, carrying that discipleship, as he called it, to the point of becoming a genuine martyr.

For myself I trust those theologians and ministers who don't use the name of God at all, use it carefully, or speak only of what the name signifies. Bonhoeffer speaks of a God beyond God, and Paul Tillich recommends the God beyond theism. Shunryu Suzuki, a Zen master, never used the word God, as far as I know, so devoted was he to spiritual emptiness. All of these seem to be efforts to avoid turning God into an idol, a disastrous mistake that can be made easily.

Idol is a difficult word. It can be an image through which we glimpse divinity, or it can be an object that is worshiped and therefore stands as a block between us and the other. We need images in the former sense, but they can easily become idols that point to, rather than beyond, themselves. The whole point of a religious image is to give us a window onto eternity. An idol blocks the awesome possibilities of vision and the corresponding passionate embrace of life.

It is always tempting to make God in our own image rather than the other way around. We feel the need for a certain source of security, and so we design a God tailor-made for our purposes. Then we defend this image against all others. But the purpose of the name of God is to crack us open, lifting us out of our finitude and self-absorbed anxiety, and this religious enterprise requires an idea of God beyond any fixed notion we might have.

During my college years I led a double life that symbolizes the dual path of image and emptiness. I spent most of my time as a monk — meditating, praying, living in community, and studying theology. But I was also a musician, and once each week I would take a train from the north shore of Chicago to the city where I completed my degree in music composition. That train ride I now see as a symbol of my lifelong attempt to reconcile the mysteries of religion with the images of art.

Reading Jung led me to connect dream images to those of art and religion. At first his psychology of religion gave my belief new life. Once again I could see how religion addresses the very questions that haunt me day after day. Later I felt that Jung's system, not his personal quest, was too dogmatic. James Hillman's acute revisioning of Jung helped ease many of my problems and brought me back to the realm of dream, art, and religion. But Hillman's work, at least on the surface, offered no positive way of appreciating my "negative" theology, the imageless, pure divine spirit. I still felt divided, still on a rail line between the monk and the artist.

Even now I'm a monk at heart. I'm drawn to the inexpressibility of such things as the meaning of life and the reality of God. When I first read them many years ago, the words of the *Tao Te Ching* burned themselves into my imagination: "The Tao that can be named is not the eternal Tao." I want spirit as pure as it can be even if I also have an appreciation for images.

Some people use religion to protect against life's challenging mysteries. Others find an opening there to pure vitality and absolute responsibility. It isn't always easy to tell the difference, but sometimes the former betrays itself in anxiety. Recently I listened to an intelligent and passionate Christian speaking persuasively about his belief. But there were two things that made me think he was using religion as a shield: one was the tone of his voice—pinched, anxious, and too insistent; the other was a simple statement he made. He quoted the Bible to support a point, and when the person in conversation with him pointed out that his interpretation of that passage was only one way of reading it, he said, "I'm telling you what is there in the Bible, not what I understand by it." He was refusing to consider the subjectivity of his belief. He wasn't able to reflect enough on his attachment to give it its necessary emptiness.

I suppose it makes sense that religious belief would be insecure. After all, it attempts to formulate the unformulatable. Frequently it makes the nervous claim that it possesses the truth pure and simple.

The insecurity behind such a superior statement is plain for all to see except those in need of airtight delusions. But this common spiritual arrogance gives religion a bad name. The theology of many traditions demonstrates that religion can be just the opposite: it can joyfully honor God without proving either God's existence or the validity of a particular path to God.

To avoid defensiveness in belief, it may be helpful to return to the ancient teaching that God is ineffable and basically unknowable. We may talk freely about God and yet at the same time understand that our language and ideas are severely limited. Many people feel insecure with such an open-ended idea of God. They may not have discovered how mystery offers its own kind of security.

Defending against mystery, people turn belief into fact, a mistake Chögyam Trungpa aptly described as "spiritual materialism" and Bonhoeffer labeled "a positivism of revelation." We parade our belief while underneath lies a serious doubt that we don't even admit to ourselves.

Now is the time to take Bonhoeffer's advice and recognize once and for all that human beings have come of age. We have created a world of science, technology, philosophy, and art that gives us almost everything we need. Bonhoeffer's strong recommendation is that we shouldn't leave the scraps that are left over to God and religion. Rather, we could find God in the midst of this culture—not in its weakness but in its strength.

Bonhoeffer challenges us to enter fully into this life but not to take it on its own terms, which are generally limited, anxious, and ambitious. We can enjoy the secular achievements of the age and yet not succumb entirely to their lure. Many of the philosophers I follow recommend taking the route of deep secularity as a path to the mysterious and the divine. Everything points beyond itself and has infinite depth, but we have to enter life as generously as possible to find its religious dimension. We have no idea, for instance, what the miracles of modern technology would be like if they were animated by a strong religious vision rather than neurotic secularism. To take a simple example, I can imagine road-building that respects established communities, nature, and beauty while at the same time gets us where we want to go. But we have a ways to go before we understand that building a road is a theological endeavor.

Many religious traditions go to great lengths to explain their faith intellectually, but their real lure is in the beauty of their rites and images. When Gerard Manley Hopkins claims that "the World is charged with the grandeur of God," I take it to mean that we can glimpse God in the electric beauty of nature and art. That is how I became aware of the "Thou" in nature on a day in Galway when I was lifted out of my usual state by the simple shimmer on the sunlit sea.

For me beauty is the primary proof of the existence of God. Beauty is sublime, transcendent, and fulfilling. It takes us to the very edge of our capacity for knowledge. And when it is not sentimentalized, it embraces the twisted, the painful, and even the cruel. Artists show us often disturbingly that even in our darkest and lowest natures something of beauty remains. The world considered without its beauty is a world perceived without its God.

During Bonhoeffer's last days when he was being carted from one prison to the next, suffering the separation from his family and his fiancée, facing almost certain death by execution, his comrades took note of his good humor, his kindness, and his appeal. The beauty of his person seemed to come out more than ever as his cruel fate unfolded into tragedy. He wrote uplifting and challenging theology and poetry full of hope and yet not unrealistic. He demonstrated personally that mature belief in God is not defensive or depressing and not in any way escapist. It is not bought at the price of any failure in ourselves or in our world. Nor does it make up for our failure to love and believe in ourselves.

The most mind-bending paradox is that this mature belief doesn't need to be explicit. God can remain not only unspeakable but unnamed.

A life given wholeheartedly to secular claims of beauty and human need may be the most religious of all. What really matters and what reveals the presence of God is the emptiness, the open-endedness, the trust, and the surrender.

Note

1. Dietrich Bonhoeffer, *Letters and Papers from Prison,* ed. B. Eberhard Bethge (New York: Collier Books, 1971), p. 281.

Jesus said, "I will give you what no eye has seen, what no ear has heard, what no hand has touched, what has not risen in the human heart."

Gospel of Thomas

20. *Jesus the Imagination*

BECAUSE I HAVE BEEN a Christian all my life, I want to write something about Jesus. If I weren't basing this book in my own spiritual processes, I might also present the Buddha, Mohammed, Laotzu, and other spiritual figures. I try to revision the image of Jesus now not only for my fellow Christians but for others, too, as an example of how all figures of devotion might be deepened.

Like millions of Christians I have lived most of my life with the echo of Jesus' footsteps and the rumbling of his words always in the background. One of the benefits of attending church regularly is to hear the stories of Gospels told over and over until they become a steady percussion deep in the memory, maintaining the rhythms of Jesus' cutting and comforting words.

His teaching is not a code of beliefs to be enforced and sanctioned but a living vision of how life might be. I hear a similar pulse of deep storytelling in the writings of Rabbi Harold Kushner and Rabbi Lawrence Kushner, and I envy their congregations who have heard those stories and commentaries all their lives. I'd like to spend many years apprenticed to a Sufi teacher who would do the same with the wonderful traditional stories of Islam.

My short-lived departure from regular church attendance and my subsequent studies in the world's religions had an effect on my idea of who Jesus was and is. I became less interested in the historical Jesus and in the churches that seem to idolize him. I became drawn more to the mystery of his presence in human spiritual history. I have come to see him as a meaningful and timeless presence through which I can make sense of a chaotic life and find a consistent vision. I am now interested in the Jesus of William Blake—the eternal Jesus, the Jesus of myth and imagination.

Like my notion of God, my idea of Jesus has become more transparent. I see life through his eyes rather than focus my attention on him. Yet I have the strong feeling that I am more Christian, more Catholic, more a follower of Jesus than before when all of this was more explicit. It feels as though my Christianity has come to infuse every cell of my being and yet at the same time has grown less visible and tangible. The color of Christianity in me has also blended with the different hues of Buddhism, Greek paganism, Renaissance syncretism, Sufism, Taoist emptiness, and Judaism. This is not a watered-down or diffused Christianity but a richer, more complex spiritual vision, one that acquires strength by not being defined in contrast with other visions.

I have no trouble believing that Jesus is the Son of God or that divinity is to be found through him. But it is difficult to understand how we moved from his plain teachings to the trappings of huge churches. His first followers were fishermen, tradespeople, and housewives. Today he is represented often by powerful, austere men who ignore the simplicity of his life and instead busy themselves with an imperial organization.

When I hear others speak in favor of Christian simplicity, it sometimes sounds naïve and sentimental. But here I am having the same thoughts. I think what motivates me, if I may indulge in some self-analysis, is a typical midlife reevaluation of what is important. Like Emerson I can't help thinking that much theologizing and church-making is a distraction that prevents us from establishing a much-needed religious attitude in our world. Life is short. Needs are pressing. The teachings and modeling of Jesus are not all that complex except perhaps at the mystical level. Perhaps it is time to abandon Christianity in favor of the Christ.

In a Blakean fashion I would describe Jesus as a new and radical imagination of human life. He lifts us out of materialism and narcissism, both of which can be fatal to human community. He teaches a profoundly ironical way of life: The first shall be last. Turn the other cheek. Love your enemies. Let the one who is innocent cast the first stone. If we heeded these challenging and paradoxical lessons, the world would be a radically different place.

Jesus argues strongly against rigid tradition and ecclesial authoritarianism. He demonstrates that healing is a mystery. He is absolutely forgiving, yet he is not a pushover. He can get angry and become an activist in the face of injustice. He is a complicated figure who always goes against the crowd, but the institutions who take his name are not nearly as paradoxical, complicated, or radical.

I prefer the image of Jesus as an enchanter and a magus, one who knew the power of language and sign and the persuasiveness of charisma and personality. Somehow he could open himself to the point where divinity flowed through him and out of him. In this openness, his very being as a conduit for a greater will, he is a perfect model for the religious person. His teachings deliteralize life, soften the ego to near extinction, and open up a wide imagination of what life and humanity and culture could be.

Certainly there are many dimensions to this extraordinary divine person. One that is not treated with the seriousness and substance it requires is Jesus the magician. In my book *The Re-Enchantment of Everyday Life* I tried to make the case that we can now leave behind the age of reason and in an intelligent way restore a sense of mystery and ways of magic. In that spirit I would also like to reconsider Jesus the miracle worker and healer. I see him as a leading image for a new era of enchantment. He lived as though he knew the hidden powers of nature and how to use them for the benefit of humanity. This Jesus, the esoteric Jesus, the magus, the gentle healer inspires me to imagine a radically different kind of existence where, it is true, conventional values would be turned upside down.

As a follower of Jesus taking lessons from his portrait in the Gospels, I want to take medicine beyond the mechanical and the technical. I see deep ties between Jesus the healer and the dream-healing god of the Greeks, Asklepios. Following his lead I'd also like to reimagine power and authority in government and business emphasizing a philosophy of deep community and justice. Listening closely to his philosophy of a kingdom of heaven, I'd like to restore a sense of the invisible and the imaginal.

Some see Jesus as the great authority, the one who possesses a truth that no one else can access. According to the Gospel writer John, he said, "I am the way, the truth, and the life," but it isn't necessary to take these words as exclusive. The word John uses for truth is *aletheia,* an unveiling and an unforgetting. The Greeks imagined truth not as provable reality but as a deep remembering of the nature of things, so subtle as to be expressed in poetry rather than dogma. In the Greek meaning of the word *truth,* Jesus is the route to deep remembrance about what is important and how things are. In this sense his way is indispensable, but that doesn't mean you have to be a Christian to pursue it.

I see no anxiety in Jesus, but his followers are often full of it. Any human act founded in anxiety is essentially weak and even neurotic. Jesus offers an alternative way of being, an attitude that is not worried about self. His nature is essentially holy, which is the opposite of neurotic. His compassion derives from profound empathy and a refusal to accept the usual condition of social divisions and hierarchies.

The Gospels are mystery texts. Some scholars worry about their faulty historicity, saying they are contaminated by the theological interests of the writers. But as sacred texts they make sense in an entirely different reality. They present the story of a man through whom divinity radiated. His entire life was in counterpoint with the eternal and mysterious, and this approach was full of power. His absolute kindness and his miracles are closely connected to each other. He wasn't paranoid about other people or about God. He was utterly undefended and so could be unusually, perhaps uniquely, open to the life that flowed through him. Isn't that what he always said, that he was here to do his Father's will and not his own? Understood without moralism, that simple statement could be the basis of a religious existence and a precious route out of egotism.

William Blake said, "The Hebrew Bible & the Gospel of Jesus are not Allegory but Eternal Vision or Imagination of All that Exists."[1] I take this to mean that Jesus demonstrates how to live in a state not conditioned by temporal logic and purpose. He shows a way to reimagine existence radically where we come into this world not to defend our egotism and separateness but to express our commonality with nature and with other human beings, where we are not anxiously trying to improve and succeed but rather embody the eternal realities of beauty and love.

Blake adds some other rich images to describe Jesus: "All Things are comprehended in their Eternal Forms in the Divine body of the Saviour the True Vine of Eternity." "The true vine of eternity" is a good phrase for the mystical Jesus. The timeless mysteries show through in Jesus' person and actions like sap in a vine. To be connected to Jesus as inspiration and model is to have a means for healing the rift in the soul between the temporal and the timeless, the understood and the mysterious. This is the Dionysian Jesus, the source of the sap, fluidity, and intoxication of life.

Blake describes Jesus as a fire in which we are heated to the point of transformation. This alchemical image presents Jesus not as a rigid standard or an object of idolization but as a transformative factor transmuting our very natures. To enter religiously and mystically into his mystery is to always be in a state of transformation, fire instead of plastic. If we imagine ourselves as fire, then our lives, with their ambitions and goals, are never fixed. We are always witnessing the consummation of a self and the arrival of new reality.

When he was in jail being punished for his homosexuality, Oscar Wilde wrote about Jesus in the way of the earlier mystics, as a figure of transforming love. The Wilde of his prison writings is not the wit and dandy of his plays but a mystic consumed with a new vision. He tells how he read the Gospels in Greek every morning and found this practice refreshing, as though he were reading about Jesus for the first time. He says, "I see this continual assertion of the imagination as the basis of all spiritual and material life, and I see also that to Christ imagination was simply a form of Love, and that to him Love was Lord in the fullest meaning of the phrase."[2]

Jesus, Wilde said, loved the sinner as a model of holiness. We sin — contradict our values, betray our vision — as we scramble to unfold our given natures into life. Moralists demand that we live according to standards and propriety, but Jesus neither taught this way nor modeled it. He was the supreme individual whose individuality fulfilled itself in a radical sense of community. And is it too much to say that Wilde went to prison for his sexuality the way Jesus went to the cross for his spiritual passions?

Jesus truly is the resurrection and the life. When in rare moments I can see him as the Blakean fire in which my defenses are burned away, I am momentarily transformed. I glimpse my essential connection to my fellow humans and to nature, and I see how the divine might be incarnated in me, a simple person struggling as much as anyone else. I can understand how I might be part of the mystical body of Jesus, an extraordinary tendrilling vine that ties me to eternity.

To appreciate the radical religious reality of Jesus I had to explore other religions, enter deep into my emotions and those of others, learn in the depths of my private thoughts that faith is not fact, and listen to the voices within me and outside me telling me how I must behave, sin, and resurrect. I've had to learn that my body is the Jesus-body, my life the fire of love rather than the rock of self.

If one can say so without being irreverent, Jesus is yet another example of the Holy Fool. His wisdom contradicts worldly wisdom, and in the eyes of his world he was a fanatic and a failure. But in the story of his resurrection he gets up from the pratfall of his crucifixion. His way is not one of ultimate tragedy but of divine comedy.

Notes

1. William Blake, *Complete Poetry and Prose*, p. 554.
2. *Complete Works of Oscar Wilde* (New York: Harper & Row, 1966), p. 930.

I am the necessary angel of earth,
Since in my sight, you see the earth again.

Wallace Stevens, "Angel Surrounded by Paysans"

21. Taking Angels Seriously

*I*HAVE CHOSEN THREE WAYS to describe the very pinnacle of spiritual experience: God, who may or may not be a factor in the lives of the reader; Jesus, who may or may not be a figure of devotion; and now angels, who may or may not play a role in the reader's religious imagination. Again I take them as models for similar issues that anyone pursuing a spiritual life might encounter.

It is as difficult in modern times to take angels seriously as it was not to a thousand years ago. Since that period, which isn't all that long ago, we've had a remarkable shift in sensibility. The air has been cleared of all kinds of spirits and demons, only to be replaced by germs and viruses and chemicals. Fortunately we still don't live in a vacuum, but now we allow into our atmosphere only those things we can see with physical eyes. The closest we now come to seeing the invisible is to peer into a microscope to perceive what is out of ordinary range but still accessible to the senses.

With the revival of a spiritual sensibility toward the end of the twentieth century, naturally angels made a comeback, but like so much of that spirituality, for the most part they were given a sentimental welcome. Books and television programs presented them as cute and wholesome, although this characterization falls far short of the way angels appear in sacred literature where they perform tasks of real spiritual value for persons and societies.

The Gabriel who appears to the Virgin Mary and challenges her with the message that she will be the mother of God is a figure of great strength and importance. His presence is a continuing and eternal reminder that our lives and our cultural history are always on the brink of new and life-changing revelations. The same angel gave Mohammed the material of his religious revolution, which has transformed a major portion of the world.

Many have pointed out that painters once pictured angels as powerful representatives of the Godhead, immensely potent in their holiness and numinousness, but they now appear in paintings as cherubs and putti, little bodiless beings who swarm the heavens like bees. I, for one, am not offended by what Rilke called these bees of the invisible who produce spirituality the way bees make honey, but I never want to lose sight of the vast substance, relevance, and theological importance of the great angels.

One of my favorite angel painters is Piero della Francesca, who reminds us of the incarnational aspect of angels, their human side. His angels are robust, serious, and substantive, their bodies as solid and imposing as their beautiful and transcending wings. There, in fact, lies their mystery: the angel's amphibious capacity to be seriously involved in human affairs and yet possessed of the wings that emblemize its proximity to the divine. An angel is a go-between connecting time and eternity, the human and the more than human.

Today people ask if angels are real or only symbols. To this key question I would answer: neither. Indeed, the only way we can appreciate the reality of angels theologically and spiritually is to find our way out of this modern dilemma and discover that liminal place where spirit resides and religion happens—the place somewhere between or other than literal fact and symbol.

If we insist that to be real angels must be sighted and their presence proven by some measurement of the senses, then we are back in the modern dualism where a thing exists only if we can kick it. In that philosophy even the reality of so spiritual a thing as love is finally proven not by human experience but by the detection of genes and blood flow. Biofeedback confirms our reality. Applied to theological matters this amounts to spiritual empiricism, which is not only an oxymoron but is a sure way to weaken the religious imagination.

If we take the other side of modernism, its rationalistic reduction of all poetic thought to abstraction, allowing theology only as metaphor, we have also lost angels. What if someone treated you as a metaphor? I place angels in this scheme quite plainly: angels are real, as real as anything, but they are neither facts nor metaphors. We will never invent infrared goggles that allow us finally to perceive these hovering entities. We don't need goggles anyway since all it takes to recognize an angel is a healthy imagination. For millennia people have had all the equipment needed to sense the presence of an angel.

We live in a world full of spiritual realities. Love and sadness, to name two examples, are not mere emotions but spirits that we can sense in the atmosphere, and you don't have to have a talent for seeing auras to observe them. We simply have lost the ability and habit of treating them as real presences. Psychology has subjectivized them and personalized them to the point where they have been demoted from spiritual entities to feelings. They are now an aspect of us or projections, but not real in themselves. Angels, too, are unreal only to those who have a seriously truncated view of reality.

You don't have to give up one iota of intelligence to believe in angels. I have no doubt that at certain moments in my life I get unexpected and unexplained support, comfort, and safety from some spiritual presence. I have no trouble believing that I have a guardian angel. The mere fact that I am alive today is evidence enough for me if I needed it.

When my grandfather drowned while holding me up in the air on the underside of our little boat as it floated upside down in the rough waves of the lake, my life was being protected not only by the love of my grandfather but by something in life that wanted me to survive. Is it naïve to say such a thing? Only if you insist on being the center of a universe that you can explain away. Only if you have surrendered your imagination to the mechanistic requirements of modern rationalism.

Who am I anyway to question the reality of angels? For millennia they have been described seriously and in some detail by religions. Do I know better because I am smug in my mechanistic worldview in which there is no room for spiritual entities — what the brilliant Thomas Aquinas called separated beings? What an impoverished world we would have if we insisted that all spiritual realities be dismissed because we can't see them with our physical eyes and can't fit them into our narrow and selective view of what is real.

Angels are not just protectors, they are messengers as well. Many paintings show them with banners flowing from their mouths, using special angel language to announce the will of God. I realize how easy it is to dismiss such a statement, but it can be made intelligently. Belief in angels may be the most sophisticated and precise means available for recognizing life's subtleties. Once we get beyond a simplistic notion of God — too anthropomorphic and too dominated by spiritual realism — we can see that we all have to grapple with the divine will every hour of every day. It follows that messengers of this will are realities of the utmost importance.

Sometimes when people speak, the impact of their words is so strong and goes so deep that they seem to have a quality of eternity about them. We can sense the divine will in their force and effectiveness. Angels sometimes appear in the guise of humans, even as our friends and family members. They speak through us, too, offering messages of spiritual importance. If we can't distinguish between human and angelic utterance, then we may well be confused about how to get on in life.

Angels are not only guardians and messengers but also musicians. Paintings of angels show them playing every instrument imaginable and singing. Choirs of angels and angel harpists have become so familiar that we may have lost the importance of this idea. I have been writing positively about angels for many years, and I remember over a decade ago realizing one day that the glorious paintings of angel musicians teach that all music with the power to move us is the playing of angels. Musicians work hard developing their talents and skills to evoke this angel music. The musician, in fact, offers a brilliant example of an ancient practice known as angel magic by which certain effects can be produced in life only through the mediation of angels.

The artist's muse is an angel by another name. The muse is not visible the way trees are, but its presence is felt, and certainly its absence. Any artist knows the minute the muse goes away and when it returns. Is this merely subjective experience? Projection? Fantasy? Why not grant the muse, and therefore the angel, reality? You can't kick it, but you can feel it. Whether you allow its presence or not, it will be there, but if you don't allow it, it may not be friendly.

Allowing angels their seriousness may mark the return of a spiritual sensibility. We need the messengers in order to receive the message. We need wings to let the imagination soar. We need the music within the music to discover once and for all that the muse, among many other presences, is an angel and that life is difficult, if not impossible, without that mediation.

The God who lets us live in the world without the working hypothesis of God is the God before whom we stand continually. Before God and with God we live without God.

Dietrich Bonhoeffer, *Letters and Papers from Prison*

22. *The Hidden God Is a Personal God*

I HAVE TRIED TO REFINE the idea of God and restore the mystery. But can this empty, transcendent, profound image of the infinite allow a personal relationship? Can we pray to an empty deity in the sense I have described? Is this empty God an abstraction, so clear of projection and wish that it is too ethereal? I don't think so.

On a cloudy autumn day I was standing on a small beach at a hauntingly still and softly colored inlet in Galway. My daughter was playing with a neighbor's dog, throwing him bits and pieces from the tidepools. He jumped high each time and twisted around in a gangly circle, snapping at the tidbits in full flight. This went on for about an hour. I stood watching the water and looking at the still headland across the bay in something of a trance. Suddenly the sun broke through the clouds and made the water sparkle. Spontaneously I said softly, "There you are. You've been hiding. But now you decide to show yourself. Why?"

I've begun speaking like this only recently, in the last decade. My sense of the mystery of life and of nature has intensified, apparently in conjunction with growing older and getting a more rounded image of my life and my place in the world. I could address God and the saints and the angels when I was a child, but then it was different. Now I have studied many religious traditions and have gone through phases in my own spiritual cycles. I have felt stirrings of agnosticism and doubt and secularism, though I've never completely surrendered to any of them. The connection I feel to the unnameable and hidden creating mystery in life is not naïve, not anthropomorphic, not simply one personality to another. Now I address the other as thou, but I have no idea what kind of personhood I'm engaged with. It is enough to speak and to feel the relation. It seems completely unnecessary to understand it.

According to an old Zen saying, first you see a mountain, then you don't see a mountain, then you see a mountain. That was the way of my religious development. First I really saw a mountain. In childhood I pictured God as an old man in a heaven lying not far beyond the clouds. As I grew older, the image became more sophisticated, but it was still quite literal and of human scale. A Sufi story tells of a man who asks an ant, "Isn't your God just like you?" "Not at all," said the ant. "He only has one antenna, we have two." That sums up the notion that stayed with me for many years.

Narrow notions of God persist. I know a few Zen ants. Talk to them about the Christian idea of charity, and they say, "Oh, yes. The Buddha nature!" I know moral ants. You say to them, "I want to do something about the condition of children in the world." They answer, "Kids don't have the solid moral instruction I had when I was a child." I know spiritual ants. I tell them I'm writing about religion, and they say, "Oh, yes. Tell people to be in the light." Some people would say I'm a soul ant.

For a while I didn't see God at all. I tried to make sense of this life in purely secular terms. Like Buddha, I experimented. I looked for meaning in philosophy and art and social awareness. At one time it seemed that psychology might take the place of religion, especially when defined with depth and subtlety. Only in the past fifteen years have I gradually come full circle, mainly through a rediscovery of the writings of mystics.

Finally, I saw God again, but this time he wasn't a he and he didn't have a beard and he didn't live on the fluff of the clouds. This God was so much beyond my naïve imagining that I could rarely use the name — and usually only in the privacy of my prayers. It now seems difficult but necessary to believe in a God who is unspeakable and unknowable. Anything less is so obviously limited by our need for the familiar that it falls short of real religion.

Yet at the same time religious experience around the world shows that our connection with God is that of one person to another. We pray to God as father, mother, protector, savior, powerful one, miracle worker, creator. Religion is not a mental experience alone but one of devotion in which the heart is as involved as the mind. But is it possible to have a sophisticated idea of God as entirely other and at the same time pursue a personal relationship, the goal of much mysticism and religion?

A related question: Can we live in this advanced culture, at a time when human life is coming of age, and still be devotional? As many current writers insist, isn't it anachronistic and superstitious to be pious in a worldly age? I advocate devotional religion, traditional religious forms — radically reimagined, of course — and even magic. Am I being naïve and gullible? Am I blind to the new truths of a scientific worldview?

Often I feel like Samuel Beckett, who writes time and again that there are no adequate words and that words are killers. For all his skepticism about language he devoted himself to a life with words. I have not only devoted my life to something that can't be known fully, but I have chosen to emphasize its mystery and ineffability. For this both secular and religious professionals criticize me. Because I choose not to enter either secular empirical studies or theological abstractions, both groups consider me lightweight. Some complain that I don't use the name of God enough, and others that I'm too pious. I conclude with Beckett that words are killers and none of them are adequate.

What words can convey the profound paradoxes and contradictions that are the stuff of theology? The brightest theologians end up referring to a God beyond God, a name that doesn't name, and a science of theology as the study of that which is unknowable. Mystics are often successful in expressing paradox and mystery—the teaching stories of Zen, Meister Eckhart's knotted sentences, Sufi poetry. They don't reason us toward understanding; they take us deep into imagery.

Often we have to do two things at once: affirm and deny, believe and doubt, worship and be skeptical, relate and keep it all empty. Take back everything as soon as you say it, but give it every inch of reality even as you take it back. Consider the following passage from Nicholas of Cusa's 1444 book *Dialogue on the Hidden God* (*Deo abscondito,* a conversation between a pagan and a Christian):

Pagan: "Who is the God you worship?"

Christian: "I don't know."

Pagan: "It's amazing to see someone devoted to what he doesn't know."

Christian: "It's even more startling to see someone devoted to what he thinks he knows."

Pagan: "Can God be named?"

Christian: "What can be named is small. That whose magnitude can't be imagined is ineffable."

Pagan: "Then God is ineffable?"

Christian: "No, he is beyond all that can be named."

Pagan: "May God, who is hidden from the eyes of the wise of the world, be blessed forever."

This is a remarkable passage written by a cardinal of the church. With a few alterations it could have been written by Beckett. God is not ineffable, but he is beyond what can be named. He is hidden but can be praised. When the cardinal, the highest placed priest other than the pope, is asked, "Who is the God you worship?" he can answer, "I don't know."

I think this is where Bonhoeffer saw us going in religion and where I think we can go, at least those of us who prefer to live with a theology come of age. We can live in contradiction and paradox, we can relate to the invisible, and we can make sense of our lives precisely because they are mysterious. If we go only in the direction of secular sophistication, we come quickly to a dead end. For it soon becomes apparent that scientific and technical modes of thought deplete the soul and diminish our humanity. Many go to the opposite extreme and insist on naïve belief, cutting themselves off from the joys of secularity and participation in the unfolding of culture. The middle way is the way of emptiness and image.

To reconcile the scientific-technological vision with religion we have to go so far into secularity that divinity appears, and so far into spirituality that we no longer separate heaven from earth. God then is not an object on the other side of secular concerns but is present in the very heart of them, like Bonhoeffer's God who is to be found in the middle of the village. I don't believe that this is pantheism or panentheism — the belief that God is everything or in all things. That would be a diffuse and abstract God. No, this God is Source and Goal, Presence and Personality.

Bonhoeffer, Paul Tillich, Zen masters, and many theologians present the pursuit of God as a paradox. Leave the paradoxical and you have exited the theological milieu. God is familiar and yet completely unknown. God is Creator and Divine Lover and yet at the same time none of these. The images we use take us into the precinct of mystery, but there we are left wordless and speechless. That is why I think everyone is called to be a mystic in his own way: each of us has to find that sanctuary where we know in our bones the presence of the unspeakable.

"We shouldn't run man down in his worldliness," Bonhoeffer wrote shortly before he died, "but confront him with God at his strongest point." For me this means to give myself as fully as possible to the world in which I find myself, noticing where I defend myself and hold back.

Avoiding life in the name of pure spirit may look like religion, but it is a defense against the God of Things, the Creator. God is to be found in the thick of life or not at all.

What about monks? They obviously withdraw from life with their "contempt for the world." In practice some monks may indeed withdraw, misunderstanding the meaning of *contemptus mundi*. But as many monks have said, their purpose is to enter more fully into the world without becoming blinded by it, seeking divinity at its core. What about God-language? Do we have to speak of God to be spiritual in a secular society? I've already addressed this issue. We do not have to speak of God in order to live at the spiritual heart of life. In fact, I believe that today it is particularly difficult to live spiritually using traditional God-talk. This may be the time to rediscover the invisible and the unnameable emerging from daily experience, from nature, and from the mysteries we encounter as we try to make a livable society.

As Bonhoeffer knew only too well, even at the center of things this is a world of suffering. To be fully engaged with it means not to turn away from the suffering and challenges but to live affirmatively and joyously no matter what happens. It also entails living so far into this life as to venture close to its mysteries, discovering that life asks each of us a particular kind of surrender. At the point most profoundly mysterious, God appears briefly not as an it but as a thou. We shouldn't reduce the idea of God to the personal but expand our notion of the personal and thereby include God. If we could see the mystery in other persons, we might be able to glimpse personality in the ultimate mystery.

Prayer, a basic means of relating to the ultimate personality, is grounded and completed in an openhearted engagement with the world. If God is at its center, then we can relate to him through it, and the quality of our relationship with God will depend on the nature of our engagement in the world. The key is not to separate divine person from divine creation or to divide holy creation from the world we are discovering and developing through science and technology. The gap between science and religion betrays a failure on the part of each to be sufficiently subtle and visionary.

Seeing God as hidden and unknown and yet in the heart of life, at its best as well as its worst, personally I begin to see a way to deepen my Catholicism. I can hear a new dimension in teachings I have meditated on all my life. The sentimentality that creeps into much Catholic language suddenly disappears. The abstract propositions take on life. Problems with authority diminish. The Catholic way of life finally begins to look catholic rather than parochial.

The soul feeds on God, nurses at the divine breast. The deep soul, embedded in life and personality, needs regular doses of spirituality, nurturance that addresses its eternal side. The human dimension thrives only if the soul is connected to the divine, however that may be imagined or articulated. But as Ficino says, when soul and spirit connect, each has to be tuned to the other. Our spirituality has to be sensitive to human needs, and our daily lives have to be open to spiritual matters.

God is as much in the mess as in the beauty. If we define our spirituality only in positive and glowing terms, it will become sentimental, and then it is of no use. To be spiritual is not just to pray and meditate but also to be involved in the struggles of marriage, work, and raising children; in social responsibility and in the effort to make a just and peaceful world.

A religious attitude would help us contemplate our failures and see them for what they are—unsuccessful, inverted attempts to make sense of life. Rather than divide in our passions over the ownership of guns, for example, we could look deeply into both our worship of weapons and our efforts to be uncontaminated by them. We could see that we need the power represented by weapons, but not their dangerous presence as fetishes. We could examine runaway development as a misdirected but valid need for creative expression and the building of a beautiful world. The absence of serious concern for beauty and community in economic development simply shows that we have forgotten the religious component.

God who is unnameable is not for that reason abstract. If God is in the heart of things, we can relate to him personally either in direct dialogue and prayer or through the medium of life and the world. A broader and deeper imagination would allow us to perceive the electric charge of meaning and transcendent implications in all of creation. Such faith depends on the extent and quality of our imagination, and the purpose of all formal religion is to educate that imagination.

We can get too personal in our religious attitude, losing the sense of God's grandeur and ineffability. The chummy approach to God is unfortunately quite popular. On the other hand, we can be too mental, too interior, or too cosmic in attitude, and then religion becomes airy and speculative. Both sides of this split need deepening: we need effective forms of devotion and a critical, unsentimental intelligence about theological matters.

Only when God's mystery, incomprehensibility, and unnameability are respected do we have the opportunity to see that God is everywhere and within everywhere. Then we can relate to God as persons do—being present to each other, not excessively familiar and not merely caught up in ideas about who we are. We can talk and hope that we are heard. We can listen and hope that we understand.

VI | *Romance*

Out of the deep paradox of the nameless God comes a growing awareness of a pulsing presence in the heart of things. The world is no longer literally empty and dead. Life returns to a state of enchantment where the imagination points the way toward meaning and value. Expression here is dreamy but intimate. We stay close to mystery but find ways to express it and share it. At this point a Romantic approach to religion becomes possible, and through it the soul reunites with the spirit.

The "theologians" appropriate for this task in Western culture are such people as William Blake, Henry David Thoreau, Emily Dickinson, Rainer Maria Rilke, and Oscar Wilde. Each explored the spiritual realm with exquisite care and devotion. Each reflected, as a theologian does, on the ultimate things, but not abstractly and not without compassion for the human individual. Each was ridiculed by society as a fool, and therefore they give us a model of the Romantic out of step but close to the mystery.

What would theology be like if it were released from its bondage to philosophy? What if we studied the great literature and art, the rituals and personalities of the many spiritual traditions, instead of abstract categories and definitions? We would have to be careful not to sentimentalize religion or the spiritual life, but we would see a side of them that is invisible when the accent is on pure intellectual content.

Now we can look more closely at the soul of religion, what Jung would call its anima. Here we move away from all abstraction and treat the spirit as an intimate. Religion becomes an adventure, a lifelong search for that elusive and central radiance of what matters and what is most our own.

The more materialistic Science becomes,
the more angels shall I paint.

Edward Burne-Jones

23. *The Romance*
of Religion

ALTHOUGH THE RELIGIOUS and spiritual traditions are full of
great stories, haunting poetry, and deep mysticism, people still
think of religion as a body of beliefs, and spirituality as higher consciousness. It is difficult in a time when science is the master of knowledge to
appreciate the importance of the interior life and to value insight, intuition, and imagination. The emphasis on transcendence comes at the
cost of spirituality's soul and the romance of religion.

For twenty years I sat in small rooms in various places practicing
therapy, fascinated by the mysteries in which my clients were caught
and using everything at my disposal to find our way through them. In
Massachusetts I rented an austere nineteenth-century studio over a
little river and part of an old-fashioned vanilla and spices shop. My
landlord made the vanilla in barrels in the basement beneath my little
office, and the aroma of distillation would often seep up into my space.
More than one client sniffed and then mentioned something about the
sweet alchemy taking place in the underworld of my office. Mean-

while, in the cubicle above the sweet oils where we met, people were being divorced, experimenting dangerously with their lives, dealing with domestic violence, and dying too quickly of cancer.

Once a week I would drive over to Amherst and ply my trade in another tiny room that was a porch made over into a sitting room. The simplicity of both places satisfied my desire to accent the interior life and offer few distractions. There, too, intense dramas were taking place on the beautiful avenue called Pleasant Street.

I have never been a heroic figure in any sense of the term. I have always cherished and identified with the antihero, the person who accomplishes little, if anything, and lives more in a void than in an adventure. I often think of myself as a Beckett-like figure sitting in his ashcan and enjoying his solitude. But interiorly I have been something of a knight of the imagination and have felt at home with the challenges and emotions involved in practicing therapy. Many times I felt I was on an emotional battlefield or wandering like a fairy tale character through a thick forest of feeling and fantasy.

I like the word *practice* for this work because of its religious overtones. For me therapy is a deeply engaging pursuit of mystic knowledge. It requires of me — I can't speak for other therapists — a willingness to enter into eternal mysteries described in the great myths and religious stories. I see this calling as the simple task of inviting the soul of my client into my small physical space, there to swell like a genie into grand proportions. Myth and ritual played themselves out in those little New England rooms, and I felt that my job was to deal with the frightening creatures and stormy events that would have been invisible to an observer but were intensely present to me and my client. I learned a great deal about religion from the powerful images that drove those people to hope or despair, and I discovered with shocking immediacy how religion is lived in the deep soul.

Today writing is my spiritual practice. Now the quest for a word or the search for an idea lies at the heart of my adventures. Where once I found religious meaning in the vast and tormented worlds of others, now I delve into my own interior universe and work out my religion by writing about it. To the reader this book may be just another attempt to make sense of religion, but for me it is a trip in a tiny sailboat across an ocean of passions and mysteries.

All of this makes religion, in my case, a romantic adventure. I use the word romantic carefully. I don't mean sentimental or amorous. Romanticism is an attitude and a point of view in which imagination, emotion, and individuality are primary. I take my idea of romanticism from the Romantic poets who stressed intimacy, beauty, ordeal, the ordinary life, and nature.

I've always been attracted to pain and twistedness and have paid little attention to the abstract mechanical, financial, and ambitious concerns of the world around me. Every morning I go to the piano and play the misty music of Debussy before venturing into the cosmic and demiurgic creations of J. S. Bach. I feel completely at home in the antic poetry of Mark Strand, the profoundly revisioning psychology of James Hillman, and the mythologies of John Moriarty. I feel alive in the presence of Edward Burne-Jones and other ultra-Romantic painters, and lately I've been enjoying Chopin as never before. I've become a dreamer and a friend to dreamers.

This life of religion, by no means over or accomplished, represents my romance with meaning. It is not a sterile intellectual game resulting in mere security and complacence. In its own way it is an odyssey on the sea, a trek over the mountains, and a passage through the jungle. It continues to fascinate me and keep me engaged. It accounts for my emotional ups and downs, my thrills and disappointments.

Meaning is perhaps not exactly the right word. I don't know what the prize in religion is, and yet the adventure is without equal. Meaning is perhaps shorthand for meaningfulness, the sense that life is grounded, tethered to a worthy anchor and somehow fixed in the right spot. It is a precious thing, and to be without it is to feel lost and anxious. It is a grail, a treasure, and a damsel in distress calling for daring and imagination.

Oscar Wilde's great letter *De Profundis*, which I've already cited for its soulful theology, spells out the basics of a romantic belief. Among them he lists a special appreciation for the individual, for pleasure and sensuality, and for pain, suffering, and struggle. Many religious people choose exactly opposite qualities as ideals — collective values, mental conviction, and a healthy, virtuous life. In this sense a romantic approach to religion goes against the grain, and yet I fear that by ignoring the romantic depths we make religion too clean and abstract, and therefore ignore its soul.

People often say that suffering is valuable because we learn from it, but often this is yet another example of spiritual productivity, the idea that anything is acceptable as long as it can be turned into a positive step in the steady progress toward a self. The romantic view is different. There suffering is of value because it brings us into our humanity. By giving ourselves to life generously we ensure that we suffer the ordinary pangs of involvement. We live intimately and generously. We love and lose, bind and separate. We become attached and are forced to move on. In spite of bad health or emotional confusion we go on into life, like the Romantic William Wordsworth finding glory in the ordinary surroundings, and John Keats praising beauty and sensation and finding meaning in the emotional and physical torments of his short life.

In romantic spirituality we both enjoy and endure our individual quirks and destiny. Emily Dickinson indulges her unusual need for privacy and her pagan slant on Christianity, while Emerson leaves the comfort of his church and invents the life of an independent, itinerant preacher. Oscar Wilde pursues every pleasure, legal and illegal, and then counts his imprisonment and dissolution as part of his adventure. Romantic spirituality is eccentric and is far from the dowdy moralism that often makes religion look ordered and conventional.

There is something bloodless in the contemporary vision of spirituality as part of a general fitness scheme, that sees it only as a means for attaining a life of perfection and health. The romantic element would bring it down to earth and connect it once again with the ordinary emotions and struggles. The romantic spirit doesn't aim to resolve those conflicts but to embrace them and imagine human existence with a depth of vision not thinned out by the need to improve or save. The romantic wants life to be rich and complex.

A romantic life is deeply interior and almost static compared to the frenetic activity around us today. It is thick with images — dreams, paintings, words — and stuffed with conversation and reflection. John Keats wrote: "I have an idea that Man might pass a very pleasant life in this manner — let him on any certain day read a certain Page of full Poesy or distilled Prose and let him wander with it, and muse upon it, and reflect from it, and bring home to it, and prophesy upon it, and dream upon it — until it become stale — but when will it do so? Never —"[1]

The autobiography of Saint Thérèse of Lisieux has a similar tone. The reflective young woman who died at twenty-four describes the minute details of her interior life as different from that of active people she admires. She says that eventually she discovered that love, and not intellect, is the way of the spirit, and she confesses to her foolishness — yet another holy fool. In true romantic fashion she says that religion must have a heart, and her calling is to that heart. She quotes her mentor, John of the Cross, saying, "Descending into the depths of my own nothingness, I was then so raised up that I attained my goal." My motto for this book has been the psalm: "Out of the depths I cry to you, O Lord." *De profundis* — out of the depths we find the union of soul and spirit.

Romanticism is in tune with the process of deepening because it places value on emotional complexity and intensity, which it uses as raw material for the imagination. I can't help contrasting this sensuous approach with the cooler, whiter, plainer development known today as spirituality. In many cases contemporary spirituality could be defined as religion stripped of its romanticism. It opts for clarity and awareness rather than absorption in the sensuous details of a world rich in meaning. It works at fabricating a highly idealized sense of community rather than getting lost in the complexities of actual, unpredictable, and highly individualistic people.

Abstract spirituality moves away from this world into utopias and sheltered communities, but a return to romanticism might bring us back to the particulars of the life we are living. William Morris, Edward Burne-Jones, and others like them invite us to find spirituality in the intensification of this life's beauty rather than in its avoidance, in the pursuit of justice and the making of a humane, colorful, and passionate world. Morris was one part craftsperson and one part social reformer, and he saw the one supporting the other. The intense colors of his wallpaper and decor reflect his passion for a more just society.

The great romantic poets of the nineteenth century wished to create an alternative to the industrial toughness and rationalistic edginess they found developing in the culture around them. They wanted to make room for the soul, for the deep, mystery-filled peculiarities of both nature and human personality. William Morris once outlined the principles behind his work, which we might take as guidelines toward restoring a romantic shade to our spirituality: "The aim should be to combine clearness of form and firmness of structure with the mystery which comes of abundance and richness of detail."[2]

The Romantics were also interested in dreams and esoteric sources of knowledge. They resisted the tendency in their time to render life abstract through dissection and analysis, processes carried to their extreme in our day. They placed value on impressions and sensations, and found intelligence in the mists of reverie. They departed from the tradition of treating theology as abstract philosophy or defensive moralizing.

When you look closely at spiritual movements of the past and many in the present, you find a preoccupation with truth, order, and personal integration. It sometimes appears that the reach for spirituality is a reaction against the complexities of modern life. The other side of this streamlining is sentimentality—the fostering of unreal relationships and communities and the overvaluation of a leader or an approach.

A romantic element would heal this split, offering a kind of reflection that doesn't oversimplify and emotion that is tougher than sentimentality. It would foster diversity and individuality, which are prerequisites for community. And it would reveal a spirituality rooted in the deep, rich entanglements of a life lived and lyricized rather than explained.

Notes

1. Robert Gittings, *John Keats* (London: Heinemann, 1970), p. 191.
2. E.P. Thompson, *William Morris* (Stanford, Calif.: Stanford University Press, 1976), p.106.

I sing of a maiden that is makeless [matchless].

Renaissance carol

24. *Eternal Maiden*

RELIGIOUS IMAGERY IS FULL of young women who portray a certain way of blending soul and spirit, a vibrant and delicate montage of qualities that plays a role in every life. The Virgin Mary; Artemis and her many lovely manifestations such as Daphne and Atalanta; the young Persephone among her flowers; Quan Yin; the dakinis of Tibet; Krishna's gopis; Saint Thérèse of Lisieux, who called herself "the little flower." In their tough delicacy these figures add considerably to the romantic tint of the spiritual life.

In the past few years I have been watching my daughter transform from a little girl into a young maiden. I see it in her eyes, which are becoming brighter and more perceptive; in her face, showing the promise of her womanhood; and in her body, becoming long and firm. Her moods are intense and her will strong. One minute you want to crush her with your love, and the next do battle with her. Above all, whatever she possesses seems indescribably precious, and the mere thought of any violation of that preternatural beauty is painful beyond endurance.

I look at her and feel blessed to have such a treasure in my life, and yet at the same time I see something universal and timeless in her. I know that countless other little girls have metamorphosed into young maidens, so much so that the mystery of this inviolate thing, this precious tenderness, transposes from the personality in my home into a priceless quality that lies in the very heart of things. I look at her and I behold one of the spirits that makes us all human.

If there is a *puer aeternus* that bestows youth forever, there is also a *puella aeterna* that gives us and our world our delicate and invincible beauty. They are not the same, but they are our youth, our evergreenness, and our always gangly beginnings. Gradually they metamorphose into our deepest strength. In religious myth the Greek Kore, seized by Hades as she is picking flowers, becomes mistress of the depths. The Virgin Mary, young and innocent, agreeing to an outrageous proposal by an intrusive, unwanted angel, turns into the sorrow-filled mother of God. Artemis and her nymphs enjoy their purity, integrity, and self-sufficiency, but their physical powers are unmatched.

The Romantic painters loved to depict maidens playing by streams and gathering at coves by the sea and alcoves in the woods. These are all anima images, to use Jung's language, as are the girls. They are representations of interiority and fantasy, important aspects of spirituality not always appreciated.

In a hard, insensitive world it isn't easy to understand the power and strength of the fragile maiden. We think we have to be tough, smart, and by all means not gullible. We plan on becoming worldly wise and getting ahead and making money. All the while the tender maiden, loved by the romantic, stands in a bath deep in the woods and gathers honey there and avoids sex. What could be more irrelevant?

But from another point of view this maiden's values strike a chord. A young man literally decides one day to use honey instead of sugar in a cup of tea, a choice that represents a new life experiment and an entry into Artemis. A mother suddenly thinks of gathering a group of fellow women in her home to explore their femininity. They discuss their fears for their own Persephone nature. A man realizes that his delicate sensitivities, though entirely different from the rough and capable men around him, are worthy. The girl archetype, the tender but life-enhancing spirituality, may appear one day as a possibility, a further step in the soul's metamorphosis.

A face of the soul is feminine and young, tender and full of hope. It makes no difference if it is the soul of an old man or a young girl. In those perceptive hands and blushing cheeks resides the eternal maiden who keeps us fresh and poised. Without her spirit we do too much, strive too hard, lead and force excessively, and take on the hero's tasks with unnecessary fortitude. She is one face of a romantic approach to religion. She is religion's tenderness and promise. Intellectually she is open and eager, but she resists being made into anything other than the pristine thing she is.

Like the puer, the maiden is potential: the virgin ready to conceive and the Maid of Orleans prepared to follow her voices. My daughter is ready to be a woman, but not for a few years, and that is the archetype —eternally young, eternally poised. I talk to many young men and women who are thus placed in their lives, and they feel embarrassed. They have been told that they should be doing something, anything, rather than standing idle and merely ready.

This spirit of the maiden plays a major role in the spiritual life. I saw it in some of the young men who were in the seminary high school with me. The blush on their cheeks betrayed the mark of the maiden who is ready for any precious gift that life has to offer. As so often happens in the spirit, gender is not etched in sharply and fixed. Of course I saw it, too, more directly, in many nuns who seemed never to have entered the world but were always on the edge, forever waiting. I had a cousin who was a nun, and whenever she visited our home, I felt as though the little prince had arrived. I don't mean that she was too precious or unreal but that she seemed to live by rules and habits that had nothing to do with life as I knew it. She was from another world. She was strong and capable but preternatural, more at home in Eden than Detroit.

These days my daughter plays with girls her age and size, and often they look like sisters or even copies of each other. The nuns, too, almost always went around in pairs, another interesting aspect of the archetype they embodied. Twin girls in my daughter's school are charming and mystifying in whatever they do. The twinning of the archetype takes it out of the ordinary and the literal, raises it a notch in fantasy, and gives the maiden resonance and poetry.

I've known spiritual people who, though strong and complicated, shine with the strong glow of this eternal maiden. They are difficult to reach because of the mistiness of maidenhood that surrounds them. It makes them seem unreal and therefore prized. A person of a different temperament may be confused and angered by the archetype and wish to seize it, exploit it, and even crush it — as has been done to many nuns and other young women.

I explored this theme in *Dark Eros* — the young maiden, Justine in Sade's fiction, who becomes the object of harsh and corrupting intentions on the part of those whose perspective is exactly opposite — teachers, bosses, husbands sometimes, and even rapists. Any spiritual searcher who has this spirit strong in her or his psyche might be careful lest it entice some leader to try to torment it and literally corrupt it. Such a person needs to be especially vigilant and strong.

The world doesn't appreciate the young maiden as a way of being. It accepts the boy with some reservations, especially the boyish futurists who populate the computer world and are successful in the stock market. With their boyish looks, high-pitched voices, and unlimited enthusiasm they play a significant role. But they may be awkward in the boardroom.

The maiden doesn't have much of a place. When I go to New York for encounters with the media, I meet many tough young women whose voices are deep and strong, sometimes artificially so, and whose manner is swift and businesslike. Professional women often take on this persona of capability, dressing formidably and speaking forcefully, an attitude that hides the maiden. But visit a spiritual community and the maiden is everywhere: extremely sensitive to the environment and health and purity of all kinds. In the boy spirit, people pursue their vision and ideals, but in the maiden spirit the world is a green garden to be handled with delicacy.

Some may judge the maiden fantasies as irrelevant and out of step, and perhaps the danger of spirituality from this angle has a tendency to create islands of peaceability and perfection cut off from the rest of the world. Yet the cultivation of these Edens can make a life and a community so appealing that the world notices them. Certainly Emily Dickinson brought a strong sense of the maiden to her Amherst homestead and to the unusual life she made for herself. Her words and her image continue to impress and challenge. They aren't as brittle as they may appear at first sight, and in that way she shows that the maiden can enjoy a certain kind of power and strength.

The poetry of Rilke contains some of this maiden quality. He speaks from a self-contained world that has an elaborate and deep interiority. As the culture moves farther away from the values of the soul in its art and academic life, Rilke appears more anachronistic and perhaps old school. But his delicate imagery and subtle perceptions take strength from their interiority that oddly makes them seem more grounded than the tense rational and political attitudes of many current writers.

Perhaps because I am so captivated by her images, I see a strong presence of Artemis in maiden spirituality. The idea of doing everything naturally, keeping the genders distinct if not separate, remaining aloof and protected from the roughness of culture's busy centers, even dancing with natural grace rather than with Aphroditic sensuousness — all these are signs of Artemis. It was her task to care for nine-year-old girls, and so it makes sense that there is an overlap between Artemis and the maiden.

There are many ways to live an archetype. One is to identify primarily and thoroughly with her and find in her ways a lifestyle and source of meaning. Another is to cultivate this spirit as one among many, getting as much as possible from her without making her the defining form. At their best, archetypes flow through like light passing through a shade and blend like watercolors on a rough patch of natural paper.

There are at least two ways not to live the archetype. One is to forget that she is a spirit, gossamer thin and mobile, and instead turn her into a literal caricature of herself. A person can become nothing more than a fragile maiden or live just the shell of this image so that it doesn't have much life or depth. Another way is to ignore or disparage this spirit altogether as irrelevant, weak, or even a sickness. In this latter case we have to take care lest the repressed archetype returns as a problem and a danger. I've seen this autonomous, crazy maiden in people who hallucinate her and are tormented by her.

Artists of the past painted hundreds of versions of the Annunciation in which they contemplated the image of the maiden, the one who sits privately in her innocence, reading and thinking, and then draws sharply away from the angel and his message. This delicate young woman has a major role to play in the course of human civilization. Are we modestly going to accept the invitation to new and mysterious life that comes unbidden at regular intervals, or are we going to trust only ourselves and heroically pursue our own plans and designs? The maiden of the Annunciation is every one of us waiting to see if we are going to live this life or avoid it.

The maiden is a moment of expectation and readiness, vulnerability itself waiting to be impregnated. When we seek some spirituality for ourselves, we may be called to this particular kind: a caretaking of our privacy and our delicate world so that it will be ready when the message comes to transform the whole. Maybe the message doesn't come to any one individual but to the many maidens cultivating their expectancy. This is a spirituality of promise, a vestal purity and readiness that is complete and meaningful in all its unfinished openness.

They conjured the spirits of demons and angels and implanted
them in likenesses through holy and divine rites . . . statues
ensouled and conscious, filled with spirit and doing great
things . . . statues that could make people ill and heal them.

Hermes Trismegistus, Asklepius

25. Venerating Images

AN IMAGE IS A POWERFUL THING. The non-Romantics among
us may prefer numbers and abstractions, but those who live
from the soul know the importance of images and know not to reduce
them to ideas and interpretations. Being a romantic in the age of rationalism and technology requires that you be eccentric, outside the circle,
a holy fool. We romantics bask in images and fight off those who would
squeeze all of life's meaning into a few facts and rules. Our religiousness is defined by our willingness to remain in the mistiness and the
mysticism of images, looking for a deeper spiritual intelligence.

It is impossible to imagine the religious traditions without their rich
horde of images: the great stories and characters, the personalities, the
temples and cathedrals and mosques, the plainchant and the hymns
and the ragas, the statues of Buddha and the saints, the robes and ceremonies, the holy objects and the processions, the oratories and kivas
and painted tepees. These images are not there to sharpen the intellect
but to absorb the person, heart and soul, into a special sacred vision
and a thoroughly holy way of life.

But a temple is not an art gallery. It is not a place to view pictures but to venerate them. If we could understand this difference, we might grasp the contrast between the spirit and the soul of religion: the spirit seeks enlightenment while the soul seeks connection. To be in the presence of a sacred image is not to be instructed, to know something one didn't know before, but simply to be the receiver of a transforming radiance. The effect on the devotee can hardly be seen, measured, or explained, and yet veneration is the quintessential religious act.

When we venerate an image, we acknowledge its inherent holiness. Several religious traditions teach that a holy statue or painting is not a mere picture of a holy figure but an evocation of the deity or spirit. In the statue we meet the saint or the goddess and are affected by it. In India special rites mark each stage in the making of a holy image, the last one calling on the spirit to take up residence in the object. In the passage from the Hermetic text *Asklepius,* a key passage in the revival of natural magic in Renaissance Europe, we see a similar approach: special rites call on the spirit to inhabit the image and work wonders from it.

In India the sight of the holy figure is called *darshan,* and in Christianity a similar attitude of honor to saints is known as *dulia.* These are technical terms for a special spiritual recognition that an image is a presence rather than a symbol. It is, moreover, a presence beyond the kind that humans can achieve. It is the presence of something not impersonal but preternaturally personal—not less personal but more. And so statues and paintings have been honored as healing and bountiful presences.

Today people are devoted to many things: television, work, money, sex, sports. Who is more a devotee than the follower of a local sports team? Modern forms of devotion are strong, but they're largely unconscious. The devotees don't realize that they are caught up in a religion of sorts when they set their schedules around a favorite television program or pay a large sum for a seat at the football stadium. The large part of religion takes place without the devotees' awareness.

The unconsciousness around secular forms of devotion goes hand in hand with the intellectualization of the spiritual life. Human beings are instinctively religious, and when they turn away from explicit forms of spirituality, they transfer their devotion to objects they don't perceive as being religious. The celebrity today is the saint of yesterday without the complication of holiness. The television of today is the altar of yesterday without the sacredness of genuine religion. In this context even the image has been secularized, and we think our task is to interpret and study and analyze it.

The religious traditions can return us to a proper idea of what devotion, sainthood, and sacred image are all about. They teach us veneration, which is the artful alternative to obsession. When we venerate an image, we allow it its greatness, something that can contain us, can take our small problems and give them greater context. As the Indian and Hermetic philosophies indicate, this larger contextualization of our "selves" within a greater image can be healing, and this kind of healing goes with holiness. The enlargement of the self into deep community and a soulful life is in itself healing.

I first discovered the importance of sacred images in my third year of high school. Father Gregory O'Brien, who had a most unpriestly sense of humor coupled with an extraordinary holiness and liturgical sensitivity, attacked our sickly sweet chapel and transformed it. He carted away the wedding-cake altars and mawkish statues and even ripped the many-layered plaster off the walls, leaving the bare red brick that had been hiding there for decades. Then he put up wrought-iron gates and plain altars of wood and statues of strong and austere virtue. This shift in visual aesthetics, along with the solid music he selected and the reverent liturgy he conducted, ruined me forever. No longer could I practice a skin-deep religion and confuse sweet illusions with tough spiritual realities.

I had always been attracted to images in church, but now I knew that images could have an intelligence as well as an emotion. For the first fifteen years of my life I was a sentimentalist. I remember pinning roses to a sheet behind an altar and at Christmas stringing garish blinking lights around a crèche. But Gregory O'Brien showed me that the spiritual life lies hidden behind such saccharinity. I learned the lesson that has inspired me ever since: if the surface of religious practice is too sweet, the internal parts offer little nourishment. But if the appearances are strong and provocative, the whole religious experience can reach into the marrow of the soul.

It makes all the difference if the images we use to express our spirituality address the serious concerns of our lives or conjure up a means of escape. Images continually feed the imagination. If they are shallow or mere ideological expressions, then our spirituality will be equally thin. We may be drawn toward images that merely comfort or sustain our illusions. Images in a church building or a spiritual magazine immediately alert the reader about the substance of the spirituality: is it too sweet, too lofty, too human and personalistic, or does it represent a serious and profound intelligence about the spirit?

Today many painters try to represent the new spirituality in an aesthetic that is a combination of romance, science fiction, and soft eroticism. In many cases this new genre is superficial, especially when compared to medieval Christian images and classic sculptures of India or Africa. It isn't the antiquity of the old images that impresses me but the austere depth of the vision they evoke. In contrast the new "spiritual" art conceives of spirit as something superhuman rather than of another order altogether. Ancient images take us to the sublime and the awesome, while contemporary spiritual images often push us only a short step beyond our circumstances, into a super-realism rather than into a world profoundly within and beyond.

Sometimes religious imagery goes in the opposite direction and aims at realism, defending against the absolutely spiritual. Many churches are filled with images of natural, literal, and realistic images of the spirits and saints. They betray the shallowness of the piety and disclose a lack of appreciation for the awesomeness and otherness of the holy. Here it is presented too close and too human, as though the imagination weren't able to penetrate these narrow limits.

Why is it that people of the past were able to capture the holy in their art? Look closely at the image of a saint on a medieval cathedral. You see the stylized beard or hair and the unnatural lines of a gown that reflect the Gothic or Romanesque evocation of a separate reality. Today we often find sacred art pulling the spiritual into human categories instead of the other way around. These images shrink our spirituality, whereas they have the power to expand the self into a soul.

JUNG MADE A REMARKABLE effort to restore religious and spiritual issues to psychology and to deepen our way of dealing with images. In his understanding a true symbol participates in the mystery to which it points. It is not merely one thing standing for another. Privately, as we see in his extraordinary autobiographical writings, he treated images with incomparable intelligence and piety. But his psychological theory has given rise to less subtle and increasingly modern methods of categorizing and interpreting. His devotion to the soul and to the image has split into the secularizing of his system and the canonization of his person.

In the 1970s in the journal *Spring*, James Hillman published a series of essays on images. He took issue with Jung's lingering reduction of a symbol to a particular meaning. Even when carefully defined, the word *symbol* encourages superficial deciphering and dictionary definitions. Hillman argued for giving as much attention to preserving the dense integrity of an image as for teasing out its implications and meanings.

In my own writing about myth, disease, and religion, I discovered that you can track an image a long way by studying its history, etymology, and its appearance in art, and you need not come up with a final interpretation. I found that by following an image closely I became educated by it in relation to the mystery it pointed to. Eventually I realized that the purpose of living with images is not to understand them but to be taught by them, not to reach a conclusion about them but to let them take you to a new place. My study of Narcissus, for instance, has led me to live in this myth continually, noticing it everywhere, almost daily seeing more of its subtlety. It has saturated my imagination. It has become me as I have become it.

I also found that once I began to pursue my fascination for an image —Acteon, Narcissus, Daphne, Godot, Marilyn Monroe—my work with it would never come to an end. In book after book, essay after essay, I found myself taking one more step into the few images that had captured me. The more I have thought and written about Artemis, for example, the less I know what her stories are all about—not from ignorance but from an appreciation of her complexity and subtlety—and the same goes for the other figures that keep popping up in my thoughts.

My friend, psychologist and writer Ronald Schenk, once took me to the Mark Rothko chapel in Houston, where we sat in the stillness of an artist's sanctuary, and I saw how modern paintings can be presented as objects of contemplation and not just criticism. Having been at the chapel, when I now visit the Tate Modern Museum in London, I sit in the Rothko room, surrounded by his awesome canvases, and in spite of the crowds, I can sense the temenos his genius provides, a chapel without walls in which I can still be infused with spirit.

In modern times we favor treating images as spectacles, objects on show. Or, at the lowest level, we often esteem them for their rarity or financial value, an indication that we have lost a sense of their inherent value. On the other side of this development, we crave images. We can't get enough of movies, magazines, and television stories, all of which tend to be so shallow that they increase the craving and offer little of what we need. Bad images are like junk food: they give the illusion of supplying what we need. We are addicted to them because in most cases we don't make them well or use them thoughtfully.

Venerate is a Venus word. The loss of the capacity to venerate images goes hand in hand with the loss of a Venusian sensitivity, which is an essential component of spirituality. Even Christianity, which has a morbid fear of all things explicitly associated with Venus, has allowed her beauty to play a central role. The great churches and liturgies and the wealth of art that Christianity has inspired over the ages honors Venus, although officially the church fails to understand her necessity.

By venerating images we participate sensually and emotionally as well as intellectually in the mysteries of faith. Entering them ritually and artistically, we know them profoundly, and they become a portion of who we are. For me, a Catholic, the Mass has been a powerful ritual all my life. It begins by inviting me to think of my failures. Then I hear the traditional stories that teach and, even more important, shape my imagination of life. Then in the holiest part of the rite I experience ritual union with divinity. When the conditions are right, this ritual, repeated over and over, allows me to live as much in the eternal as the temporal.

The deepening of my own spirituality has gone hand in hand with my increasing love of art. As I write, I am listening to a Mass by Arvo Pärt, and I feel strongly that I am present to two worlds—the task at hand and the deeply interior life of my soul. Pärt accomplishes in sound what I would like to achieve in my life: a fundamentally new interpretation of ancient sensibilities and aesthetics. If I could embody Christianity with the devotion and imagination with which he renews ancient music, I would have solved the problem of institution versus personal spirituality. I would be inventive with my spirituality without abandoning the tradition.

I have learned much about images from my life in music, my studies in psychology, and various theories of image. But this has all found body and immediacy through my wife, who is a serious painter. I see both her struggle and her effortless way with images. I see how closely they are tied to her beliefs and her way of life. I see her loyalty to her imagination and inspirations, and I see how her artwork is a form of spiritual practice, although she might not agree with me about that—and all of this confirms my idea that images are the most important element in anyone's spirituality.

I have several of her paintings in my writing studio. One close at hand is a colorful rendition of the reclining Buddha. The Buddha seems to be there in person, and I can't imagine parting with this image. On another wall a woman with long, dark, frizzy hair stands against a light-blue and green split background, her pubic hair and face more articulated than any other part of her body. For several years now she has been there in front of me as I have written page after page. She is a participant here. If there is such a thing as an anima image or a muse, she is one.

As we notice the presence of the art images around us, we may come to see everything as an image. Every room has a dream quality if you only look for it. Every conversation is carried on the wave of a myth, a deep story or set of images that may not be at all conscious to the people involved and yet defines precisely what they are doing. Once we enter that world of imagination with a degree of awareness, then the statues and the paintings take on a new reality. They are no longer symbols to an interpreting mind, but images that have a presence not much different from our own.

The capacity to be in the presence of an image is a requirement for a religious life, because images are mediators between the divine and the human. Hillman says that words are angels, and the same could be said of all images. Angels mediate between this world of time and the other of eternity, and that is precisely the role of images. They relocate the focus of our thoughts and attention away from practicality and ego and into the realm of the timeless and the deep soul.

There is a kind of spirituality that overflows with images. Go into an Italian, Spanish, or Mexican church, and you are surrounded with images that have an extraordinary vitality about them even if they aren't all perfect and noble. But there is another fantasy of spirituality that is just the opposite: it prefers stark simplicity, abstraction, the well-defined word. There is beauty and necessity in the austere approach, but I think the deep soul is represented most appropriately in a cornucopia of images. All that variety and color is like rich earth that nurtures with its richness; it gives body and ground to the spiritual life.

An old Greek story tells how Aphrodite, Venus's Greek counterpart, stirs a statue to life by placing a butterfly on it. The Venusian spirit continues to bring images to life, and where that spirit is present, there are no dead symbols or lifeless rituals. Wherever we venerate, we are evoking this life-enhancing spirit of Venus. We are reconnecting the body to the spirit through the medium of the soul, an ancient formula offered to anyone seeking a spirituality that has blood and vitality.

The gods are nameless and imageless
yet looking in a great full lime-tree of summer
I suddenly saw deep into the eyes of gods:
it is enough.

D. H. Lawrence, *The Body of God*

26. *Nature Spirituality*

IN ANCIENT TIMES VENUS was the patroness of sexuality, beauty, and gardens. She is a goddess of both the soft, comfortable, civilized life and the wilds and beauties of nature. Those who worshiped her could see, through her image, the awesome spirituality in ordinary things of beauty and in nature. But lately we have been increasingly cut off from nature and therefore have felt the diminishment of our spirituality.

When I wish to understand how nature can be a source of spirituality, I have only to turn to my neighbors, the New England writers, who in the last century worked out their own vision of a natural religion. Emerson says in *Nature,* "It seems as if the day was not wholly profane in which we have given heed to some natural object."[1] We are part of nature, and yet nature far transcends us and so opens up a way toward an intimate kind of transcendence.

I know the arguments that nature means different things to different people at different times and that cities are as much a revelation of the spirit as natural places are, and yet still I would urge the importance of natural places and objects in the spiritual life. It is easy to romanticize and sentimentalize nature. We may overlook the fact that it is as fearsome as it is inspiring. But even in its frightening power and its threat to human life, it is a source of spiritual realization. As Emerson says, we have only to give attention to some aspect of nature to make a day holy.

Thoreau's contribution to the idea was to focus on the specific natural environment in which we live and move. Know your seasons, your animals, your birds, your trees, and you know not only a great deal about yourself but also the particular path to transcendence available in the place where you live. And we all live in particular places. There can be no abstract spirituality. The ultimate paradox taught by many religions is that the absolutely sublime is to be found in the absolutely ordinary. The universality so loved by the spirit can be discovered only in each locality.

Emily Dickinson adds the idea that we can have a personal relationship of friendliness to nature. She assures her mentor Higginson that she is not too solitary; she has her hills for her friends. At the same time she recognizes the gulf between nature and ourselves — nature's transcendence:

> But God be with the Clown —
> Who ponders this tremendous scene —
> This whole Experiment of Green —
> As if it were his own!
>
> "Entering the Kingdom"

The roots of spirituality depend on just this sentiment, this realization that nature far transcends the human capacity to exploit, control, and study. Dickinson has what could truly be called a devotion to nature, and from it, from the particular natural world of her garden and the hills and fields around her home, she found her meaning and filled out her religion.

A contemporary New England poet who is also well known for her reflective life with nature, Mary Oliver, writes:

The dream of my life
Is to lie down by a slow river
And stare at the light in the trees —
To learn something by being nothing
A little while but the rich
Lens of attention.

Attending to nature is a spiritual exercise whether or not it goes by that name. It is a particular kind of contemplation. Not empty, except that the lens is still. Not full, because there is no agenda. It could be part of a spiritual practice, and indeed in some instances it is the major part. But this ritual asks for an attitude not congenial in a world given to action. Being a lens is far different from looking through one. How many awards for research have been given to the lens through which the expert made her discovery? To be a lens is to live in a certain way, to be a means rather than a subject, and transparent rather than stuffed with a self.

No one has appreciated the deep values of nature more than Thoreau. Here, from *A Week on the Concord and Merrimack Rivers,* is one sample among hundreds of his formulations of this mystery:

The winter is lurking within my moods,
And the rustling of the withered leaf
Is the constant music of my grief. [2]

Thoreau here echoes ancient ideas connecting the human being to the natural environment. Boethius, author of the *Consolation of Philosophy,* said that the seasons of the year are the music of the soul, and those seasons mark the rhythm of a human life as much as the timing of the sun and stars. Taking the whole of life into us is a step on the mystical way; it helps give to the ego the background and context it requires so as not to be the dominant thing in a personality or a life.

Reflecting on the connection between nature and spirit, I can't help but quote one poet after another. Nature translates directly into poetry. The connection between the poet and the natural world is often, though not always, a close one, and that tie may instruct us in the practice of spirituality. We can see the poetry of our lives when we attend to nature, when we become more a lens than a tool, and the perception of ourselves as poems is a step in the direction of the spirit.

The Greeks and others who practiced nature religion knew that each element in nature has a different aspect. It is one thing to enjoy a colorful sunrise, quite another to sit through a powerful storm. The Greeks saw Pan in nature's constant vitality and Artemis in nature's resistance to the human presence. They felt the dismembering god Dionysus in a grape and the sexual Aphrodite in the beautiful shimmering sea.

This power of nature to show us the particular qualities of the gods and goddesses contributes something essential to the life of religion. Nature not only reveals that God is present in the world in which we live, but it also teaches us the different kinds of spirituality that make up a devout life. Nature then is not a commodity but a source of self-reflection and contemplation. It becomes part of the community in which we live, giving us its wisdom through its own ways of expression. We need to protect it not out of sheer duty but because our spiritual existence depends on it.

The church in which I was brought up generally ignored all these issues: it did not encourage a life with nature as a way of getting closer to God; it did not teach the different ways in which spirituality might be cultivated according to the different aspects of nature; and it came late, when at all, to the heightened moral consciousness about protecting the natural world. Yet it did give us Saint Francis, a figure who has often been sentimentalized but who offers a good model for nature spirituality. And it gave us Teilhard de Chardin, a visionary criticized by the Vatican who found an astonishing spiritual vision through natural science. But as a society influenced by the same philosophy that has given Christianity its moral shape, we have not yet reconciled nature and spirit. We still think of these two aspects as separate and in many ways antagonistic. As long as that battle rages, we will not enjoy the fullness of the spiritual life.

Early on, Christianity defined itself against paganism and was especially reticent to espouse sexual freedom and acknowledge nature's sanctity. Worry about sex and neglect of nature, two aspects of the same anxiety, have weakened this religion, indeed crippled it. Anyone can reach such a high level of spirit that sex and the natural world may appear to be enemies, but for a religious tradition, otherwise so full of wisdom and beauty, to stumble on this basic issue is a scandal. This central anxiety, which infects the whole of the moral program of the religion, is still evident and still causes confusion and suffering among those looking for spirituality on the model of Christ.

In therapy people sometimes told me how angry they were with their marriage partners. I was interested to see that in their dreams they took out their aggression on animals and plants. In some cases I interpreted this inner nature as the person's human nature—nature understood here as the wilderness of the soul, the animals of the imagination, and the plant life of the person's interior world. Somehow this wilderness was a threat and a challenge that needed to be beaten down so that the person felt morally fit. But this pattern goes out into the world as well. It is readily externalized and lived out in relation to actual animals and natural places. Behind our mistreatment of nature lies yet another kind of spiritual anger rooted in the thought that nature is a threat to the deepest aspects of the self, and indeed almost immoral.

Our dealings with nature are more complicated than they appear to be. They are as much about ourselves as about our world. Therefore the protection of nature requires a caring attitude toward our own inner wilderness, our passions and urges and instincts. The outer division between nature and culture is reflected in an inner division between natural desire and ego anxiety. I think desire is the ultimate issue: How can we respond positively to our deepest desires and yet remain virtuous?

I myself am only slowly coming to the realization of how the renewal of spirit is dependent on a radical reconsideration of nature. How we deal with nature is tied in with how we deal with the untamed soul and its passions. That is why sexuality and nature are so closely connected and why they pose a problem for any religious attitude that seeks domination over passion. Whatever the facts are, we tend to imagine sex as a biological urge, a raw intrusion of nature that interferes with our controlled quest for spirituality. What we may finally have to achieve is a more complex, individual, and livable definition of moral virtue. Ideology has invaded our sense of morality, and so among many spiritual people you find moralism instead of ethical sensitivity, and by a short circuitous route that moralism turns against nature.

At first sight it is confusing to hear of conservative church groups arguing strongly against environmentalism. One might think that people so outspoken about God's act of creation, especially in the face of science, would be motivated to protect that creation. But I suspect that the worry over the unleashing of human passion is stronger than any conviction about the spirituality implicit in the natural world. Creation is usually a spiritual abstraction, a pure idea that can be discussed for a lifetime without any reference to the natural world. This abstraction is far less demanding than the sexual passions and harmonizes easily with a purely spiritual religion, a spirituality lacking soul.

The world out there, the clouds and rivers, the land and the animals, is highly unpredictable. It can feed and give pleasure, but it can also kill violently. Those who imagine God as a father protector only may find it difficult to imagine that nature could be a revelation of God and a source of spirituality. Indeed, they might go so far as to see it as evil, as something to conquer once and for all, just like the human passions.

But we have come to a point in the development of our social morality when it is time finally to heal this wound in human life—to find peace with our inner wilderness and discover our deep kinship with the natural order. A daytime walk in the woods or an evening stroll by the sea could provide us with the secret of our deepest identity if we realize that what we are looking at is somehow mysteriously us. If we look further, we might even see traces of a divine presence. Nature is not the only source of transcendence, but it is indispensable.

Nature requires from us a natural religion, which may or may not coexist with an institution. Hidden among all the roadways and billboards and buildings is a holiness native to the material world, and hidden among all our beliefs and morals and anxieties is a natural religious impulse. The two desperately require each other.

Notes

1. Emerson, "Nature," in *The Portable Emerson,* ed. Carl Bode and Malcolm Cowley (New York: Viking Press, 1981), pp. 283–84.
2. Henry David Thoreau, *A Week on the Concord and Merrimack Rivers* (New York: The Library of America, 1985), p. 307.

Our attitude toward [dreams] may be modeled upon Hades,
receiving, hospitable, yet relentlessly deepening, attuned
to the nocturne, dusky, and with a fearful cold intelligence that
gives permanent shelter in his house to the incurable conditions
of human being.

James Hillman, *The Dream and the Underworld*

27. *Dream Practice*

To GROUND OUR SPIRITUALITY we are in search of anima, the presence of the soul and its vivifying romanticism. We are looking for
ways to blend soul and spirit into a vision and way of life that are as
deep-seated as they are transcendent. If these two are not connected,
spirituality may well be incomplete and extreme. The soul then can't
give ballast to a spirit that tends naturally to soar and drift. One of the
most direct ways to glimpse the anima is through dreams, and, indeed,
dream work can have a central place in spiritual practice.

An example of the mysterious role that dreams can play in the search
for meaning is from my experience as a teacher. In the mid 1970s I was
a professor of religion at a large university where the students were
often more interested in preparing themselves to make a high salary
than to have an education. A few stood out as exceptions, among them
a young man who took several of my courses, including a class on feminine figures in myth. He was the only man in a class of thirty. One day
he came to me for advice about his future. He was trying to decide
whether to go into business or, like his father, become a golfer.

I asked him to bring me a dream. He told me a dream that I

recounted, without mentioning his name, in *Care of the Soul*. He was flying in a small aircraft that he couldn't control. It kept swooping up and down. He discovered that when he looked into a large rear-view mirror attached to the side, the plane would level off for a while. He was frightened but was able to control his flight.

The young man, whom I admired a great deal for his charm, his intelligence, and his big heart, went on to become a famous golfer. Now I think it's appropriate to mention his name, Payne Stewart. Whenever I saw his picture in the newspapers or on television I felt proud of this fine man who could reflect on his progress — the mirror in his dream — and therefore was a model athlete. But in the prime of his life he died in an airplane that for hours was out of control, weaving up and down, the newspaper accounts said, and finally crashed.

I don't remember many sessions that took place during twenty years of practicing therapy when I didn't focus on a dream. At first I tried to harness the dream for the arduous work of cure, but there came a point when therapy lost some of its heroics, and I let the dreams more calmly color and guide the work. This I now believe was a turn toward the spiritual. I stopped being so psychological and began to practice more as a representative of spirit, more a guide than an intepreter. I let the dreams infuse my work with particular mysteries, never to be fully sorted out. The effect was to shift radically from the task of figuring out a life to becoming a person of depth, someone who could track the progress of his life without correcting it or explaining it.

Now that I'm no longer a full-time therapist, I don't spend my waking hours with dreams. In our family we occasionally tell our dreams at breakfast, and if any of us has a reaction, we mention it. Later in the day or week the dream might come up again, and there might be a small discussion. It isn't unusual to talk about dreams from long ago, especially when events bring them to mind. We treat them as enduring presences or signs rather than as puzzles to solve.

I no longer deal with dreams professionally. I've given up all the theories that I studied over the years — Fritz Perls, Freud, and Jung. I'm still influenced by James Hillman's extraordinary book *The Dream and the Underworld,* in which he recommends letting a dream take us down into the unknown rather than try to decipher and explain it. The move away from theory has helped me appreciate the mystery of dreams more and see them as part of the spiritual life rather than an aspect of psychology. Payne Stewart's dream doesn't prove any theory or satisfy the desire to understand. It strengthens the mystery and increases wonder about the connection between life and dream. Nowadays I sense my own life more as a mystery, as the wall between dream and experience grows thinner every day.

The role of dream work in spiritual practice is not to get clues to the meaning of the personality but to take another step into the misty world of ritual, mythology, theology, and mysticism. I feel strongly that we are all called to be mystics in our own way, and attending to our dreams without intellectual heroics can enhance the development of a mystical self. While we are attending to dreams, the focus shifts and the very sense of self broadens and deepens. The important thing is not what you do to a dream but what the dream does to you.

I learned long ago that anytime I mention dreams, people prick up their ears and want to talk about them. Dreams have a magic about them, and whatever our theories, we continue to be curious about them. But without guidance and education in the interior life, people are quick to interpret dreams, analyze each other, and even give advice based on them. In the dream groups I led, I usually asked people to treat the dream as an image and to forego the thrill of telling each other what is wrong with them. In some instances I asked people to write their dreams on a sheet of paper without signing them. Then I would distribute the pages, and we would treat the dreams as entities in their own right, not the private possession of the dreamer. This helped take some of the psychology out of the dream work.

During this shift in focus I noticed that in therapy my clients and I became more like equals facing a common challenge. I allowed the dream under discussion to color my mood and thoughts and even to take the lead. We might return to a powerful dream again and again over many weeks. Some people decided to make paintings or poetry of their dreams and present them that way. They became so familiar with dreams that they didn't want to spend a therapeutic hour without one.

Religion and spiritual practice teach us the importance of getting our interior images out into the world in some way. When Black Elk, the Sioux mystic, had his great visions, he painted the images on his tepee and clothing. He literally wore his dreams on his shirt. Many powerful works of art have come directly from dreams, such as Igor Stravinsky's *Rite of Spring*. This kind of dreaming the dream onward increases the mystical reality in which we live our everyday lives, and I assume that being so connected with the deep currents of the soul, we stand a chance of not acting out so often or feeling the delirium of not knowing what is happening to us on the inside—a condition endemic to modern society.

Once I moved away from excessive interpretation—I never fully gave up the effort to read a dream, I merely tried to do it as cautiously and respectfully as I could—other traditional ways of dealing with dreams came into play. I took them as divination, prognostication, a medium for connecting with the dead, and a foundation for spiritual practice. In other words, I abandoned the psychological agenda and returned to my first calling—priesthood. To deal seriously with dreams, while abandoning the modern identity of researcher or analyst, may require adopting the persona of seer. I think it is possible to drift away from modernism enough to adopt this unconventional role without loss of intelligence.

Dreams play a major role in the Bible where they are usually seen as a means God uses to speak to men and women. When Abraham told King Abimalech that Sarah was his sister and didn't mention that she was his wife, God appeared in the king's dream to warn him not to wed

Sarah because she was already married [Genesis 20.3]. God appears in a dream to Jacob and tells him to leave the land he is in and go home [Genesis 31.10]. Joseph interprets several dreams but repeatedly says, "Do not interpretations belong to God?" [Genesis 40.8]. God appears to Gideon and Solomon in dreams [Judges 7.13; I Kings 3.5]. Daniel interprets the king's dream after being shown the dream and its meaning in a vision from God [Daniel 2.26], and in the New Testament Joseph receives divine instruction in a dream [Matthew 2.19]. Each of these instances shows us how a dream connects heaven and earth and heals the rift we usually feel between our transcendent lives and the depth of our emotions and life progress.

Dreams play a significant role in other religions as well. A person may discover his or her calling to be a shaman in a dream of dismemberment and renewal. In Greece and elsewhere dreams were part of incubation rites of healing as in the temples of Asklepios. It's well known that Native American young people would go into the wilderness in quest of visions and dreams that would initiate them into adulthood. All of these uses of dreams could be followed today.

In none of these instances is the dream explained and then applied. It is taken as a real presence, as an icon to be heeded in the context of life and death. The idea is not to take the dream literally and do what it says. We always have to be poets to every aspect of our lives and appreciate forms like narrative, parable, lyric, and myth, all of which appear in ordinary dreams. As part of our personal religion, we could welcome the dream into serious discussion and in that simple way form strong ties between ordinary experience and timeless mystery.

In a magazine interview Jung once said, "All dreams reveal spiritual experience, provided one does not apply one's own point of view to the interpretation of them."[1] I can use all the knowledge I have about images, myths, symbols, and the arts to read a dream onward, staying as close to the original imagery as possible, while at the same time feeling its impact. The difference between conquering a dream with a con-

vincing and definitive interpretation and reading its imagery for insight
or epiphany is not always easy to spell out, but it is crucial. The question is: Are we going to be hunters carrying our big guns of analysis? Or
are we ecologists getting to know the flora and fauna of this mysterious
territory?

The night before I was to appear on a national television news program I had the following dream:

> I am standing at the top of our steep driveway. A red pick-up truck
> comes up the hill and almost reaches the top when it begins to slide
> back. It picks up great speed as it is going backwards down the hill.
> At the bottom it hits a bump and goes sailing into the air. The driver
> is a woman who was a student of mine many years ago. I expect the
> truck to flip over backwards dangerously, but instead it lands hard
> right side up. Silence. Another woman rushes over to the truck, looks
> inside, and begins to wail. I'm still at the top of the hill, frozen, afraid
> that the driver has been badly injured or killed.

The theme of this dream is familiar to me. I am in a high place in the
terrain and the truck makes a harsh descent. As I have already con-
fessed, I am a flyer and a person familiar with lofty attitudes and projects. I'm also afraid of heights. In this dream, I'm afraid when I see the
truck's descent. It looks like death. But apparently everything is all right.
No one gets hurt, no one dies. In life, the driver was an artist I once
knew who was not too confident of herself. Reading the dream with reference to Jung and Hillman, I first thought of the woman as an anima
figure, while I was in the position of the spirit, high on the hill.

In the television studio I had an hour to wait alone in the green
room. Staff kept walking in offering me food and seemed puzzled to see
me sitting there doing nothing. I was thinking hard about my dream. I
imagined how it would feel to be on camera with my anima more present and visible. During the interview, which was conducted by a sensitive and intellectually acute woman, I did feel the presence of the

anima, but not with the intensity I had hoped for. Still, when the program was over and I had gone home, many people commented that the interview had had a special poignancy.

This dream makes me think of my own task in getting spirit and soul together. At the time I could apply it to my immediate situation, and now I can generalize about it. Now I'd like to think more about the specific person who was driving the truck and how her spirit plays a role in my life. Yet the dream captures a central theme of this book: the necessity to deepen our spiritual outlook and restore some of the humanity and feeling that only the lower soul can provide. It gives me emotionally vivid imagery of descent, regression, danger, and survival.

Attending to dreams over many years, a person can gradually live more in imagination than in fact and in that way move closer to his personal mystery. A person steeped in dreams goes to an art gallery or to the theater and recognizes the atmosphere, the setting, and the characters. He has been there in dream. The same person could go to a temple or church and feel at home, because a great portion of religious experience is of the same nature as dreams. Dreams teach us how to live in that deeper place where religion does its work, and in that way they prepare us for that tenuous fall toward bliss that is posted with images. But if we are not familiar with the language, we may not find our way.

Note

1.   C. G. Jung Speaking, p. 71.

The person who is his own master knocks
in vain at the doors of Poetry.

Emerson, *Journals*

28. *The Sacred Irrational*

T HE MONASTERY WHERE I lived for a number of years had a brilliant,
warm, and funny professor of dogmatic theology, who taught his
courses in Latin, which he spat out at a ferocious speed. He would stay
up far into the night writing up his notes, in Latin, and then, he told us,
have a breakfast of hot peppers, sausages, and eggs. He would come
into the class full of energy, belching his lessons, and present the dry
theology with such wit and humor that we would laugh our way through
hours of classical distinctions and propositions. I came away with an impression of theology as fascinating, but not nearly as rational as it looks.

Indeed, religion in general is the most intelligent and least rational
way of making sense of life. I was often confused when, as a student, I
read Erasmus, Thomas à Kempis, or some other spiritual writer speaking out against the intellect and "in praise of folly." Why this anti-
intellectualism? I wondered. But now I understand the complaint differently. They were not against rationality, but rationalism. They didn't
trust the pure intellect to find its way to divinity. They were against an
excess of mind.

I, too, am concerned that we are losing touch with the soul of religion and spiritual depth by emphasizing understanding and consciousness. I have made it my life's work to write about the sacred mysteries in a way that I hope is intelligent but not excessively intellectual. Freud said that the mind can be a defense, and only late in life have I come to see the value of that observation. People are often impressed by intellectualism, but genuine insight that we can live by is something else altogether.

Religion is a mystery, which can be appreciated by the senses and the intuition as well as the mind. Pianists know that the fingers have their own intelligence, and spiritual teachers recognize the intelligence in an image, a ritual, or a sacred story. These sacred forms of expression can take us out of the stream of reasoning and measuring that occupies the secular mind. They allow a special kind of knowing that resists rational formulation but offers depth of perspective.

About an hour's ride outside Dublin, in a region full of ancient sacred sites, you come to a famous neolithic center of ceremony and burial at Newgrange. This awe-inspiring place offers a powerful example for all that is indirect, cyclic, and mysterious in the spiritual life. At the entrance to the chamber lies a huge stone carved with spirals spinning in several directions. These spiral images have been interpreted in many ways, but I think they portray the nature of religious knowing. It is not a straight line of reasoning leading to a clear answer, but rather a spiral and a labyrinth taking you deep within, where you learn important lessons about human existence through the atmosphere, the shapes and textures, and the symbols.

When we want to signal that a person is not quite right in the head, we make a little circling motion with our finger next to the brain. This is how I read the Irish spirals and knots, images for an intelligence that is deeper and more mysterious than what can be found through research and analysis. To get to the core of religion we may have to set aside secular methods and learn how to work with and trust the less direct routes of traditional forms such as ritual, story, and contemplation.

The stories of Jesus usually take the form of parable and paradox. Zen teaching tales leave you hanging or surprised. Sufi stories circle back on themselves or are full of subtle insinuations that only a master could sort out. Rituals, too, are full of hidden nuances, like the mysterious design of Newgrange that allows the sun to enter the chamber only on the winter solstice, when it lights up a special altar stone. What kind of technology is this, and what are we supposed to learn from it? Why do we have to get tied up in knots in order to see through earth to heaven?

The modern attempt to understand the world in which we live occupies the mind, not the whole of the person, and keeps us separate from the world we're studying. We come to it as though from outside, making it an "it" rather than an "us." But religious ways of knowing engage us completely. They draw us in and help us see with a different eye. They lead us to be thankful and appreciative rather than just informed. They inspire wonder and take the ego out of our curiosity. Most of all, they teach that the mysteries outside of us are identical with the mystery of who we are.

One spring day, with my family and several friends, I crawled through the narrow passageway at Newgrange and felt myself in a different dimension. For a few moments I left the ordinary world and felt safe and comforted in the womblike inner chamber. Some people complain that the place has been desecrated as a tourist haven, but I felt the magic. I can only imagine what it was like thousands of years ago to enter that holy place in the midst of ritual and within a worldview far more intimate with nature than ours.

Plato taught that there are four ways of escaping the restrictions of rationality for a more intense way of knowing, four useful kinds of *mania*. Sometimes this word is translated as "frenzy," but I think it would be better to consider it more along the lines of artistic inspiration with a touch of madness, a state of mind in which the person is open to creative influence. The four irrational channels mentioned by Plato are those of the seer, the lover, the artist, and the mystic. They are all similar in the way they work, and so to understand the religious impulse we might also study the mentality of the artist, the psychic, and the person in love.

To read signs the clairvoyant has to achieve a considerable distance from ordinary approaches to knowledge. The lover has to allow himself to be taken over by his passion. The artist needs to find a deep source of images. And the spiritual person can find what he's looking for only in a special susceptible state. The low, tight passageway at Newgrange takes the visitor to a place of special learning, a haunting, cramped schoolroom of the soul.

I was taught quite differently. I studied philosophy as the base for theology, spending years trying to make logical sense of impenetrable mysteries. Fortunately, the monastic life also emphasized meditation and liturgy, which offset the tendency to explain. But in recent decades I have seen my church favor clarity over mystery, shifting from the sacred language of Latin to flat English prose, changing from the lofty chants and complex polyphony to folk songs and even popular music — all in the name of relevance. At the same time, fortunately, priests have learned to appreciate the importance of performing ritual with care and have become sensitive to gesture and other aspects of liturgical performance.

An artist may have to live an alternative lifestyle to be open to inspiration. Similarly, a person interested in spiritual development may have to dress differently, establish a special rhythm to the day, live in a place set apart and decorated differently, or go to a church or temple with an atmosphere so different from the usual that it invites spiritual awareness. It takes a peculiar frame of mind to perceive the unusual truths of religion.

The modern world is quickly losing its special retreats where a person can shut out time and attend to spirit and soul. Nature is disappearing or being shut away by commerce and private ownership. Ministers and priests are locking the churches or selling them to businesses. Two of the monasteries I lived in during my youth are now conference centers. In the center of Dublin there is a beautiful old church that is now a tourist information center. Whenever I see this splendid building, I feel a mild shock. I'm happy to see there's a way to preserve the building, but the contradiction between the architecture and the business carried out there says something ominous about changes in culture.

The contemporary idea of intelligence follows the general tone of the times: we trust in the mind and in facts, and so we imagine education to be a mental process. Millions of college students are learning how to do research studies, using numbers and charts. Medicine prides itself on being "evidence based." Much of professional psychology is carried out in a laboratory. All of this represents a materialistic approach to knowledge, which creeps over into the arts and religion. Soon we will have lost the Platonic ways of knowing altogether, and with that loss the soul will be dangerously impoverished.

The spiritual life cannot be reduced to numbers and research studies. It requires methods of learning that are not only foreign to the secular sciences but often exactly opposite. Some are tempted to give spirituality respectability in the secular environment by applying the methods of business and science, but the loss of deep, non-rational knowing in that approach ultimately defeats the religious purpose altogether. What is needed is a new appreciation of the nonrational without sentimentalizing eccentricity or a magical view of life.

At the personal level, giving a place to the Platonic madness of religion might mean strengthening intuition and trusting other less rational forms of knowing. In my family we read signs in the world for indications of what to do next or where to go. Sometimes we follow our bare intuitions and see where they lead, not ignorantly but cautiously and interpretively. Like many people, we also read ordinary events as signs —a missed plane, a silly mistake, a wrong turn.

I consult the *I Ching* sometimes to steer my thinking in new directions, and at crucial times I read tarot cards for a similar shift in focus. I pray and meditate and listen to special music. I nurture my eccentricity and refuse to buy into current notions of what is prudent. I trust my intuitions and those of my family and close friends. Such faith is a form of Platonic madness—it can't be proved, but it offers confidence and emotional security.

I don't want to swing toward the nonrational in reaction to the intellectualism of the day. I'd rather explore the many traditional ways of nurturing the imagination—the tarot cards, and so on—while taking full advantage of science and technology. I don't want my intuition to eclipse other kinds of intelligence, but to complement them. In matters of meaning and values, though, I put more faith in the nonrational.

Nonrational is not the same as irrational, and everyone knows how susceptible to folly spirituality and religion can be. It takes emotional grounding and a sure intelligence to steer a course between silly experiments and excessive prudence. You can't get it perfect every time, but you can certainly be intelligent and inspired simultaneously. I have found it useful to study religions closely and to become acquainted with ancient traditions of magic. I've discovered a wisdom and common sense in these largely neglected sources, and they give me guidance.

Personally I am wary of mass enthusiasms, and I want to choose my own nonrationalities, ways of adapting the Platonic forms of knowing that appeal to me and suit me. People tell me I must visit the temples of Greece. After all, I have studied this religion and often write about the gods and goddesses. Yet I don't feel a need to go there. I'm sure it would be enriching, but that's a different thing. People want me to walk the labyrinth, visit a zendo, do the enneagram, find myself on the Meyers-Briggs test of personality, do a particular kind of yoga. I'm sure these are all excellent resources, but it's important to me that I find my own way into religion, trusting my intuitions and following my own angel. When I consult my muse, I find that I'm a spiritual minimalist. I don't need much beyond my library, my family, and my home.

I know how fascinating the spirit can be and how it can easily make a person crazed. Jung warned against this danger many times and suggested that a person caught by the spirit look for grounding in the traditions, in a daily practice, and in the ordinary life of family and home. He said that not only do leaders and teachers become inflated by their proximity to spirit, but their disciples, too, fall victim. As useful as Jung's suggestions are, I think a more direct approach is necessary as well: doing everything possible to be spiritually intelligent as well as spiritually enthusiastic. Knowing that spirit can be dangerous is a start, and then following through with a watchful, even somewhat skeptical assessment of spiritual resources might keep us sane.

People caught in the extremes of spirituality don't want to hear that it can be the source of evil. It is of the nature of spirit not to be self-reflective. It tends toward action and literalism. It takes its own imagination of reality as plain fact and angrily defends those facts. And so spirituality often has two layers of defensiveness—a belligerent attack on those who don't agree, backed up by a refusal to think about that belligerence. People seized by the archetype of spirit may be thrilled to be possessed and free of self-deliberation.

The more absorbed a person becomes in a spiritual enthusiasm, the more blind he may be to the damage being done to him and those around him. Blindness is an apt image, because the light and energy of spirit can obliterate the potential danger. I've rarely heard a spiritual person, leader or follower, say, "I must be careful because I could be wrong or overly excited by what I've learned and discovered." Usually, quite the opposite, the person seized by spirit can't restrain his enthusiasm and his desire to convert others to his point of view.

If I sound ambivalent in this book about my Catholicism, it is because I have been both blessed and wounded by it. I don't know if it's possible to escape the wounds of any spiritual method or community, but I do know that it's important not to be naïve about spirituality and inflict pain and suffer domination in the name of some exalted belief.

This is where soul and spirit join forces for the good: soul offers a degree of self-possession, while spirit keeps us interested and energetic.

I find C. G. Jung's ideas on the anima useful in this regard. Anima is the face of the soul, he says, its presence and ambience. Anima shows herself in moods and a certain inward kind of reflection. It's also evident in the intimacy and interiority of relationships. Spiritual practice is incomplete if it doesn't attend to these anima elements, even though they may offend the wish for rationality. But I know from much personal experience that spiritual leaders often try to minimize anima values. I was kept from my family for years due to this mistaken notion. I've taught many young people who have told me stories of their spiritual leaders taking them away from home and family, if only for a few weeks, to indoctrinate them. Being enveloped in a family is one way to nurture the anima.

Another way, of course, is through intimate or sexual relationships, and spiritual leaders often want to have control over this aspect as well. The arranged marriage, sexual restrictions, warnings against intimacy —these all work against the anima. In Ireland I heard several stories of husbands and wives, one Protestant and the other Catholic, trying to preserve their love against the negative attitudes of family and spiritual leaders. The ideal of the pure race and religion is yet another way of defending against the anima, which, after all, is the soul, the archetype of life.

Spirit needs soul just as soul needs spirit. The images, sounds, and gestures of traditional religious ritual are essential to the learning and initiating that is part of spiritual learning. They are full of anima qualities and give spirit its body and soul. Belief is not only a matter of intellectual understanding but also of memory, sensation, art, and atmosphere. Belief has a soul as well as spirit, and addressing the soul is as important to religious knowledge as any attempt at clarity and understanding.

In all things we need to get soul and spirit together, so that our ordinary human lives will be inspired and instructed by the spirit, and our spiritual lives will enjoy the fullness of our humanity. My impression is that the spiritual life tends toward an excess of spirit and a minimum of soul. I think the proportions might be better reversed. Religion could be mainly a matter of soul, but given vision and excitement through a measure of spirit. The challenge is to find heaven while remaining beings of earth.

VII

A Holy Life

Returning to a romantic view of spirit restores soul to belief and practice. It adds the intelligence of the heart to what can become an abstract and ethereal spirituality. Ignoring the anima makes spiritual devotion too sweet because then the heart is the repressed element, returning in an exaggerated and clumsy way. When the soul elements are neglected, they return to plague the spiritual life as inane pieties and unwholesome attachments. But when the soul is represented well, spirituality recovers its depth and its ties to ordinary life. It loses its wounding edge and becomes humane and tolerant.

The result is an ongoing way of life that is deep, intelligent, and compassionate. I don't call it a healthy life because a person need not be physically or emotionally healthy to have spiritual depth. I'd like to call it a holy life, by which I don't mean pious or overly religious. Holy means not motivated by any anxiety about self, a style that is open, relaxed, and both grounded and transcendent. A holy person is one who has broken through all anxiety about the ego and is fulfilled in the abundance of vitality that streams through.

I'm aware that holiness is not in vogue. Parents never say that they wish their children would become holy people. But societies less secular than ours have honored holiness and understood its importance. They have recognized the essential need for a life of radical compassion and spiritual sophistication.

Holiness may appear foolish in the eyes of the world, but I imagine it as a postmodern version of health and intelligence. Ultimately we may need another word for it because of sentimental notions that might accrue to it now. But I foresee a new flowering of spiritual vision grounded in a sense of mystery and radical sense of community, which together might explode our current puny notions of self, breaking finally into intelligent and legitimate holiness.

The place where my body will be laid is
the center of the earth and from there God
will come to redeem all our race.

Book of Adam

29. *In Every Sacrifice, God Is Born*

I N MANY RELIGIONS SACRIFICE is the most effective way of invoking the divine. In early societies it was symbolized in the killing of
an animal or the pouring out of a precious liquid. Today we might feel
the sting of sacrifice in personal decision-making or strokes of fate. In
all these cases sacrifice is an emptying out of personal will so that the
spirit can have a greater presence. In everyday life certain losses and
surrenders may signal an opening of the self that serves the purpose of
sacrifice in the religious sense.

The most painful sacrifice I ever made was at a tender age—to leave
my family and pursue a religious calling. It was not a difficult decision
because I was so enthusiastic. But it was painful at the time and continues to be disturbing in memory. I relive that parting every day as I
realize how far I am from people I love and how much life I was not able
to share with my family. I still don't know, almost fifty years later, if it
was the right decision or even if it was a good one. I do know that for all
my confusion about it, it was a major turning point in my life and was a

real sacrifice. In the confused thoughts and passions of a thirteen-year-old, I wanted to transform my ordinary life by offering it to religion as I knew it.

It is possible to stumble across the sacred already in existence, as in an old moss-covered oak in the thick of a virgin woods or in a hoary statue of the Buddha that has been resting in an ancient temple for centuries. But sometimes the sacred has to be brought into being through art and effort. In ancient times people sacrificed an animal, placing their prized possession and important food in the hands of divinity rather than using it for themselves. They gave up something they cherished to make room for the holy. Religions teach that when the sacrifice is genuine and pure, the spirit has no choice but to be enticed by it and be present. Sacrifice is a quid pro quo or, as scholars say, *do et des:* I give something up, I get something in return. The word *sacrifice* means to make sacred, and it is still the primary way to sanctify a life.

I don't think it is necessary to intend sacrifice for it effectively to take place. I certainly didn't mean to make a sacrifice when I left home, but as the years go by I see that is exactly what it was. Life gives us plenty of opportunities to make sacrifices. Getting a divorce or changing jobs may entail the kind of sacrifice that increases the holiness of one's life depending on how we deal with it. Sacrifice and sanctifying are natural processes available in every life.

Today it is easy to dismiss the importance of sacrifice. We may consider only the giving-up part and not the sanctifying element. The very idea of sacrifice may seem anachronistic. Only primitive people kill animals in the name of their gods. Or the idea of sacrifice may go against all that seems reasonable in a secular world. Why give up the very things one has worked for and achieved? What good is an attitude of self-denial? These sentiments are full of worldly wisdom, but they overlook the profound insight of religion: The giving up of ego transforms the person radically, placing him in a much vaster notion of what it means to be a human being. It puts him in touch with the incomprehensible mysteries that shape life regardless of our awareness and appreciation of them.

Many psychologists today say that it is important for a person to feel empowered. For them sacrifice might seem disempowering and therefore undesirable. But sacrifice doesn't have to be accomplished in a masochistic spirit of self-deprivation. It is more a graceful and creative acquiescence, a willingness to let life happen and flow through us. It makes room for a selfless power that is not intended to bolster the ego. Sacrifice doesn't make us feel self-important, but it can offer an increase in personal power, a strength that derives from being close to the source of life.

A modern person may find it difficult to imagine living from a place other than the ego. Secularism and ego go together, and it may seem only prudent to do whatever is possible to be a conscious, evolving, and successful individual. But the religions teach a different set of values with a focus on eternal concerns and radical community. They promote a different notion of self—if the word *self* is appropriate at all. They suggest that a person might feel profoundly fulfilled by being a receptor of life rather than a doer and achiever, a conduit of power rather than the originator.

When in the past people killed their precious livestock for the sake of religion, they were doing something both symbolic and literal. The animal represented what they considered valuable, and they were willing to give it up for a divine blessing. Giving over what they most prized, they felt a great loss. If sacrifice is a mere formality, it simply doesn't work because the emotional sting indicates a letting go of something felt as precious.

Every sacrifice transforms the person in a small way, and bit by bit life becomes holy. By allowing a greater will to have a role, the person is deliteralized, made into something less centripetal. Even the mystic, so interiorly absorbed, looks beyond the self for meaning. Sacrifice chips away at the self, allowing the deep soul to take over. The need to insist on our own existence gives way to a more relaxed appreciation of the life passing through us, achieving its own ends, which, mysteriously, create a fuller version of self than what we might have created from our own designs.

But sacrifice works this way only if the one receiving our surrender represents the infinite. Sacrificing ourselves to another person or an ideology is as demonic as real sacrifice is holy. I once attended a conference where different leaders were demonstrating their theories and exercises. I happened to be sitting in the audience next to Joseph Campbell, well known even then for his tapes on mythology. We had been chatting before the program began, but we weren't discussing what was going to happen. After a few minutes of prepping the crowd, the leader asked everyone to stand and shout "No" while extending a stiff arm and clenched fist. Automatically the audience rose from their seats except for Campbell and me and just a few others scattered around the room. Without planning a protest we remained seated. We were being asked to give up our will to a crowd mentality, which is a bastardization of sacrifice.

It makes all the difference in sacrifice to whom the offering is made. Is it to the person of the leader? People sometimes give all their money and maybe their lives to a charismatic teacher and the emotion of the moment. Or is it to an infinite and absolute object of worship? Ultimately God is the only worthy object of sacrifice. That statement could also be turned around: when we find a worthy object of sacrifice, we have found God.

When I meet former clergy and nuns and monks who are angry at themselves and their churches for having given years of their life to religion, I wonder to whom they sacrificed so much. To their parents? To their own success? To the church? Even marriage is not surrender to another person but to the great mystery that is matrimony. The trouble in marriage vows in which the woman is asked to obey her husband is not only the gender bias. No human being deserves such absolute obedience.

The sacrifice also has to be genuine and complete. In ancient times King Minos promised to sacrifice the pure bull Poseidon gave him, but he reneged. He substituted a good but lesser animal, and for generations his family was hounded by murderous bulls. There is a lesson there for anyone inspired to sacrifice. It is all or nothing. A tepid, mediocre sacrifice is worse than not making a sacrifice at all. What we think is a sacrifice may ultimately not be the thing that most represents what is valuable to us. We give something up in the name of sacrifice when what is really being asked of us is far more subtle and unexpected. The Minos syndrome is quite common in the spiritual life.

The essence of jealousy may be nothing more than a failure to sacrifice. The jealous person believes that he has given himself completely to the other, and he is distressed when his partner doesn't surrender completely to him. This sacrifice of self to another *person* is the key mistake, the first step toward jealousy. The only worthy object of sacrifice is infinite—life, fate, God's will—and the ultimate sin is to confuse the human for the divine. Anyone consumed with jealousy needs to find religion and discover that love is holy and infinite. He has to learn how to let life flow unhindered, acknowledging a will greater than his own.

Secularism might be defined as life without sacrifice. In a wholly secular society we strive for complete understanding and control. We study everything in existence exhaustively. If there is anything left unproven, we believe we have failed. We want to fix everything, prevent every disaster, and make life safe and predictable. And yet the more secular we become, the more intractable our problems seem to be. Things get worse, not better. We have yet to learn that the only humanism which is ultimately effective is religious humanism, a combination of human effort and divine influence.

Sacrifice is essential because without it there is no space in our thinking or in our life work for anything beyond our knowledge and control. Sacrifice creates a felt vision in which great mysteries play themselves out. In a way we are their subjects, their pawns, and yet by allowing them their influence, we become more than we are otherwise capable of being.

This is the "more" I mentioned at the beginning. I believe we set ourselves up for depression and disillusionment when we don't move toward this greater degree of being, and the only way is to give up the jealous possession of the life we know and understand. The resulting humility is not the intentional putting down of oneself but a simple acknowledgment that our humanity is only fulfilled in the emptiness we carve out through sacrifice. We are called to sacrifice many times a day, but religion teaches that we can do this well only if we find ritual ways of expressing that sacrificial attitude, preparing ourselves for those moments in life when we are asked to take up less space than usual.

The more uncertain I have felt about myself,
the more there has grown up in me a feeling
of kinship with all things.

C. G. Jung, *Memories, Dreams, Reflections*

30. *Ethics: A Way to Spirit*

*T*HE SACRIFICE OF SELF — that is, the making sacred of the personality — naturally leads to a life sensitive to all that is not the self,
which is one way to define ethics. Whenever I studied ethics in school,
I always found it a cool, distant, abstract system of principles and rules.
Of course I always knew it was important to live ethically, but the
subject itself never had much passion for me — until recently. I have
begun to see that I have been deeply involved in ethical issues all my
life and that finding my way toward an ethical lifestyle is to find a spiritual identity.

The religious institutions often present ethics as charting the minimum that we should do. Largely it is a classification of thou-shalt-nots
according to a highly selective list of values. It is generally negative and
hardly inspiring. My eyes were opened when I first began to speak to
businesspeople about bringing soul into their work. I realized that dealing with ethical issues could be the beginning of a soulful commercial
enterprise, but it wasn't easy for these business people to see the
connection.

I also began to realize that my personal life was full of ethical decisions that rarely came up in the ethics I learned in school: how to handle the ending of a long-standing and intimate relationship ethically; how to earn a living in a corporation that stands for questionable values and gets its money unethically. Is it all right to subordinate the quality of your work to personal ambitions, to work only for the money and to prey on people's insecurities? I see now that narcissism, the concern for personal identity and value, blocks a deep moral sensitivity and that the outcome of an ethical life is profound involvement in community.

I have also been challenged by people whose lives are much more ethical than my own, who make extraordinary efforts on behalf of nature, animals, children, the sick, and the underprivileged, who risk their lives and their freedom on behalf of their vision. I have come to see that ethics is not a listing of negative and minimal standards but a calling, a personal philosophy whereby we are sensitive to nature and the human community, and from that sensitivity conduct a caring way of life. Ethics is a way out of confinement in a self-absorbed personality.

Ethos, from which we get the word *ethics,* originally meant a place where animals frequent. When we herd together, how do we behave? Do we look after one another? Do we take care of the place where we gather—the land, the city, the drinking water? Are we welcome here? Can we be ourselves? These are basic questions of human existence, and how we answer them and live them has everything to do with our ethics.

Ethics is usually considered the product of spirit alone. We assume we are ethical because of universal principles, personal character, and a strict upbringing. We think of discipline, duty, and demand. But Jung feels differently. He senses a closer kinship with everything when he feels uncertain about himself. As his narcissism dissolves, he begins to feel connected to people and things, and therefore takes more responsibility. We might call this the soul of ethics, the capacity to respond to the world around because we're at ease with ourselves and our empathy can reach out gracefully and broadly. Ethics is simply a facet of a radical sense of community.

In contrast the moralist is quite certain about himself, and he believes that he is more ethical than anyone else. In recent years one of the main criticisms directed at me by certain church groups has been that I don't advocate absolute moral principles, that I am a moral relativist. There is nothing I can say in response. If I were to define ethics as a work of the soul that is based on communal feeling rather than responsibility, I'd be criticized no end. Emerson wrote in his topical notebooks, with an edge to his words: "I fear that what is called Religion, but what is perhaps Pew-holding, not obeys but conceals the moral sentiment."[1] Pewholders, I've noticed, are the very people who don't want to hear about the soul.

I feel the way Jung does: the older I get, the more uncertain I am about the formulations of truth and morals I received in my youth. There was a time when I thought I knew everything and had the right slant on every issue. Now life is so subtle and complex that I stew in my reflections as people around me take sides.

I also question the certitude I have felt all my life that I am inherently good and on the side of right. I realize now that there are many more effective and more risky ways in which I could contribute to the human community. It is difficult to be bourgeois and middle class and still live ethically because the moral life demands resistance to the questionable values of the culture as a whole.

Recently after a lecture someone asked me quite seriously, "Are you a bodhisattva [one who returns from his or her own realization to be of service to others]?" I thought about the question and answered, "No." I used to have an exalted view of myself, thinking that I was ethical to the core. Now I realize that I will never have such a honed sense of community. I don't have sufficient openness of heart, and I lack the courage. This is not false humility but a dawning realization of what an ethical life really is and how far I am from it. This discovery doesn't discourage me but only places me more deeply in my imperfection.

Ethics is a way of recognizing that although we are each alone in this universe, we are all alone together. We can make a good life not only by protecting each other but by being creative together and taking our pleasures from one another. If I feel the urge to write a good book, I need generous neighbors who will read my words and respond to them. If someone makes a special effort to add to the beauty of human life, I, being a member of his or her herd, can receive that gift with understanding and appreciation. And this is an ethical consideration. We are all herding around the pond in need of rest, nourishment, and revitalizing.

Human life finds fulfillment in service and in making a contribution. That effort of adding to the common joy in living is an ethical deed. I believe the churches have sold us short when they have presented ethics as the minimum and as a collective, universal requirement. Ethics is an opportunity, not a demand. It is in the nature of things and is not only for those who follow a system of morals.

Businesspeople who have been led into the ethical narrows of believing that financial profit is a worthy motive in life fail to notice the self-destructiveness in that philosophy. In the tight confines of their own part of the herd they may appear practical and appropriately self-interested. A life in finance and commerce can be profoundly rewarding, but it has obvious dangers that stem from a narrow view of the meaning of business and its place in society. Seeing ethics as an opening to soul suggests that a morally aware approach to money would be infinitely more satisfying in the long run than an unethical one.

Business is a powerful way, second perhaps only to politics, of being in the center of community life and finding meaning by advancing the life of the community. The goods and services that business provides are not only literal but also symbolic. They represent an exchange of talents and a response to need. But if the opportunities for involvement are great, it follows that the ethical vision has to be all the more acute. Any business-seeking soul need only become exquisitely ethical for the rewards of soul to follow.

The more we get from community, the more we owe it. Politicians and business leaders, so directly engaged in the activities that foster community, need an ethical sensitivity of extraordinary proportions to do their job well and enjoy its deep personal benefits. These are the people, of course, who are also in a position to fall the hardest and the farthest. But we are all in community, and the reciprocal law of soul and ethics affects us all.

The emphasis in theology on sin and rules has obscured an important aspect of ethics: making a contribution and doing no harm adds substantially to a religious life. Ethics carries the religious spirit forward and deepens its connection to the soul. Each ethical decision and action initiates a person into community and fosters the development of character. Having gone some distance into the complexities of morality, our vision expands. Gradually we move toward the holy through action and attitude rather than mere consciousness.

Ethics is a defining element in the path to spirit and not just an offshoot. As we struggle with ethical decisions in our own lives and in society, we are discovering important insights into the nature of things and our relation to the world and each other. Gradually, step by step, we become more refined in ways of being together and making sense of life. Our defenses against dialogue and commonality fall away. Sitting back comfortably and trying to divine these insights as a purely intellectual effort is too easy. It doesn't touch the emotional life and is usually stillborn.

All my life I've heard religious people advocate high ethical principles, but with some outstanding exceptions I haven't seen them take the lead in the great moral issues of the time. Often their ethics seem connected to their anxieties, such as their overriding concern about sexual morality. As a whole they don't inspire an ethical approach to race relations, bigotry, the natural environment, and violence. In many cases they stand in the way of ethical advance.

Why this ethical temerity and shortsightedness among people dedicated to the highest values? One reason has to do with the psychology of the religious organization. It has its own insecurities that must be addressed honestly and seriously. The narrowing of ethics among the churches is often an expression of their particular neuroses. Religious communities have not only a specific devotional focus but also certain anxieties that show themselves in an obsession with particular moral issues. Catholicism's fixation on sex is the obvious example for me.

Another reason is a faulty understanding of the role of the religious tradition and its theology. If the main purpose is the maintenance of the tradition, the size of membership, or adherence to dogma, then the resulting ethical vision will be severely limited. These are all forms of narcissism, which distorts the ethical life. The spiritual side of ethics is its transcendent vision, which leads to real concern for others, an appreciation of diversity, and a steadily increasing imagination of community.

In our moral decisions we need intellectual and moral leaders to give us fresh vision and encouragement. We also need friends with whom we can discuss our values and interpretations of events. We could use the wisdom of spiritual leaders as well, but we have to sort out moralistic anxiety from ethical maturity. When we do find a wise leader—and there have been many—we can learn from that person how to embody the ethical spirit. Spiritual leaders such as Shunryu Suzuki, Paul Tillich, Abraham Heschel, the great founders of feminism, Rabbi Lawrence Kushner and Rabbi Harold Kushner, the Berrigans, Mary Robinson, the actor Martin Sheen, Jesse Jackson, and Father Thomas Berry help us find our way to an ethical and therefore a compassionate life.

The soul in ethics, in contrast to the spirit, relies less on principle and more on the voice of conscience. The impulse of conscience is not made up merely of learned rules and admonitions. It is not a superego, although we may indeed hear voices of caution that are suspiciously familiar from life—a mother's fear, a father's warning, a teacher's caution. The deep voice of conscience is not aimed at producing guilt or standing in the way of life. No, conscience is a presence more like a guardian angel or a guiding daimon. The word could be translated as "companion advisor" (literally, "knowledge alongside"), a knowing presence that sees more than we see. It counters the thoughtless pursuit of passion and appetite and sometimes urges us toward the courageous display of compassion.

Sitting in a cold, damp prison, Thomas More tried hard to hear clearly the precise direction of his conscience because it stood alone against the reasoning of his accusers and even the pleas of his family. He expected that God would give him the strength to follow it, and he knew that the "peril of his soul" was at stake. At the end of his life this confident loyalty to a familiar voice of the soul gave this man's life its meaning. It defined him. His very identity depended on the strength of his ethics, which was inextricable from his faith.

So it is with all of us. As More said, for each, conscience is individual, and choosing to be faithful to it, after a life of cultivating it, makes us who we are. If we betray conscience or become numb to it after a lifetime of neglect, our individuality will get lost in conformity. We won't know who we are because we will have consistently betrayed the voice that shapes a unique life. But working out our lives in dialogue with the challenging voice of conscience, we become more than we could ever imagine ourselves to be. Surely that is what happened to Martin Luther King, Jr., who found a powerful identity by responding to a call to social activism.

When we finally understand that ethics is an affirmative way of being and that it can heal a troubled soul, we might move more courageously toward our individual destiny as we are guided emotionally by our compassion and our increasing vision of community. Annoying negative concerns about good and bad fall by the wayside. Splitting hairs about purely intellectual interpretations of ethical principles are revealed as distractions from what is more accurately a passion for the good. Too many people get scruples over minor issues while the really important ethical concerns are neglected.

Ethics is a form of soul care because it clears away significant obstacles to the movement of life. Conversely, failure in ethics is always a signal of some fundamental anxiety or blind spot about the nature of things. Any effort toward living ethically is a way of caring for the soul, and anyone seriously interested in living a spiritual life might first consider, honestly and deeply, the state of his ethics and the positive call of his conscience.

Note

1.	Emerson, *Topical Notebooks,* vol. 3, p. 270.

Mari and her young daughter Sita emerge from the doorway of their mud house. They each carry small metal bowls of white powder ground from parboiled rice. Mari paints the curves of leaves and vines. It is a lotus vine — serpentine and sensuous, bursting with budding and open flowers — the centrifugal symbol of the goddess that protects family and home.

Stephen Huyler, *Painted Prayers*

31. *The Inner Life of Rice*

WHEN ETHICS IS DEFINED positively as a creative and communal way of life, it quickly bleeds over into aesthetics. The good and the beautiful are like sisters: the ethical person sees the potential for a beautiful world and works to clear away the obstacles. Both values express a vision that reaches beyond the self and contributes to community, which is the heart of spirituality.

In his remarkable book *Painted Prayers,* Stephen Huyler presents images of women in India painting designs on their houses as a petition to the goddess Lakshmi for the safety of their families. They paint images of peacocks, lotus vines, pyramids, and elephants in a pigment made new each week from rice powder and cow dung. With their simple ritual painting they teach many lessons about family spirituality and the role of art.

Huyler quotes a farmer's wife as saying, "How can I know what is outside my house? Anything might be out there! So I paint my house inside and out." Jealousies and envies are out there, these people say, and violence and illness. We in our modern homes and businesses know that our world is full of dangers, but we try physically to protect ourselves with bolts and locks on our doors and iron screens pulled unseemly across storefronts. If we could reflect on these locks and screens as the paranoid poetry of our lives, we might realize how literal and mechanical are the ways we protect ourselves.

The Indian woman splashing rice in beautiful natural forms on the floors and walls of her simple house sees more deeply into the reality of the dangers that threaten. She wants to please the goddess who offers protection. Her response to evil is religious, and in her simple act she reminds us about a number of central issues: that the purpose of art is to serve and give body to religion; that evil is not as concrete as it may appear; that it requires measures which are spiritual; that the home should be a sanctuary where anxiety eases; that even a home needs devotional images to keep it tranquil.

Those pictures made from rice and dung on the walls and courtyards of ordinary poor people demonstrate a spiritual sophistication that we in the so-called more developed regions are losing. Our methods are physically complex but often philosophically shallow and naïve. We no longer have the imagination to see the spirits that inhabit criminals in moments of mad transgression or that drive executives and government leaders toward corruption. The tendency today is to interpret evil psychologically and to rely on therapeutic strategies to deal with it.

Modern life is sophisticated about material and mechanical things, but it is curiously naïve about the invisible world. It would be outrageous to invite a theologian to offer input on the design of a building or a home. We have forgotten that a house is a refuge of the soul. It would be pushing the limit to expect modern people to paint their houses and patios with ephemeral images of great spiritual forces. Yet for millennia people have used images for protection and as a way of sanctifying their immediate environment.

The rice-painting women of India are using the pale color of rice to transform their homes from secular physical shelters into places of spiritual significance. They are baptizing their environment, transforming it into a place full of an imagination for the sacred. For them the sanctuary of the home is not a metaphor understood by the mind but a reality created by concrete and powerful paintings. Living in these homes they are fully immersed in a spiritual point of view. The modern way is to use sacred images as decoration or instruction rather than to permeate the environment completely with a transcendent vision.

Whether intended or not, our homes and public buildings are images. When we build them, we are largely unconscious of their deeper meaning as images, but we are guided by an underlying, subliminal myth. The heavy row of locks and the electronic security systems tell a great and sad story about life in the modern sophisticated West. The iron gates pulled across storefronts at the end of the commercial day indirectly hint at the spirits that come out after hours. The graffiti that plasters every blank wall and flat surface is not all that different in style and method from the rice paint drawings of elephants and peacocks that stare out from the walls of rural India, and yet there is an essential difference: the one is an expression of a dark and crude repressed religion, while the other is the manifestation of a joyous and explicit religious sensibility.

We tend to think of religion and spirituality both as forms of consciousness, but the rice paintings portray religion as a concrete way of life that takes the spiritual seriously into account. In these rural communities evil is as real as anything else; it is not imagined as a failure in upbringing or a social injustice. It is not, as Jung often warned, the absence of good but a negative presence in itself. As such it requires a concrete response, not mere sociological analysis. Spirit is real for these people, and yet it is not literal.

It is said of Michelangelo that he merely revealed the figure waiting in the marble to be released. The Indian women similarly show what is contained in the simple material of rice juice. In their hands the rice is treated as a sacrament. Its inherent and potential sacredness comes out in the quick and sure fingers of women who are not artists as much as worshipers. In religion generally the most ordinary things—bread and wine, sprigs of herbs, a bowl of water—are revealed as having a profound interiority. Their sacredness lies in their multiple layers of meaning—the whole world in a grain of rice, eternity in a day's painting. *Hoc est corpus meum.* This bread is my body. Rice juice transforms an ordinary home into a chapel.

Bread and rice are staples, as basic as a felt and lived fear of evil. A religious imagination transforms them, accenting their symbolic power. In the context of ritual they bring to light primal forces that drive and shape us—not distant, not overinterpreted, not abstracted, not hiding behind technology. The rice-painted house presents a spiritual intensity that might cause a visitor to pause before entering. Both psychologically and spiritually human beings need such power to deal with the forces that threaten.

When my family built our house, we tried to give it a primal quality and a timeless appearance, but it was difficult to convince the carpenters and builders not to lace it with meaningless ornament that I felt weakened its power. I wouldn't want to have an unfriendly home, but to keep it honest, it has to be primal, and if it is primal, it shouldn't be too easy to enter. A visitor, alert to the spirits of the place, might well hesitate, stop, and look before knocking. Fear and trembling are an important part of a spiritual culture.

It makes sense to have the image of a gorgon, dragon, or threatening lion at the entrance of any building. Walking into any significant space is to confront the challenge of a new world with its opportunities and its threats. Those images also echo the zodiac, a circle of animals that surrounds and makes sacred life on earth. They remind us that a building is also a beast, and anyone who confuses it for mere space is setting himself up for trouble.

If religion is not in place at home, it won't be strong anywhere else. Church is a model, an example, and a source of instruction, while home is the cradle of religion. With our families we are the first priests, the bishop, and guru. *Cathedra* means chair. Where we sit is where we have our power. The Holy See is actually a holy seat—the words come from the Latin for chair. The chairs in our home are sacred and represent our Holy See. A good part of our lives takes place at home, and we need religion there as much as in the world around us.

To sit at home with authority over our lives and with security and belonging is to perform one of the greatest of all religious acts. There we establish our beliefs and preside over the precious education of our children. From there we author our children, our lives, and our thoughts. Safe in our homes, we find sanctuary from the evil spirits that roam in the night hours and in unpainted places.

Most people assume that religion means church, a body of beliefs, a tradition, and an organization. But these are only the means by which religion, a fundamental attitude and posture in life, may take form. There are other ways, including the simple and ordinary piety of the home. Our devotion there, our traditions, and our faith and loyalty constitute another place where religious feeling takes form and shapes life.

The rice painters also demonstrate the role in religion of giving form to spiritual intuitions and presences. Taking external images seriously also allows us to live in relation to our inner images, those figures of dream and waking fantasy, those voices and presences that give us dimension and fill out our rationality. We can derive wisdom, guidance, and power from those figures of the deep imagination who don't ask to be figured out and understood but only acknowledged and heeded.

Many religions offer a variety of ways of imagining these inner presences, such as spirits of ancestors or guardian angels. The Iroquois, for instance, like so many religions that acknowledge a numinosity in nature and things, honored a power they called *orenda,* which was received from a sky spirit.[1] Orenda, mana, grace—this widespread notion of a spiritual power within things and operative in human life infuses the most ordinary things with a spiritual sheen and power that gives the whole of life a dimension far beyond the measurable and the knowable. Secularism doesn't lack orenda entirely—it is able to work some magic—but it could be much more effective if it reconciled with the religious impulse.

I stare thoughtfully at Huyler's marvelous photograph of a thatched-roof house. A beautiful basket lies empty in a corner. A woman, no doubt the artist, stands framed in the doorway as in a classic painting. The outer walls of the house spin with sunlike lotuses and vines showing the vitality, the embrace of nature, and the rootedness of lives deeply connected to the dharma, the Tao, the absolute way of things.[2] In these ordinary people, artists of rice, we behold the essence of religion and the secret of living without fear.

Notes

1. Thomas McElwain, "Asking the Stars: Seneca Hunting Ceremonial," in *Earth and Sky: Visions of the Cosmos in Native American Folklore*, ed. Ray A. Williamson and Claire R. Farrer (Albuquerque: University of New Mexico Press, 1992), pp. 260–77.

2. Stephen Huyler, *Painted Prayers* (New York: Rizzoli, 1994), p. 41.

The future of religion lies in the mystery of touch.

D. H. Lawrence, "Future Religion"

32. *Sensing the Holy*

WHEN SPIRIT IS SPLIT OFF from soul, life is dangerously divided. The beautiful seems to have little to do with the meaningful, or the spiritual with the sensual. But the romantic person understands that the sensuality we usually think of as merely physical also engages the holy. Sensuality is as much a route to spirit as good thinking and good living.

During my monastic years it was the custom to go on retreat one day each month and for a week each year. These were periods of silence, study of the spiritual life, fasting, and contemplation. But what do I remember of those retreats? The substance of talks and reading? No. I remember the smell of flowers and the taste of grapes that grew on the paths where I walked and meditated. I remember the haunting chant of the *Veni Creator* that began the retreat and especially the *Te Deum* that ended it. I can still smell the incense that clung to my clothes during the closing benediction.

I don't remember a single idea or lesson from those retreats, but I would want to go back on retreat just for the sensuousness of it all. Maybe the silence and free time allowed me to open up in a special way to the physical presence of the world. I made a retreat from ordinary life to find meaning and instead came to my senses.

Several centuries ago philosophers described spirit as a vapor or an ether thinner than air. Alchemists pictured it as a unicorn horn coming to a vanishing point or as the vaporization of liquids. These images have direct relevance to our contemporary experience of spirituality, and from them we might learn not to make it abstract. Spirit may not be visible, but it can still be felt and heard.

At its best, spirituality is the most sensuous area of experience, and it aims at an intensification rather than a diminishment of existence. I often wondered why I had to spend two full years studying philosophy in preparation for the priesthood. Why not art or theater or gardening? The accent on definitions and dogmas indicates that people think of religion as having to do with meaning rather than experience. They think that the religion specialist should be a good thinker. Most priests have to be good at presenting ritual, counseling troubled people, and running the church business, and yet they are trained to be philosophers.

There came a point in our history where we began to doubt the existence of a spiritual realm. We became enchanted with the physical domain and our ability to measure it and manipulate it. We abandoned spirit to the churches, tolerating them but turning more and more to a materialistic viewpoint. We began to live in a new way, in a universe divided between mind and spirit. You see this dualism even today in talk of body-spirit medicine and in the accent of the new spirituality on the supernatural rather than the earthly.

I fear that our current interest in spirituality is often a reaction to materialism. We go in the opposite direction and look for miracles, engage in naïve praying, and withdraw from the complexities of an embodied life. We return to perfectionism — the ideal of a lean body, an obsession with health, and an elitism of community. Even when spirituality is self-consciously sensual, as sometimes happens today, it is often an idealized sensuality, which is still more idea than sensation.

Rather than a vapor constantly rising out of lived experience, spirit becomes an otherworldly atmosphere, hardly perceptible, floating and soaring, detached from the human plane. It gives rise to all kinds of beliefs in remote and magical worlds, having no relationship to scientific knowledge and little connection to the effort to work out social conflicts. It takes us above this world rather than deeper into it.

Christian monks used the phrase *contemptus mundi,* which appears to mean contempt for the world. But as Thomas Merton explains, it really means a withdrawal from life in service of the spirit, without any judgment against ordinary life. But this is a subtle distinction that only a thoughtful thinker like Merton could make. Spiritual leaders are often seized by a passion for an alternative vision, and they don't take the time to reflect and make these important distinctions. They may rant against what they see as a sinful or merely unhealthy society, and they may recommend a contemptible escape from it. Of course there are exceptions, such as Rabbi Michael Lerner and Marianne Williamson, who place spirituality in the very thick of community life.

In my childhood the nuns and priests weighed me down with rules and limitations on my enjoyment of the body, and I was made to feel ambivalent about sex. Today's leaders are more sophisticated about these things, but even now, using different language, many still preach a spirituality not fully engaged in the struggle to make a humane society. Spirituality can become otherworldly not only by promising heaven but also by separating itself from the issues and problems of our time. Even the idealizing of sex that one sometimes sees in the new spirituality is a kind of spiritualization of matter, a subtle sign of the old split between body and spirit.

Spirituality is always at risk of becoming anorexic. The word means no appetite, and indeed spiritual teachings often seem frustrated with human appetites. They deal with sex by setting up confining rules or finding ways to keep it clean and one-dimensional—only an expression of love, esoteric and ritualistic, flawless in technique. A certain approach to spirituality aligns itself with a movement in culture toward purity in eating, lifestyle, and body type.

In one of my books I told the dream I once heard in therapy from a sensitive anorexic woman. In the dream a horde of peasant women were cooking great quantities of food at long tables. There was garbage everywhere, strong smells, and heavy, sweating people. All these images horrified the dreamer who tried to live up to an ideal of sexless, bodiless, clean, and pure existence. I thought the dream showed her the route toward her healing. But the dream didn't offer her the image of the lovely goddess, the blemish-free, thin woman portrayed in the art of her spiritual magazines. She wanted to be the perfect bronze Diana, but the dream women, so full of life and soul, represented exactly what she despised. Years later I wonder if this dream could also be a healing image for contemporary spirituality, which seems preoccupied with an anorexic ideal, free of ordinary appetites, and dedicated to a purified body.

One of the things I love about images of the Buddha is that so often he is presented as heavy, fleshy, and happy. In the statue of him I have on my desk, he is smiling as monks climb all over his body. I trust that image of spirituality — in no way severe, full of body and pleasure.

Could the anorexia of spirituality be the reason that the churches have not been taking the lead in protecting the natural environment? Is nature too messy, too physical to appeal to a loftier attitude? Is it undignified to live as a body surrounded by other bodies? If so, then this is a major problem and a sign that spirituality has been cut off from its roots in the material world. It confuses physical fastidiousness with purity of intention.

Sensuousness has its own intelligence. Couples may discover that they can't be together because they can't make love. A farmer has unusual gifts that perhaps are not appreciated by an idea person who doesn't know that sensation is a kind of intelligence. A farmer knows more about human life than the average person because he lives with animals and plants and observes their lives and their direct relation to the weather and the moon and the sun. Our loss of local farming goes hand in hand with the devastating abstraction of everyday life as we try to distance ourselves from our animal nature.

Sensuality can be subtle, as in music. You don't have to understand music or know all about the performers and composers to enjoy it. Yet music is part of our intelligence and serves the spirit by directing our attention to eternal things. I recently sat in an audience listening to Indian musicians play the sitar and tabla and was pulverized by it, taken away, completely caught up in the sonorities. While writing this book I listened over and over to the preludes and fugues of Dmitry Shostakovich. They helped me think and write. I didn't have to pay attention to the form of the music. Its sensuality inspired me to reflect directly on the nature of things without becoming too analytical in my thoughts even though those pieces are particularly well crafted.

Sensuous revelations are richer, more complex, and more mysterious than the revelations of intellect. It may not be obvious how our spiritual lives benefit from a week's respite by the sea, but there is no doubt that the ocean can give us far more knowledge than the book we are reading as we sit in the sand. I don't mean to leap in a direction away from the mind to romanticize the body. I want to counter the philosophical undercurrents of the time in which we tend to equate knowledge with abstraction. In this context, sensation may appear primitive and prior to knowledge. But in fact it is the most direct and most precise form of knowing.

A sensuous experience not only stirs the emotion but can waken memories and turn the imagination in a certain direction. Much poetry is nothing more than sensuous experience giving rise to image and language. Poetry dreams the sensation onward. When I get stuck on a certain passage in my writing, I put on a piece of music, such as the Shostakovich, and find my way toward the right-sounding words. As I write, I listen closely to the music and read a few lines from a favorite writer. During the writing of this book I have had a novel by Jamaica

Kincaid at my side. I turn to her not for the story, as good as it is, and not for its meaning and the ideas it stimulates, but for the sensuality of her words. In one sitting I will open her book to any page and read two or three lines, and I'm inspired for another hour. This use of sensuality can be a way of life.

Eons ago spiritual traditions discovered the importance of the senses to the life of spirit. Why else would they build cathedrals filled with such strong images and haunting spaces? Why else did the ancient Egyptians make their sarcophagi so delicately beautiful? Why do the holy people of India build intricate and massive temples and statues of the Buddha and the saints except with the knowledge that the sheer explosion of sensuality draws people closer to God than anything? Why do monks chant when they could be praying freely and intimately in the free space of their minds?

Through a life of sensation we take in what the world has to offer and what an artist has beheld in trance. This is the most appropriate way to inquire into the mysteries and search for the presence of God, because analysis only takes us further into our own reasoning while the senses carry us into an undiscovered, unfiltered world. The senses not only reveal the cold facts of the physical universe, but they also grasp the secrets of the spirit.

As life becomes more distant and abstract, we are in danger of undervaluing the gifts of sensation. This change in values leads to secularization and the weakening of religion because the spiritual is not abstract and cannot be quantified. God far transcends reason, but he is well embodied in the sensuous world. To know the creator we have to know creation firsthand and not through the secondary means of logic.

The brilliant Irish theologian and mystical writer John Moriarty says in *Dreamtime,* "Jesus the Christ is he among us who is most incarnate. . . . He has enabled us who, hitherto, were only on the earth, to be of the earth." So often we have taken religious teachers to be pied pipers leading us out of this earthly life rather than further into it. This is a crucial mistake in spirituality, a defensiveness hardly noticed in the thrill of escape. The spirit is not apart from the body but, rather, is revealed through it and in it.

God is in the flutter of the butterfly and the sweet aroma of the honeysuckle, in the steam rising from the pot of potatoes on the stove and in the smells and sounds and passing light in every room of the house. God is also in the negative, horrific sensations — in the explosion of the bomb and the firing of the pistol. All these sensations are there to be read theologically if we have the holy imagination to recognize them. Otherwise they are mere impressions lost to consciousness and reflection.

The holy person is the one whose senses are at their peak and whose imagination is ever ready to notice the slightest sign of the divine presence revealed momentarily in the most mundane of sensations. He is the one who doesn't feel the need to analyze all of experience either for a greater ego or in defense against the thick, fertile, and ineffable torrent of vitality that streams at us every moment. She is the woman who can live as a body among bodies and in a world that has a body that is an extension of her own physical being. Allowing the physical is equivalent to inviting the spiritual because God is in the details, in the colors and aromas and textures.

I am in the fever of love.
His left hand beneath my head,
his right arm holding me close.

Song of Songs

33. *Religious Eroticism*

SENSUALITY IS SISTER to eroticism, but people tend to think of both as opposed to spirituality. This unnecessary split is perhaps the one most damaging of all to the spirit, the emotions, and ordinary life because desire and pleasure offer life its impetus and give us a reason for being. Desire moves us forward, and to be suspicious of it is to question life itself.

Life flows in two streams: eros and logos. Logos is the meaning, whether articulate or mysterious, and eros the force that keeps everything connected. It is essential to have a sense of what is going on (logos) and to have the desire (eros) to proceed. Logos can take familiar and ordinary forms: study, research, analysis, meditation, and the quest for meaning. Eros may be found in the search for a partner, the making of a home, or the desire for sex. At their best they work together like yin and yang, but usually one wins out over the other. Sometimes the preference for one causes a reaction in the other: The more we rationalize life, the more compulsive desire grows. The more materialistic we become, the wilder and less reasonable our ideas and thoughts.

In modern life we are good at certain kinds of mental activity—research, invention, and analysis—but not so good at the erotic. Today sexual confusion seems almost a natural part of life, and many people feel such vague longings that they wander aimlessly trying to find out who and what they love. Many, in the early decades of their lives especially, seem driven more by the search for a satisfying sex partner than by anything else, and they may not realize that the actual longing runs much deeper than sex. It is not just a partner they want but the feeling of being alive.

All of this may sound abstract, but it is very real to me. I was fifty before my desires sorted themselves out. For years I looked for ideas that I could live by and that could fuel my work, and during that same time I felt overwhelmed by unstable and disconnected sexual longings. Eventually a sense of personal cohesion began to emerge from all the chaos and painful attempts at a settled life, but what surprised me was that this sense of what was mine had much less ego in it than I had anticipated. I had to discover what my nature is, who I am by birth rather than intention, and to whom and what I am called. I had to find the particular qualities of my own soul and give up surface goals that I mistakenly thought were primary.

I remember clearly as an adolescent how satisfying it was to entertain sexual fantasies that rose up in my imagination without any effort. But when those images grew tired or were absent, I felt a similar enjoyment with thoughts of being someone special. The logos of my existence — my identity, if you will — expressed appropriately in adolescent narcissism, matched the mysterious sexual interests, which clearly pointed to a larger meaning. Both fascinations had to do with my congealing into a person.

Well-intentioned teachers tried to make me forget my erotic nature and to consider it incompatible with spirituality, but in the depths of my feelings and private fantasies I never believed this. I was convinced enough of the validity of my Catholic education to feel considerable guilt for my loyalty to eros, but it always seemed that the guilt was a small price to pay.

As time went on I felt sexual desire transform into a focus on pleasure as a rule of life. I studied what interested me. I wrote in the style I enjoyed. I taught in a manner in which I would want to be taught myself. I found a way of making a living that, for all its risks and problems, is essentially a pleasurable one. I learned that the challenges of being a husband and a father can all be borne if I tend to the pleasures in parenthood, even if at times they seem small in proportion to the struggles.

During the last twenty-five years I have been a listener, hearing the woes and longings of many people. They often tell the story of their erotic lives, though they wouldn't use the word. They recount their marriages and divorces, their affairs and their separations, their longings and their fears. Many have been persuaded to tame their sexuality in the service of pure spirit, and of course they have found themselves squeezed between their wish for virtue and the strength of their passions. They come to therapy because of the discomfort in that tension between ideal and desire.

I no longer believe that to be spiritual one has to be sexually reserved. We can be ethical in our relationships without perceiving sexuality as a devilish instinct working against spirit or as the primary obstacle to morality. This dichotomy shows not only how much we misunderstand and mistreat our sexuality but also how skewed our notion of the spiritual often is.

People sense a certain victory in conquering their appetites and fail to notice how this repression creates a backlash of depression. Rather than feeling virtuous, we might be better off simply being ordinary, imperfect humans doing our best to find our calling, be available to others, and pray in times of distress. Being virtuous in the ordinary sense is different from acting maturely and morally; it is more focused on the perfection of the self than on responding generously and sensitively to life.

Many religious people seem convinced that if they control their sexuality, even in marriage, day after day, year after year, this constant suppression will make them more godly. But year after year the neglect of their erotic lives has negative effect. They may become depressed, confused, angry, and moralistic. And they may have trouble being married. I've seen many cases where one partner, simply trying to be a good person, feels obligated to be sexually restrained, while the other feels quite the opposite. The marriage suffers unnecessary tension and only with extreme generosity and good luck survives.

The imagined antagonism between sex and spirit is for many a personal tragedy and wounds the very marriages and families that religious leaders want to save. It seems they don't understand that generous and openhearted sex can generate profound joy, and it is this joy that holds a marriage and a family together. There is no escaping the complexities and frustrations of living together intimately, but they are bearable and workable if they rest on a strong support of joy, which can be nurtured by loving and happy sex.

The fear of sex among many religious people often plays out as a reaction formation—protesting too much. I have a pious friend who I believe is typical. He often preaches sexual purity, but he is preoccupied with sex to a degree far greater than that of less anxious people. If you tell him you went to Greece to see the temples, he says, "Don't they have nude beaches there?" If you tell him you saw a good movie on cable television, he says, "I've never seen such sexual filth as on cable." The spiritual person's obsession with sex, though often critical and negative, may show how much that person needs sexual comfort and acceptance.

If we can imagine spirituality not as the pursuit of perfection and high virtue but as a generous embrace of who we are and what life asks of us, we might see how sex contributes to religion rather than takes away from it. Finding our way to sexual maturity requires getting many things in order: power, control, physical ease, love, generosity, ethics, and some wisdom about gender. All of this is prelude to good sex and spiritual development. The two go hand in hand, and eventually it may be revealed that one profoundly enhances the other.

We might even come to understand how God is sexual—in the

sensuality of the natural world and in the intimacy with which the divine is present in life. In my dream church I would have the Song of Songs painted in colorful, glorious calligraphy on the walls everywhere as a reminder that love and sex are the very basis of a spiritual life and, as the mystics of many traditions say, that God is, more than anything else, a lover. I'd include the extravagant poems of D. H. Lawrence, the etchings of Eric Gill, and the temple carvings of erotic India.

A clue to making peace between sex and spirit can be found in the art and mythology of many religions. The Greeks worshiped gods and goddesses who were plainly sexual in many different ways, from the beautiful Aphrodite to the lusty Priapus. In India the sexual aspect of the spirit leads the worshiper deep into the principles of creation and destruction that account for life itself. The American Indian figure of Coyote shows the craftiness of the sexual impulse and the fear people have of it, and yet he is an attractive and ultimately creative force. Even in Christianity artists picture the Holy Spirit in the form of a bird impregnating the Virgin Mary, and mystics write about their experience of God in sexual language.

In these inspiring images, sex and spirit are in the same business. They are both involved in the unfolding of life, and sometimes it becomes clear that they are two sides of a coin, the most basic kind of creativity seen from two different points of view. But of course most people don't see this connection because they don't reflect enough on the meaning of their sexuality. They accept the limited ideas they get from popular psychology, that sex is mainly about communication and satisfying an urge. The religious literature shows, though, that sex is a far deeper factor and plays a significant role in the spiritual life.

My experience as a therapist tells me that if we were to distill all sexuality to its essence, we would be left with pure vitality. When conditions are right, sexual behavior can make us feel reborn, alive, at the beginning of a glorious life. Of course sex can also lead us into despair and to feeling sullied and used up. Everything has its shadow.

The literature on sexual dysfunction often uses imagery of constriction, nervousness, performance anxiety, fearful memories, and the like to portray the problem. In the broader picture these images imply a resistance to vitality and an unwillingness to allow life to flow. But isn't this equivalent to resisting the divine will? God is in our sexuality, and paradoxically maybe that is why we try so hard to restrain it—because God, vitality itself, is present in sex as nowhere else.

Not getting deep enough into the challenge that our sexuality presents, we turn sex into a fetish. It becomes a meaningless act that decidedly does not offer joy or vitality. Because it now lacks its inherent value, we try to get from it what we need through repetition and exaggerations of method and technique. And the more it acts as a fetish, the more hidden is its spirituality.

The spiritual healing of our sexuality requires several challenging tests. We have to find a way to let life move through us without undue interference, to get the ego out of the way, to find a way of imagining God as sexual and certainly not antisexual, to see that our particular sexuality is part of our calling in this life and that it is God-given, and to be loyal to it at all costs. In the end, working our way through the maze of our precious sexuality, we may discover that it is a direct path to spirit.

VIII

Practice

The spirituality of everyday life requires a livable, inspiring philosophy and daily attention. In all traditions, spiritual practice zeroes in on a particular method for transforming life according to one's spiritual vision. It begins in being a student or an apprentice, and it involves some kind of structuring of life.

The great and lesser religious traditions tell marvelous stories about learning the mysteries. Jesus' followers sit at his feet and listen to one striking puzzle after another. The Zen student is baffled again and again by the insistence of the teacher on mysteries. The Sufi teacher tells funny, romantic, and incomprehensible tales to students who may be looking for a plain lesson.

A similar inscrutability surrounds prayer. It takes many forms, and any attempt to limit its range of expression kills it. Prayer is full of mysteries, and yet it, too, requires craft and thoughtfulness.

Religious traditions teach an important lesson: the more mysterious the insights and the deeper the prayer, the more we need technique, method, and a studied practice. It doesn't do to improvise our spirituality or to keep it feathery and amorphous.

Yet it is obvious that method quickly turns into habit and teachings into dogma. How do we give form to our spirituality without making it rigid? How do we find companions in our efforts without creating a stifling organization?

It has often been said that religion is by nature liminal, neither here nor there, always on the line between two positions and never in one or the other. Here is another hint on how to practice regularly without getting stuck: look for the places in between; don't let the paradoxes collapse into logic and certainty; and don't let any one community become the only authority. The trick is to create a structure that is living and flexible and always open to reform.

For the Greeks there was no moment
and no place where people could not
be confronted by a god.

K. Kerenyi, *Zeus and Hera*

34. Crafting a Soul

MAKERS OF CRAFT WILL TELL you that their sometimes laborious work is a spiritual practice. And many a spiritual teacher will tell you that spirituality requires craft. You can become skilled at prayer, technically trained in meditation, and schooled in spiritual aspects of music and art. Spirituality doesn't grow like a flower; rather, it comes into being like a temple or an illuminated manuscript, through hard work, imagination, and skill.

There are several books on the market—and I have considered producing one myself—that use words and photographs to explore monasteries from several traditions and from long ago. It is curious that not only the life and personalities of the monks but the buildings they made and the things they created still fascinate. These monasteries are often simple in their materials and design, especially compared to the great temples and cathedrals, and yet their beauty and awe remain. Today we emphasize the teachings and the moral precepts of religious traditions, but at another time it was equally important to craft the soul and spirit, to translate faith into the simple beauty of the things and places where holiness was sought.

Today when almost anything can be made with machines and computers, craft is easily romanticized and idealized. But I think we idealize craft in reaction to the dead relationship we have with most manufactured things. As we all know, a thing can have life in it if it is made well or if it shows signs of the hand and the imagination that put it together. Today those qualities are becoming scarce.

Recently I came across in the magazine *Fine Woodworking* an interview with the master cabinetmaker James Krenov. What he says about making a cabinet could be applied to the spiritual life. You have to get acquainted with the wood, he says, "a wood's colors; its hardness or lack of hardness; whether its grain is ornery or not. It's a very personal thing, and not everyone pays such close attention. But if you do, you are more in harmony with the wood and the work. And the results flow from this harmony, even though it is connected with periods of stress and doubt." I can imagine a Zen master using almost the same words. Krenov's reflections also echo the teachings of the *Tao Te Ching*, which advocates a life in harmony with things:

> Blunt the sharpness,
> Untangle the knot,
> Soften the glare,
> Merge with dust.

The concrete loss of self achieved by getting lost in the material lies at the very heart of spiritual practice, and it can be accomplished without any explicit reference to a religious language or institution.

I do a little woodworking, and I wonder sometimes why I do it. I don't have many tools, and I'm not terribly skilled with the ones I have. But I do love to touch wood and carry it and cut it. I love to notice its infinite range of colors and see how the application of oil or wax brings out latent hues and markings. The whole of wood is ornery to me, not only its grain. It doesn't cut as expected, and no matter how carefully I make them, marbles easily roll off my cabinets. I have made table legs so crooked that the pieces could easily pass for experimental art.

I love the solitude, concentration, and the creative expression involved in woodworking, and there is no doubt that it teaches values and encourages contemplation. Many people believe that you have to get far away from this world to be spiritual, but woodworking teaches a different lesson: it is possible to be so close to the material and the work that soon you find yourself a novice in a new monastic endeavor. In the Gospel of Thomas, Jesus says, in a phrase that inspires me in many different ways, "Split a piece of wood and I am there." When I literally split a piece of wood and smell the pristine aroma of the virgin pulp, I know that once again my senses have detected the presence of God. I also find there my original self and my entire world in microcosm.

The same spirit draws me to the work of Eric Gill who created a community in the 1920s in which workers went through a ritual initiation, accepting the idea that craft is accomplished for the glory of God and the benefit of neighbor. Gill was a passionate man full of contradictions: extremely erotic in his life and art, and yet dedicated to living, even dressing, like a craftsman monk. His unique spirituality, a challenge to anyone trying to understand virtue and morality, combined Christian piety with pagan eroticism and reverence for work and objects.

Some of my books are set in type that Gill designed those many years ago, and I feel his influence in my own attitude toward work. Everyday work and craft form a major part of my spirituality, and I think my spiritual life would diminish more from loss of that work than from loss of church. My ideal is a lived spirituality, subtle rather than gross, integral rather than applied, indistinguishable from secularity rather than its opposite.

Gill spent thousands of hours carving his elegant alphabets into slabs of stone and then making some of the most erotic etchings known in the Western world. And both his calligraphy and his erotic drawings have a strong spiritual quality, as though one influenced the other, so that his alphabets are almost otherworldly and yet sensuous, and his erotic images carry you upward into sensuous spirit rather than downward into impure sensuality.

I feel frustrated knowing that my published writing doesn't have much of the eroticism and humor that are so much a part of me. I can't seem to get either into the words except obliquely, and then it seems most readers are not aware of those qualities in me. In unpublished snippets of fiction and fanciful writing I let it pour out. My lectures are embarrassingly comic. The fact that I'm drawn so powerfully to a character like Eric Gill, a master of eroticism, must say something about me as well. And yet — a constant frustration — I continue to write with a persona that is not nearly as sensuous. But I don't want to judge myself harshly on this point. Maybe I am called to a private kind of eroticism that seeps into my public life quietly and unnoticed.

In his bright and erudite reflection on music, *Piano Pieces,* pianist Russel Sherman writes about spiritual factors in composing and performing music: "When we play, this gentle, uneasy, fluctuating, nameless, stark condition of wonder infiltrates the tone and diction of every tone; without it no fake bluster of certitude, no glib assurance of set formulas can compensate or cover up the existential void. This doubt, born in fear and trembling, is not a liability; it is a sign of a contemplative wisdom which is unafraid to admit fear into its poetic construct, and which is the indispensable prelude to conviction and faith."[1]

Sherman's statement could also be the advice of a spiritual master — and maybe it is. Everything we do in the spiritual life has to include wonder. Faked certitude, glib formula, and the cover-up of doubt all weaken or destroy our spiritual efforts. He reminds us that fear plays a role in faith and that there is no need to pretend that we are above fear. All of this is inherent in craft, in what artists often call the honesty in their work. It is also inherent in other forms of spirituality, even the way we live our lives.

To pursue both the craft of spirituality and the spirituality of craft we have no choice but to go our own way. By its very nature craft has a strong personal element and may not be understood and appreciated by others. Usually it is not the convenient way, and for some reason today we are charmed by conveniences. I remember once as a child while spending a summer on the family farm I noticed that the outhouse didn't have a lock on it. So I took out my pocket knife, one of several interesting and heavy objects I kept in my jeans pocket, and carved a homely sliding lock. Apparently I have had an interest in craft from the beginning, even though I never had much skill.

For many years I lived in the thick of Shaker country in the Berkshires and western New York. There almost every day I could see signs of Shaker spirituality, yet another version of monastic life, in buildings, barns, and furniture. Somehow these industrious and pious people understood that spirituality resides in the world around us, not just in nature but in the world we craft as well. You can look at a Shaker wood joint and see in its plain elegance a secret about how life can be lived. You learn how the process of creation continues in a highly spiritual, highly sensuous appreciation of the divine craftsperson who not only made the world but crafted it with simple proportion, beautiful lines, and the best of materials.

Note

1.   Russel Sherman, *Piano Pieces* (New York: Northpoint Press, 1997), p. 133.

The most powerful prayer . . . is that which proceeds from an empty spirit. . . . An empty spirit is one that is confused about nothing, attached to nothing, and has no concern whatever in anything for its own gain, for it is all sunk deep down into God's dearest will and has forsaken its own.

Meister Eckhart

35. An Instinct for Prayer

HUMAN BEINGS HAVE a natural impulse to pray. One of my favorite forms is to sing or recite the psalms of the Bible: "Like the deer that yearns for running streams, so my soul yearns for you, O God." When I was young and chanted these words every day, they didn't penetrate very far into me. But today, closer to the end, tenderly tied to my children, aware of the need to turn from self to the unnamed God, the psalms give my words sentiments that I could not find on my own.

The obvious reason to pray is from need, but we also turn to prayer in thanks, praise, blessing, and remembrance. Prayer doesn't require belief in a personal God but may be an expression of absolute dependency and an appreciation for the mysteries. Prayer requires being in dialogue with life, having at least a vague sense of the other who defines us.

Of course we labor under the illusion that only humans can and should talk to each other. To the scientific eye the world doesn't have personality. We have looked into molecules and atoms and neutrons and have seen only empty space. There is no one there. No one to pray to. No one to listen to our prayer. To pray, many conclude, is to talk to yourself or to stand in front of the mirror of your projections.

But this is only one myth about the way things are. We see what our imaginations allow us to see, and we are always looking through the filter of a myth that we take as true and obvious. The microscope is an extension not only of the eye but also of the myth through which the eye sees. If we can't imagine God, we will not see any signs of divinity.

But it is possible to see differently, to reject the scientific myth as the only possible screen for experience. Opening up the pores of sensation —or the doors of perception, as Blake called them—we might sense more in the world than can be seen with the literal eye. We might perceive the world's beauty, its presence as a whole and in parts in relation to us, and our family relationship to it. We might sense a stirring there, a spark—scintilla, the ancients called it. We might sense, as Meister Eckhart said, an eye looking back at us as we look into the world.

One day many years ago my wife came to me early in the morning to show me her home pregnancy test. I looked closely and saw the faintest mark indicating a positive result. It was the first indication of my daughter's presence in the world and in my life. That little mark felt momentous. Months later the doctor told me to look as she was being born. I saw red hair, only red hair, and she was not yet born. Another sign of her presence. Now I look at the pond at the bottom of our hill and at the fullness of life in that pond, and I think I glimpse a spark not entirely different from the signals of my daughter's arrival. I don't know what that spark is, that scintillating that is hardly perceptible. I can only imagine. But whatever it is, I can talk to it and come to it for consolation, just as I found "proof" of God's existence in the scintillating Galway inlet.

Prayer is foremost a way of being. Sometimes it finds its way into words, but even when it doesn't, it makes life a dialogue. I don't know how other people are, but I am always talking inwardly to presences that I take as real—my dead grandparents, an animal, existence itself, or no one in particular. I find myself in the midst of that otherness, and I talk to it. I talk to the trees that are so tall and green and branching around our house. I'm in awe of the stones that stick up from the earth around us like hints of eternity in a world of change, and I connect with them, as Jung did as a young man.

Many people today are trying to prove that prayer works. It is an attitude that I can't appreciate. What does it mean to work? Is prayer effective when we get what we want? Is prayer only petition and worth the effort if our prayers cause some change in the physical world? Are my wishes the measure of prayer's effectiveness?

I simply trust the impulse to pray. It is strong and sometimes overwhelming. Besides, people all over the world pray. It is clearly a natural instinct and therefore can be trusted as valuable. I can understand those mystics who withdrew into a closed room or a cloistered building for the sole purpose of praying.

Prayer makes us holy. It represents our awareness that we live in at least two universes: the world of the senses that we control — ego — and the world of mystery and timelessness that far transcends our abilities. By keeping these two universes connected, prayer makes holiness possible. Modern scholars talk about prayer as performance language. It doesn't merely express, it accomplishes something, and one of the things it accomplishes is holiness.

Prayer also helps hold families and communities together. The intention to be a family or a community is not enough. But the recognition, expressed in prayer, of a deeper source of connectedness is effective. People come together mysteriously. They may not know exactly what they're doing. Prayer acknowledges that mystery, and so appropriately we pray at weddings and funerals, before meals, and at gatherings. That is why lovemaking, too, is prayer.

In another context I've quoted the composer Monteverdi, saying that there are three passions: love, anger, and prayer. I prefer to think of prayer as a passion, as a way to take life on and respond to it as fully as possible. Prayer doesn't arise out of meekness and need only; it expresses our strength and is a sign of deep intelligence. We pray because we can stretch beyond our narcissism, knowing that our life is a grace and that the mysteries we are born into ask for acknowledgment.

The way we pray depends on how we imagine God. If we use the name of God, it is fairly easy to pray since we sense the personality of that which is beyond comprehension. If we don't use the name of God, we can still pray from the awareness of a creator or simply a presence in the very marrow of life, a presence not clearly defined and yet still sufficiently other to allow dialogue.

Prayer can be subtle and sophisticated or plain and simple. I use many forms of prayer that come mainly from my childhood. My mother, who is an expert at prayer, taught me well, and I also learned much in the monastery. When an image comes to me of a friend or relative who has passed on, without thinking I say a Hail Mary. Whenever I hear an emergency siren, another Hail Mary. When my daughter was injured, I prayed so fast and hard I had no mind for anything else.

This approach to prayer may appear naïve, but life not fully explained has a basic simplicity about it. To be in touch with invisible presences need not be naïve; on the contrary it may represent a vital and sophisticated religious imagination. I don't have to know how prayer works or prove to myself or anybody else that there is someone or something on the other side of the dialogue. It is enough to sense the impulse to pray, to have some imagination of a holy other, and to act on that awareness in simple ways.

Religious traditions have created a vast culture of prayer—words, songs, gestures, objects, places, times, and formats. Prayer is the soul of religion because it comes from the heart and is often expressed beautifully, as in the words of the psalms: "I place all my trust in you, my God; all my hope is in your mercy." These simple words could transform a political party if they were seen for their subtlety and intelligence.

In Sophocles' *Oedipus* the chorus teaches Oedipus how to pray to the eumenides, the kindly gods of the earth. To these gods he should pray silently, they say, with no shouts or display. The prayer of the deep soul is appropriately quiet and reflective. It is inspired by deep feeling, and it makes sense to perform this prayer more with reflection than with formality. Part of being a religious person is to know when and how to pray.

I was taught as a monk to pray without ceasing, to see every moment and every action as a prayer. I can see now that praying at all times takes us out of the relentless streaming of life and into eternity, and this is a good way to prepare for death, which, as a form of the eternal, is an aspect of living. If we don't pray, how can we be ready for death?

Prayer lies at the heart of Hindu tradition and is summarized beautifully in the words of Ramana Maharshi: "When you pray for God's grace, you are like someone standing neck-deep in water and yet crying for water. It is like saying that someone neck-deep in water feels thirsty, or that a fish in water feels thirsty, or that water feels thirsty."[1] These powerful words remind us that from a holy imagination everything is grace, everything is godly, and therefore prayer is the most natural and available thing in the world. If we don't pray, it must be because we are inhibiting it in some way, for it will flow of its own accord.

In the library of our house, high above the door, we have painted a brief prayer from Nicholas of Cusa: *Ubicumque me verto ades* — Wherever I turn, you are there. This, to me, is a reminder of the omnipresence of God and the ubiquity of prayer. We need to be reminded, not to pray, but that we are praying.

Prayer connects me to the depths and heights of the world in which I live. If I don't pray, I live as though life were wafer thin and purely horizontal. But when I pray, I bring to bear the vertical dimensions, which offer meaning and value. Everything that is done in the practical world is completed by prayer. All the effort finds its value in being tied to the mysteries.

Prayer is a means of breaking through the limitations of secular discourse and thought and of a too narrowly circumscribed world. Prayer is a kind of intellectual sacrifice in which we give up the illusion of self-reliance and extend our need for another to the very limit. It enlarges the sense of self and world, and makes connections between them.

Meister Eckhart describes prayer at its best as a sinking down into "God's dearest will," a lovely phrase which of course can be taken naïvely but might also be understood as the affectionate and benign source of our lives. I would say that prayer at its best requires from many of us that we give up all naïve notions of God, emptying ourselves of all intention and manipulation, all expectations and demands, and exposing ourselves to the absolute but affectionate emptiness.

At the same time I think we can come to prayer with a strong sense of need, and that is also an expression of the deep soul. It should be possible to do both: sink into God's dearest will and be full of the thoughts and emotions of our need. There is a difference between demanding that life unfold as we expect it and feeling the most profound anxiety in the face of tragedy and danger. Like Job we beg for some understanding without demanding it, and like the psalmist we pray, "*De profundis clamavi ad te Domine* — Out of the depths I cry to you, O Lord."

I should think it obvious that prayer emerges naturally out of anxiety, fear, and depression. These extreme emotions don't weaken prayer at all; in fact they reveal the connection between our deepest turmoil and our highest yearnings for transcendence. What else satisfies the longing that rises up from despair and anxiety? Not the easy explanations and encouragements of psychology. Not the equally anxious attempts of friends to spur us on past our anxieties. Prayer acknowledges fear and takes us beyond it. What could be more elegant?

People of simple faith may never consider the importance of emptiness in religion and yet make it part of their faith. Some people don't question the theology with which they have grown up, and yet their faith matures over time into something approaching absolute. The prayer that rises out of this kind of faith is also powerful and not as naïve as might be supposed.

Nicholas of Cusa is an example of one who can be intellectually sophisticated and at the same time search for simple ways to be pious. "Whoever seeks God might remember that in God's name is contained a certain path for seeking God so that God can be groped for."[2] The point in this intellectually honest approach to prayer is not to grasp but to grope. As in all matters of religion there is no final certainty and no final outcome. Through prayer we approach the mysteries, but we don't conquer them.

The mystic advises us to pray always, to simply be aware of the grace that permeates everything at every moment just as the water permeates the lake. There is nothing to do but stand in this water. Like fish we breathe in the life-giving nutrients that are naturally present. We understand that grace is not given apart from life but is food for the soul that saturates everything in existence.

Notes

1. Philip Novak, *The World's Wisdom* (San Francisco: HarperSanFrancisco, 1994), p. 48.
2. Nicholas of Cusa, p. 218.

Be soft in your practice. Think of the method as a fine silvery stream, not a raging waterfall. Follow the stream, have faith in its course. It will go its own way, meandering here, trickling there. It will find the grooves, the cracks, the crevices. Just follow it. Never let it out of your sight. It will take you.

Sheng-yen

36. Finding a Teacher Who Knows Not to Teach

THE SPIRITUAL IMPULSE OFTEN gives rise to special forms of teaching and learning the stories, ideas, and practices of a tradition. Even when the spirituality has not taken the form of an organization but is mainly the vision of an individual, some form of education usually takes center stage in the practice. The point may seem obvious, but sometimes it helps to reconsider the obvious and look with fresh eyes at what has become unconscious.

I think of John Humphrey Noyes who founded the extraordinary Oneida Community in upstate New York in the nineteenth century. A large number of people — hundreds — came together to live an absorbing community life, working for the common good of the group, having and raising children according to their principles, and practicing a complicated form of sexual arrangement called appropriately "complex marriage." It was all based on the genius of Noyes and his interpretation of the New Testament. He was the leader, but above all else he was the group's constant teacher.

In this book I also refer to Shunryu Suzuki, the Zen master who brought a particularly simple and direct form of Zen to San Francisco. My attitude toward religion has been shaped significantly by this man who consistently taught a spiritual approach full of paradox and devotion. I didn't know Shunryu Suzuki, and so I depend on students of his I do know, such as Michael Katz and David Chadwick, to teach me the lessons he embodied so well. When a teacher evokes the deep process of imparting and learning subtle aspects of life's mysteries, the teaching goes on.

Teaching may seem to be the simple transfer of information from one person to another, but this is its most superficial aspect. Deep emotional fantasies are always at work, and when real learning takes place, a mysterious process is underway. We all know how easy it is to learn from certain people and in certain circumstances, and how difficult when conditions change. Like any creative activity, teaching happens best when a muse is present, initiating something far deeper than the intentions and efforts of the teacher and student.

For most of my life I have been a teacher of one kind or another—at all age levels and in many different formats. And I've also been a perpetual student. The deepest influence on my teaching is the example of my father, who spent most of his career in the classroom and who is a born teacher. He never lets an opportunity for learning or teaching go by, and he always teaches in a Socratic manner—drawing out the inherent skills of the learner. I grew up watching a gifted teacher at work, and I recognize that genius when I come upon it and, rarely, when I feel it stirring in me as I talk and write.

People who are expert at their professions sometimes try desperately to teach but fail all the way. It isn't that they lack knowledge in their field or even standard skills of teaching. It just isn't in their nature to evoke the spirit of the teacher and to elicit the fantasies and passions needed for effective teaching and learning. All teaching is a spiritual activity and requires the special magic of an adept.

Teaching spiritual matters is a special case and may require extraordinary forms. When I was a child, I learned some of the spirit of my Catholicism in the confessional. In the monastery I always had a spiritual director. In many religions important insights are conveyed in special meetings between the spiritual master and the student, as in widely known formats in Zen Buddhism, such as dokusan, a private interview for instruction.

In traditional Judaism a rabbi was first of all a teacher and not the leader or hierarch found in other religions. Rabbi Lawrence Kushner, a genuine and effective religious teacher—I know this from working with him—aptly ends his collection of writings *Eyes Full of Wonder* not with an instruction but with a blessing:

> *May your eyes shine with the light of holy words*
> *and your face reflect the brightness of the heavens.*

Notice that the object of learning here is not a new pile of facts or a student able to score well on an exam. Signs of learning are shining eyes and a bright face made so by holy words and the brightness of the heavens. Taking these words seriously suggests that spiritual education requires a special vocabulary and style of teaching coupled with the viewpoint of the eternal. The intention of the instruction is obviously important as well. The teacher or program of learning that distinguishes between dispensing information and initiating a person into spiritual matters has a chance to transform the learner.

When I first started teaching in the university, I noticed that many of the athletes were failing their courses or just getting by with the aid of special tutors. I was teaching a course on the nature of religion, and I felt it would be beneficial for those students just to be exposed to the world's spiritual wisdom. So I encouraged the athletes to attend my classes. I didn't have any expectations that they would do well academically. As long as they showed up regularly, I would pass them. And I do think that many young men and women whose time was completely devoted to their sports learned the basics of a spiritual existence.

But some of my colleagues didn't approve of my attitude. They thought I was being too soft and dispensing passing grades too lightly. The athletic directors thought I was being too hard by not passing all the athletes who signed up for the course even if they never showed up. I failed those people who never appeared, and I couldn't understand why they wouldn't give themselves a chance for real learning at the slightest cost of their time and attention. A few of the athletes were profoundly affected by their exposure to ancient spiritual wisdom, and it was clear that at least in their choice to learn they were teachers of themselves.

Many of the athletes I taught became interested in further explorations in religion. I've already mentioned the example of the golfer Payne Stewart. One young man I remember was a star football player. He was destined for the heady life of a highly paid, internationally known superstar. He wanted a grade in my freshman class so he could graduate. He wouldn't attend class, so I told him that if he read the small book called *Zen and the Art of Archery* and wrote a brief, thoughtful paper on it, I'd give him a passing grade. This book speaks well to an athlete who wants to learn the basics of a religious approach to self-transcendence. But apparently he was too preoccupied with his stardom to do even that. I regretted that he made this small choice, one that probably reflected the bigger decisions he would make later.

Shunryu Suzuki takes the notion of spiritual learning to yet another level: "When you realize Buddha nature, you are the teacher. You are the teacher of your master too."[1] At its very best the archetype of teaching/learning is not split up between two people. Both teach and both learn. The learner teaches himself but instructs the teacher as well, and the teacher is always at the point of taking his learning deeper.

The teacher brings the pupil to the point where he can learn on his own, and the pupil shows the teacher how to preserve his beginner's mind. In therapy, which is as much about education as it is about healing, that clients would stop me occasionally and remind me of certain principles I had taught them. For instance, I always recommended staying as close as possible to depression, but I myself would stray at times and look for a way out. In those moments the client would say, "Don't abandon me now. Let's stay with these feelings and watch where they take me." This loyalty to the soul I considered a profound spiritual act, and I was being taught the lesson by my students.

Suzuki is quoting the Zen patriarch Dogen, and he goes on to say, rather outrageously, "And you will be even the teacher of Shakyamuni Buddha." It's like saying that you will teach Christ or lead Mohammed on his way. The point here is not to acquire hubris but rather to become absolutely absorbed in the teaching and the persona of holiness, to take the teacher in, no matter how exalted. The purpose in teaching religion is certainly not to prepare a person to defend intellectual positions but to achieve a lived level of holiness. Any one of us could become suffused with the Christ nature and become real teachers and healers. The Tao could be embodied as never before in the way we live and in the quality of our soul. We could manifest the Buddha in our composure and teach more by manner than by word.

Of course this kind of transformational education doesn't result from the mere acquiring of facts and ideas. It is closer to Plato's conception of learning as remembering, realizing the truths that are already there to be recalled and embodied in us. When we learn spiritually, we realize more vividly who we are and what this life is all about.

Like any leader, the teacher has to learn to distinguish the teaching from the teacher's own anxious needs and agendas. The challenge is to present the wisdom without forcing the student to accept it in any particular way. This, of course, is a principle routinely ignored in religious and spiritual institutions, but it still holds as the only way to keep the material to be learned holy and religious rather than ideological.

To teach in this maeutic way—Socrates' ideal of being the *midwife* in learning—requires that both teacher and student serve the process. The midwife doesn't give birth but only assists. The good teacher doesn't just present the facts, he or she assists at the birth of a self that

hasn't been seen before. Many spiritual leaders see their job as imparting teachings that are correct in light of some authoritative source. But
the Platonic way is to teach even the spiritual life with an eye toward
helping a person find the truth that is in them from the beginning.
Many spiritual teachers apparently find it difficult to trust that God
lives in the depths of each person.

Like Socrates, the thoughtful spiritual teacher works with a profound sense of irony to the extent that he presents himself as a fool. He
can only teach if he has nothing to convey. She can only assist at discovery or memory. A teacher is nothing in himself, and even what he
teaches is nothing once it is absorbed by the learner. Suzuki says, "The
moment you meet a teacher you should leave the teacher, and you
should be independent."[2] To make too much of a teacher or a teaching
is to miss the opportunity to really learn. The teacher's task is to help us
remember what we carry unrecognized in the cellars of memory. And
since the basis of learning is our own memory, we should not be dis-
tracted by the teacher's personal intentions. Teachers often forget that
their job is to waken what is in the student and not present what has
been awakened in them.

Often the wise spiritual teacher will not impart lessons but only
teach indirectly. Many Zen stories tell of students approaching a master to learn, only to be told to hang around for a while. The while often
extends to years, until eventually the students discover that they have
learned something mysterious and certainly not what they set out to
learn. Here therapy and spiritual education have something else in
common: what we think we should know turns out to be the very thing
we don't need to know, and what we finally learn is exactly what we
thought was unnecessary.

Jesus the teacher represents this mystifying approach to learning as
well. He speaks in parables and stories and almost never gives a direct
answer to a sincere question. His actions seem to be largely symbolic.
And ironically, according to his theologian biographers, he seems to

embody the old prophecies in his most ordinary actions, living in two dimensions at once, giving the impression that his words and actions are primary and the old prophecies dependent for meaning on him. He also teaches by example and by his presence.

Quoting Suzuki once more describing another Zen master: "He has no idea of helping people. What he is doing is helping, but he himself has no idea of helping people."[3] I have the same feeling. I hope to make a contribution of some kind, but if I have the intention of helping, I can't help. The best way to teach is not to intend any teaching, and the purer that lack of intention is, the more can be taught.

Paradoxically, the really good teacher is often an imperfect person. I could provide a long list of marvelous teachers from whom I have learned, but I could also show where each was wrong and misguided, where ego entered and fear obstructed. The people and teachings that have meant the most to me were often the ones most limited and lacking. Yet behind or through these learning experiences I have glimpsed the ghostly mythic teacher and the faintest of eternal teachings, and these intimations have been more than adequate.

There is nothing more injurious to the spiritual life than gross doctrine. In this area if you can spell out and explain what you are trying to say, it probably isn't worth saying. The perfect teacher and the correct teaching are particularly suspicious, for the only real learning comes through the most imperfect and mistaken channels of knowledge. This is so because a good teacher is one who has risked life and has therefore failed, and the good teaching is so full of mystery that any clear exposition is by definition misguided.

Good teachers are those people who have gone so deep in their knowledge that they know bitterly and honestly that they don't know. They speak directly from their inability to speak and teach what they know to be unteachable. They may well have found fascinating methods to impart this knowledge beyond knowing, and therefore they tend to be eccentric. If the eccentricity rises up from richness of soul, it is to be trusted, but never naïvely. For spiritual knowledge in the best of us is always surrounded by potential self-deception and illusion. The good teacher is not afraid of such things and even uses them for the benefit of his students.

In the spiritual life a good teacher is worth everything, and nothing is worse than a bad teacher. A good student doesn't give away everything to the teacher but plays his role in keeping the archetype intact. Carlos Castaneda and Don Juan, Zorba the Greek and his British teacher apprentice — these are good examples of the archetypal dimensions in teaching and learning. In these cases the student is a bit naïve, the teacher perhaps overly wise. In actual situations each has to be both. We learners have to be both simpleminded and intellectually acute, and our teachers have to be all-knowing and imperfect. Otherwise we are only exchanging information, a sure sign that there is nothing here worth learning and no one to teach it.

Notes
1. David Chadwick, *Crooked Cucumber* (New York: Broadway Books, 1999), p. 354.
2. Ibid., p. 321.
3. Ibid., p. 387.

Jesus said to his disciples, "Compare me to something
and tell me what I am like."
Simon Peter said to him, "You are like a just angel."
Matthew said to him, "You are like a wise philosopher."
Thomas said to him, "Teacher, my mouth is utterly unable
to say what you are like."

The Gospel of Thomas

37. Deepening the Meaning of Church

IN THE BEST OF CIRCUMSTANCES a church is a means of inspiring
and guiding all people in their spirituality, whether or not they are
members. A church offers ritual, a place of prayer, education and counseling, and a model, nurturing the vision and transcendent life of all
people. We all know that this living image of church doesn't always
match the facts. In spite of their best intentions, churches get loaded
down with rules and traditions, formulas and hierarchies, and they
usually serve only their own members.

Recently I attended the Easter Vigil at Saint Peter's Basilica in Rome
with my family. The cavernous and imposing church was packed with
people; cameras flashed as the pope entered (an elevated area was
roped off for photographers near the altar), and the procession included
many cardinals and other high-level clergy. But I had the feeling that for
all the grandeur and pomp, this was still a church, and the liturgy was
simple, exactly like that in any other church in the world.

In many ways I would have preferred to celebrate this particular primal rite in a small country monastery, but I was pleased to see that it was possible to evoke a sense of church in the mammoth baroque hall and in the thick of the pope's celebrity. I know, of course, that behind the simplicity of the ritual lay bitter politics and authoritarianism. I was also uncomfortable in that place of edicts and condemnations. Still, I believe it is possible for real church to shine through all the layers of history and confrontation that have obscured it.

In a famous entry in his journal in the summer of 1902, the American poet Wallace Stevens explores this territory. The passage is so rich and relevant, I want to quote a major portion of it:

> Last night I spent an hour in the dark transept of St. Patrick's Cathedral where I go now and then in my more lonely moods. An old argument with me is that the true religious force in the world is not the church, but the world itself: the mysterious callings of Nature and our responses. What incessant murmurs fill that ever-laboring, tireless church! But to-day in my walk I thought that after all there is no conflict of format but rather a contrast. In the cathedral I felt one presence; on the highway I felt another. Two different deities present themselves; and though I have only a cloudy vision of either, yet I now feel the distinction between them. The priest in me worshipped one God at one shrine; the poet another God at another shrine. The priest worshipped Mercy and Love; the poet, Beauty and Might. In the shadows of the church I could hear the prayers of men and women; in the shadows of the trees nothing human mingled with Divinity. As I sat dreaming with the Congregation I felt how the glittering altar works on my senses stimulating and consoling them; and as I went tramping through the fields and woods I beheld every leaf and blade of grass revealing or rather betokening the Invisible.

This tender passage offers many lessons on religion and church, among them the idea that the poet could sit dreaming in the cathedral and feel the haunting reality of the altar. There he could meditate his way past the gap between church and nature and see each in its own way as a revelation of divinity. In my language, he discovered the soul of religion and found it in two different places, in nature and a church. Now I'd like to suggest a third place.

The word *church* has its origins in the Greek *kyrios*, which would be familiar to Christians from the Eucharistic liturgy. *"Kyrie eleison,"* the choir sings. "Lord, have mercy." *Kyrios* is a term of honor, like *sir,* but stronger. The Greeks also used the feminine form, *kyria*, suggesting that the essence of church might have a feminine slant, its anima. *Kyrios/a* is the infinite we address as "thou," and *church* might refer then to the place or occasion where people can sense the divine presence.

Any situation in which the divine makes itself felt can be church in a less formal sense. It could be the building, and usually sacred architecture goes a long way toward invoking divinity. It could also be the rites that take place there, but ritual has to be carried out with care and a proper attitude so that it doesn't become just a means of getting a message across. Church could also be a gathering of people. Jesus said, "Where two or three are gathered together, I am there in their midst." Let's look more closely at this idea of church as gathering, the third option.

When people gather to evoke the divine presence, something happens in the imaginations of the participants. A felt spirit comes over the group, and people may find themselves bound by an invisible temenos, a sense of holy place formed by nothing more than their will to be together for serious purpose. I'm not talking about a vague feeling of togetherness but a significant evocation of community, which is a spiritual expression sufficient in itself or might also be an effective context for ritual and teaching.

Each of us has the capacity for evoking divinity, and when we gather, this potential may find expression in a communal form. I have witnessed it in homes and in the middle of a forest when people have gathered to pray or simply to reflect on their lives. Kyria doesn't require formal religion because gathering gives enough form. I remember many years ago being in a peace rally in Washington, D.C., during the Vietnam war. That was church. And with the family gathered to tell stories about a member who had passed on. That was church, too.

Gathering is important in Buddhist spirituality as well. The three jewels of Buddhism include the Buddha himself, the Dharma or teaching, and the sangha or community. In Buddhism the idea of sangha historically led to the forming of communities of monks, but it, too, is essentially a community coming together with purpose. Commenting on Jesus' statement about gathering, Thich Nhat Hanh says, "Communities of practice, with all their shortcomings, are the best way to make the teachings available to people." I don't believe this is a superficial suggestion but rather the recognition that the very archetype of community constitutes a major portion of the spiritual life. That peace rally I attended had plenty of shortcomings, but even so it was a powerful spiritual experience.

The word *liturgy* means the activity of the people. So it is not just the ceremonies that bring people into the divine presence but the gathering as well. The mere presence of people is part of the rite. We see this also in another old word for church, *ecclesia*, which refers to the gathering of citizens in assembly and gives rise to the common word *ecclesiastical*. *Ecclesia* emphasizes that a church is before all else a gathering of people.

Because gathering is an archetypal reality, the result of a deep urge and a primal act of imagination, it has considerable power, which may account for some of the fear authorities have of it. If you unleash the power of the people, a torrent of vitality pours into the stream. It is difficult to control and shape, and in reaction many leaders are tempted toward an excess of rules and sanctions, which betray the anxiety involved. If leaders of all kinds would reflect on this deeper meaning of church, they might learn to trust the vital force of the people and guide that energy rather than try to keep it in check. Repressive moves only take the life out of the religious experience and incite people to go off in search of alternate forms that still have life in them.

Church is a model. People gather there to focus directly on the unnameable object of their devotion, and from there they can find the divine presence in other forms of gathering. Families coming together are a form of church, and every dinner where the family gathers is a true communion. Every festive party is a spiritual as well as a spirited celebration. Political gatherings, school gatherings, neighborhood gatherings — they are all essential elements in a comprehensive spiritual life, and in a sense they are all church, though we wouldn't call them such.

The Gospel of Thomas inspires me because Thomas, my namesake, the courageous doubter, can't say who or what Jesus is like. He can only say, "I don't know." Thomas was a great missionary, and yet his mission begins in holy ignorance. His religious vision is empty in the deep sense with which I began this book. His honest words hint at what a church might be if it were empty in this same sacred sense.

It could still have external form, teachings, leaders, and traditions, but these would be porous and diaphanous. They wouldn't be rigid and imprisoning. They would have life only as long as we continued to bring them to life, and they would be holy to the extent that they manifested the unnameable mystery that is the object of spiritual attention. The key to resolving any conflict between institution and personal spirituality is to keep qualities of soul in each, always redefining them to keep life in them.

A person or a community can break with a church and go off in a new direction and yet still not have this essential emptiness. Reaction can be as literal and egotistic as tradition. If we must rebel or withdraw from church as we have known it, we must be careful not to establish another rigid form of what we're looking for, yet this is precisely what often happens. It is in the nature of spirit, even the most liberated, to think in hierarchies and rules. A strong saturnine fantasy colors our very notion of spirituality, causing us to think automatically in terms of structure and authority. Paternalism sneaks in because it is lodged in the base of culture, affecting us all.

There is another related word that I have not discussed in the context of gathering: religion. Many people, maybe most, equate religion with a church institution, and of course the word will continue to be used to name a tradition. But in a deeper sense, as we've seen throughout this book, religion is an attitude and an outlook in which mystery, transcendence, and unfathomable depth are taken seriously into account.

Religion is reverence, vision, piety, practice, and compassion. If a tradition serves as a good vessel for these virtues, then it is a religion in a real sense, and if an institution could truly foster these qualities, then it would deserve to be called a religion. But often ideology replaces faith, and authoritarianism substitutes for vision. Then the word *religion* comes to denote the opposite of these qualities.

The history of religions is full of reforms, heresies, and defensive reactions. Perhaps these developments simply show that the church is a living entity, growing and maturing. But I suspect that these points of growth could be more subtle and become part of daily religious experience. We are always reforming our vision, always refining our practice, and always trying out heresies — deviations from the direction we have found worthy of our belief. These are all signs of life that could be incorporated into an institution and even fostered.

The word *re-ligion* means connecting back. In our religious lives we connect with the source of our existence and the origins of time. We contact the deepest mythic and archetypal mysteries that shape our lives, and in that way we live from a profound place, as much engaged with the eternal as the temporal. With deep religion we are in touch with the currents of thought, imagery, and emotion that well up from our depths. That is why religion is essentially a healing and teaching force.

Whenever I go into a church, I know that this building, leadership, and community offer a limited embodiment of the archetypal church, the church of imagination incarnated in this place imperfectly. But a church is both divine and human. It links us to the eternal and unnameable, while it shows all the signs of passing fads and nervous self-protection. What is most important is our own vision, our capacity to see through the imperfections to the mystical reality that is accessible only to an imagination schooled in the sacred.

The current reaction against religious institutions in favor of personal spirituality is an unstable and rather neurotic condition. It presents an artificial division. Personal religious inspiration and institutions call each other into being. They are two sides of a coin. I don't mean that it is impossible to be spiritual without being a follower of a particular tradition. That is an option for some. But placing these two dimensions of the religious life in opposition betrays the fact that both are currently on shaky ground.

Perhaps we are in a state of spiritual crisis, but that, too, is a feeling and a fantasy that may always be in play. From it we may reform our private spiritual lives and reform the institutions. We may also discover new, more congenial forms of community and ritual. But beneath all the reform lies the eternal realities: the need to be inspired toward a communal, ethical, and reverential life, and the need to gather and make a culture of belief. The ancient teaching of many traditions is that if we conduct the rites, create the art, and build the buildings thoughtfully, we will be in the divine presence, the ultimate source of the vitality of our belief.

No umbrella, getting soaked,
I'll just use the rain as my raincoat.

Daito

38. Transparent Tradition

IN THE TWELFTH CENTURY the abbot Joachim of Fiore tried to imagine a subtle form of church, something not entirely amorphous yet not made of bricks and laws. He taught an approach to history so stimulating to the imagination that he was prosecuted for heresy, championed by monks, and proclaimed a prophet and a visionary by reformers. He said that there have been three historical periods: the era of the Father and law, the era of the Son and church, and the current era of the Holy Spirit, when institutions will give way to the eternal spirit of community, especially in the form of monasticism.

Dividing experience into ten laws or twelve steps or three periods is enticing in its simplicity. We are invited to fill in our own details, as did many who were inspired by Joachim. I confess that I caught the spirit when I first read Joachim's ideas and quickly turned them into something conforming to my own tastes and thought. I imagine the era of spirit as a time when the institution may still exist but will be surpassed in importance by the ideas and images of the tradition.

I expect Catholicism to survive, though I don't think the current authoritarianism has much of a future. Today you can see the retrenchment, the desperate reaching for authority, and the attempts to control people's behavior and thought. When will spiritual leaders of all stripes finally realize that spirituality and religion are not enhanced by thought control? Religion thrives when leaders offer inspiring possibilities and rich interpretations of experience; when they truly help us deal responsibly and hopefully with our mortality, our attempts at love, and our work; and when we can admire them and wish to be like them rather than follow their stipulations out of fear or contest them in rebellion.

The kind of seed that Joachim planted offers a way of imagining the spiritual life freed of authoritarianism and dogmatism. His views were revolutionary and heretical in his own time, and so they are now when we still cling to dogma as a way of preserving values. Joachim's understanding of religion rests on a remarkable degree of trust, something that is still elusive.

A few years ago my family started attending Mass at a small community in a forest a half hour's drive from our house. We loved that community and found hope in it. It was staffed by a monk priest and a student brother, both intelligent, honest, and compassionate. But after going there for three years and offering to do anything we could to keep it thriving, we were told that the fathers in authority, like absentee landlords thousands of miles away, decided to close it down. When I complained about their tactics—they were condescending and secretive about the closing—they told me they could feel my pain, but they couldn't find monks interested in keeping the community going. I thought it ironic that we lay people were passionate about sustaining that community while the monks, dedicated to the very ideal of the common life, said they couldn't find anyone interested and didn't feel any responsibility.

So I imagined an alternative. I thought the two Catholic monks could be joined by a Zen teacher perhaps and a Jewish rabbi and maybe a Muslim mystic. I foresaw the possibility of a spiritual community not bound by pre-Joachimite literalisms and boundaries. I saw a way of teaching my children Catholicism without defining it as something at odds with other traditions. I hoped that the two good monks would turn radical.

Of course this was a pipe dream, and the little home church was closed down and the community disbanded. I remember one day before the closing an elderly man who usually spoke in rather harsh tones in favor of old-time practices and ideas stood up and said, "I've been coming to Mass here for twenty years, and I expect it to continue for another twenty." I felt sad for him because he was obviously raised to trust his spiritual teachers and had to learn a hard lesson about betrayal.

My point is not to criticize persons but to point to inhumane aspects of the spirit that seizes us and moves us to do what we do. There has to be some deep soul in a spiritual group in order to foster real community. The spirit alone is interested in hierarchies, orders, rules, and traditions, and it has a tendency toward narcissism: "I need my space. I need my time. Those children and families interfere with my spiritual life." I have been in spiritual communities where the soul was well represented, and there it is possible to eclipse rules on behalf of communal need.

I read Joachim to mean that there comes a time in history, in the life of a church or organization, and even in an individual's experience, when authority and organization recede into the background and more subtle issues come forward. There follows a refining of the religion. Its poetry rather than its dogma now comes to the fore. Defensiveness and competition ease or disappear altogether, allowing the real depths of the spiritual vision to reveal themselves.

When people ask me if I'm a practicing Catholic, I always answer yes, with Joachim in the back of my mind. I practice my Catholicism in everything I do, but my ties to the organization are slender at the moment. Like so many people today I don't want authorities acting out their emotional problems at my expense. I want real spiritual guidance and example, or I want nothing at all. The hiercharchy doesn't own Catholicism. I refuse to give it away.

A person raised, as I was, to surrender ego to the will of God might say, "Aren't you placing yourself above a long tradition? Aren't there wonderful things about your church in spite of a few old-timers who can't let go of power?" My answer is that in these Joachimite days of spirit I have to meet the organization halfway. I have to use all my intelligence, accept full responsiblity, and bring my concern for community and family into my practice of religion. Otherwise my spirituality will become separate from my religion, which is a dangerous situation indeed because when that happens, religion becomes little more than an empty shell and spirituality improvises on shaky ground.

Dealing with spiritual authority I follow a formula. Authority can be a useful part of practice. The word means to author, which in turn means to increase or grow something. At its best an authority is one who can help you become what you potentially are. But authority is demonized when it turns into pressure to become what the authority wants you to be.

We can best deal with authority by first having it ourselves. We are the authors of our lives, including our spirituality. Possessing and enjoying that personal authority, we can then give ourselves to people in position and those who have special knowledge and skill to help us author ourselves. The authoring is always two-sided, and it flows in two directions. The external authority has the privilege and the pleasure of serving others as they increase in their spirituality, and the individual receives guidance and structure, two valuable items in the education of the soul.

Too often this formula breaks down, with the external authority disregarding the individual needs, responsibility, and freedom of the person. Guidance and structure corrode into dogma and institution. The liberating pleasure of education turns into the sadomasochistic gratification of dominance and submission.

The power relations among people are never pure and never free of sadomasochistic strains. But it is one thing to have bits of power struggle in our dealings with a spiritual organization and quite another to be an actual victim of domination. There can be little doubt, too, that the sexual abuse frequently found in spiritual organizations is simply an extension of sadomasochistic patterns, which are always a blend of power and sex, that lie at the core of the organization. Recent sexual scandals among the clergy highlight the humanity within religion but also indicate the profound soullessness that has creeped into religious authority.

In Joachim's time his view of history was seen as a way out of the domination of corrupt religious authorities. Today the same is true: his image of the era of spirit offers a way out of the power neuroses that have crippled many religious institutions and stifled the spiritual lives of their followers. The key idea is to live the spirit first and turn to the institution only as an aid to the spiritual life. With Joachim we can say that the day of spiritual domination is over. A new era of deep spirituality is finding its place, and the archetype and deep myth underlying our spirituality is, thankfully, shifting.

God owns heaven
But He craves the earth.

   Anne Sexton, "The Earth"

39. *Secular Holiness*

STUNNED BY A SPIRITUAL VISION, men and women leave home and their familiar worlds to enter monasteries and spiritual communities. The impulse toward withdrawal seems intrinsic to the archetype of spirit. If the movement away isn't physical, it is a matter of thought and style. People drift into a special language or way of life. They may feel only a vague urge to get away and be alone, but their retreat is an important part of their spirituality.

In spite of my tenure in a religious community, I have always wanted to link the religious and the secular, and especially find signs of the sacred in ordinary life. The first essay I ever published was called "Christian Humanism" and was an attempt to show that the Christian way and a deeply human life are indistinguishable. When I went to Syracuse University and found courses in Rilke, Wallace Stevens, and Samuel Beckett being taught in the religion department, I felt at home. I feel in my bones that it is wrong to separate the religious in any way from the secular.

The most disturbing problem I had while living in a religious order was the loss of my secularity. It began when I was thirteen and went off to the prep seminary, a boarding school built on a square of flat land outlined by a long, straight sidewalk. To us young students this ribbon of cement marked the boundary between the holy precinct of our special world and the simple pleasures enjoyed by ordinary people everywhere. When eventually I left the order, I had to struggle financially for several years, but the recovery of my secularity was a joy that far surpassed my worries about survival.

Maybe that deprivation early in my life accounts for the passion I feel for connecting the sacred and the ordinary in every instance. I know what it is like to lean too far into the religious and do without the ordinary pleasures of life. I see many people who similarly give too much to the exalted spirit and not enough to the human soul. Some seem obsessed with religion. The insecurity of their belief gets in the way of their living, and they seem driven to convert others to their beliefs and values. They can think of nothing else, and it is difficult to have an ordinary friendship with them.

But it works the other way as well, as is only too obvious: we can be caught up in the secularism all around us. Western culture as a whole has retreated from a religious point of view and has created a world based on machines, explanation, and self-advancement. But this secularism doesn't offer the secularity we need. After all, it is an ism — a psychological complex, an exaggeration, and the opposite of secularity. Secularism is a symptom betraying the fact that we no longer enjoy the fullness of secular existence.

The religion I have been envisioning in this book, so difficult to spell out, would be an antidote to soulless secularism, but it would not create a separate reality, a high moral ground from which to judge the ordinary life or certainly to escape from it. It would be based on the notion that everything pulses with a hidden vitality and emerges from a hidden mystery. The point of a holy life is to be in harmony with that underlying source.

All my life I've been attracted to religious teachings that keep the holy and the secular together. In my late twenties the visionary writings of Teilhard de Chardin inspired me. He wanted to show that evolution is not just a material process but entails a sophistication of consciousness and a radical spiritual development in human culture. He called it Christogenesis, which I might define in simple terms as the coming to be of the Christ ideal in individuals and communities. By wrapping theology and science within each other, Chardin attempted to heal the gap between the religious and the secular.

John Dominic Crossan, the brilliant New Testament scholar, was my teacher for a while, though he was only a few years older than me. In the late 1960s he was espousing the idea of "realized eschatology." Again in the Christian context, this referred to the presence of the kingdom that Jesus announced as having already been initiated. We don't wait for an actual end to this physical world but rather an end to the condition of raw, literal, competitive survival. With a religious point of view whatever we imagine in some future ideal state is already available if only we have the eyes to see it and the courage to bring it into being.

In my own evolving effort to keep religion and secular life connected, my studies in pagan polytheism came next. I learned from the Greek mythologists and dramatists to see that every aspect of daily life has its presiding spirit, its god or goddess. I was astonished to learn, for example, that the great and mysterious god Hermes represented a particular kind of spirituality for business and financial institutions, and that Aphrodite gave sexuality, beauty, and even body care a spiritual dimension.

Because I found religious depth for secular life in Greek polytheism, in my books I frequently refer to various myths for insight. This habit sometimes confuses readers who don't understand how mythology—apparently so fanciful and so far from monotheistic ideals—could be real religion. Some Catholic critics complain that because I refer to pagan myth so positively, my work is not Christian. Here and there groups have boycotted my lectures for this reason. I don't understand that criticism, but given the narrow, literal ways in which religion is taught — and most adults have only an elementary education in religion — I am not surprised at the confusion. On the surface it may look as though paganism is the enemy of a certain kind of spirituality, but an open-minded study of polytheistic religions would reveal a spirituality the equal of any monotheism.

This turn to polytheism is complicated. At the time I was poring over the Greek sacred texts, I was also reading C. G. Jung and James Hillman with considerable passion. Jung helped me take religion out of the realm of simple fact, to be accepted or rejected, and see it as a source of mysteries that live through me every day. Even today I read at least a passage from Jung regularly, though I admire Jung the theologian and the magus more than Jung the psychologist.

Jung was the first to teach me how to take figures of dream, imagination, and religion not as symbols but as presences. This is a crucial part of a polytheistic approach to spirituality. Hermes is neither a symbol nor a literal being. He is a spiritual reality, one that I encounter daily in my world. Every time I deal with money or tell a story I enter the mysterious realm the Greeks called Hermes. A special enlivening spirit moves through me. I am not in full control, and if I can surrender to the inspiration, I can be creative in my life and work. Like the ancient Greeks I can honor this profound spirit, maybe not by offering sacrifice at a temple but certainly by sacrificing my will to the presence that has stirred within me and who gives life to my world.

By recognizing the many and powerful mysteries playing out in my own life and in the culture, I became less interested in familiar ideas like wholeness and integration. As I have already mentioned, they seem to me sentimental ideals, whereas the secular world is full of many mysteries that need not be brought under a single umbrella. I wonder if all the talk about wholeness in spiritual groups is not a sentimental expression of the desire to be in control. To be polytheistic requires humility and surrender rather than control, and its by-products are not competition and missionary zeal but, rather, unlimited tolerance and appreciation for diversity.

James Hillman's early essay on psychological polytheism, rewritten in his major book *Re-Visioning Psychology,* had a powerful impact on me, too. I think I first read it in 1973 when it caused a major shift in my thinking about religion. He helped me avoid literalizing polytheism and getting stuck on the Greek imagination as a new and exclusive belief system. He also opened the door to a study I took up with considerable energy: the reworking of pagan polytheism by Renaissance European thinkers who never thought of abandoning their Christian piety even as they were captivated by the religion of the Greeks and Romans. Ever since, I have adopted a similar stance for myself, finding it the richest way to be both religious and secular at the same time.

So today whenever I read in the newspapers about some sexual scandal, I'm reminded of the mystery of Aphrodite, and I read the story as a spiritual conflict. I read the financial pages with Hermes in mind and look for the myth lying there in hiding. I read about murder and warfare, and I wonder, in the light of Greek tragedy, how we as a society are offending the god of aggression, Ares. I read about children killing each other, and I imagine that we are offending Artemis in some way. She is responsible for the protection of young people.

THE SECRET OF FINDING the sacred in ordinary life is not in applying moralisms and ideologies to current affairs but in grasping the inherent profundity and indeed spirituality of every situation. Always there lies a mystery, perhaps very much in hiding while the surfaces suggest only facts. Having the vision to perceive the mystery in all situations is an important part of the spiritual life. From that vision flow values, involvement, reflection, and action. A distinctive way of life emerges, and that is the true flowering of spiritual awareness.

Recently these ideas came up in a small way in a fascinating conversation I had with two remarkable people. They were showing me an apparatus they had had a hand in creating. It was a small system of plastic water containers filled with plants and snails and stones, the purpose of which was to purify water. And the "living machine," as it is called, worked wonderfully. What began as foul sludge ended in pure water. Like my two friends I was impressed by the mysteriousness and elegance of the process.

They told me they wanted to paste some symbols of the planetary gods on the containers to accent the spiritual and alchemical aspects of the apparatus, and they asked my advice. At first they didn't like my ideas. We argued in a friendly way. I thought that if they wanted to complexify the spirituality of their contraption, they should do more than paste labels on it. They should reimagine the whole thing. I didn't like the name anyway, "living machine." I thought it would be better to get away from the fantasy of machine altogether. I know it can be reimagined, but today the word has connotations of mechanism and materialism.

I suggested that instead of pasting a picture of Venus on ugly plastic they could make a beautiful terraced garden and call it a cleansing park or a water garden. A garden is a classic Venusian object, and it would be better to completely remake the object with Venusian values in mind than to give her only superficial acknowledgment. They picked up on the idea and quickly imagined a large garden that could do an equally effective job of purifying water.

Everything we do at home or in society can be imagined from a spiritual point of view. If you reflect on anything deep enough, it reveals itself as a mystery. The writing I am engaged in at the moment is mysterious and spiritual. It is mercurial, Venusian, saturnine, jovial, and many other things besides. Each of these spiritualities has a muse who can inspire qualities like persuasion, beauty, turns of phrase, irony, form, depth of reflection, accessibility—each of which can be traced to one of the classical deities. During the Renaissance, writers spoke of style in these terms, expressing what they called rhetoric in the language of polytheism. I see these developments not only as matters of style but as a way of honoring the spirituality of the work.

This is why I want to support people who are studying theology in the context of ordinary life. Here and there I meet a few who see the possibilities for being creative, involved theologians in the midst of culture, not plastering a layer of piety onto otherwise secular matters but offering insight into the spiritual issues of secular life. I'd like to think that the day of the theologian who is constrained by a tradition, rather than simply inspired by it, is gone. Secularity is incomplete if its spiritual dimension has been suppressed or neglected. Paradoxically, sectarian theology contributes to the secularization of life by dividing the sacred from the ordinary.

The ultimate goal of a new religious vision is a world so fully secular and so fully sacred that there would be no way to tell them apart. Yet we need an articulation of religious and spiritual vision to achieve a deeply humane secular existence. The old forms of religious teaching and ritual need to be revised radically, but most of all we need the capacity to see the sacred in the ordinary and the mundane. Then we could respond to all of life with the appropriate language and action. Our public religion could be sincere and comprehensive. We could leave behind secularism, with all its competitive jealousies, and make a different kind of culture where play, art, and prayer would be as common and natural as work and commerce. In such a world we would have the vision to care for each other and live moral lives. Under current conditions where the religious and the secular are separated, there is no effective motivation for bringing morality into politics, business, and other aspects of culture-building.

To be thoroughly secular, free of neurosis and egotism, we need a spiritual viewpoint. Secularity without spirituality is secularism mixed with religionism. It is a deadly equation. Currently, insofar as we separate the sacred and the mundane, we don't have access to the full pleasures of secular existence. Lacking a spiritual imagination of ordinary life, we are left with egotism, which screens out the full impact of nature and culture. With all our warfare, crime, and competitiveness, we have little access to the full economic and cultural richness that could be the heart of secular living.

Here is a great paradox: we need a vital spiritual existence in order to enjoy all that life has to offer. Of course the religions have often presented an entirely different point of view, but that is because in so many ways they have got caught in the split of sacred from the mundane. We have yet to see on a broad scale what it would be like to press beyond the competitive spiritual traditions and live a life saturated with spiritual vision and values, which would allow full participation in the joys of secular life.

This world is not conclusion;
A sequel stands beyond,
Invisible as music,
But positive, as sound.
  Emily Dickinson, "This World Is Not Conclusion"

40. *Eternal Life*

WE COME FULL CIRCLE NOW to the very heart of emptiness and spiritual vision: the mystery of death and life after death. Unexpectedly, perhaps, the question fits in with our discussion of practice, and it is directly related to the previous theme of spiritual secularity. I want to ask not what happens after death, though I'd certainly like to know, but rather how do we live knowing that we will die? Is there a sophisticated way to speak of eternal life?

For the past ten years many people have asked me, as someone who has explored the nature of the soul, what I think about life after death and immortality. I have always evaded the question, saying honestly that I am more concerned about the soul as the source of this life and the depth dimension of this experience. But recently I turned sixty, and I feel different already. I don't worry much about death, but I wonder about my daughter, who is not yet ten years old, and my wife, who is fifteen years younger than I, and my young godson. I never want to part from them, and so now I'm reluctant to sidestep the issue of the immortality of the soul.

My own view, as limited as any, is that immortality is something to discover in the living of this life. It can't be contained in an idea, to say nothing of a theological theory. It has to be lived every day in order to have real meaning. It is so mixed with fear, wonder, hope, and disbelief that understandably we look for a few comforting words in explanation or revelation. But it seems to be part of the human condition, a prerequisite for our very participation in this life, not to know about the afterlife with the certainty of fact. Religion rises or falls on this point: whether, in the face of the unknown, it offers comforting illusions or genuine hope.

My answer about life after death is not simple. Plato said that philosophers prepare for death by spending a lifetime in contemplation. But there are many things we can do, not just to prepare for death but to enter eternity step by step. For me the love of my family is a taste of immortality. Whatever happens, nothing could ever destroy that love. Certain raptures of beauty, too — Beethoven's *Seventh Symphony*, Stravinsky's *Firebird,* and J. S. Bach's keyboard concertos — take me away from the particulars of this life and offer a sign of what eternity might be like. A truly ethical decision, large or small, releases me from my imprisonment in self-interest and allows me to glimpse the eternity of the self.

Love, beauty, community, creativity, and even insight, things I am always after in my writing and lecturing, encourage me to go on living. They pull me out of myself and into the world, an enormous achievement because I realize that only by being out of myself will I ever discover who and what I am. This is the nature of religious ecstasy — the word means standing outside; it is not a sweet emotion but a state of being where I learn that I am more than a physical being. Each time I transcend myself in this life, I am readying for the final transcendence.

I can imagine three ways of dealing with mortality. I could decide that there is no more to life than this. Death is the end. Several people I know and admire, who are much smarter than I, take this position. But I can't help thinking that it is a bit defensive. It is like saying that you are not good at something so you don't have to do it. It closes the question. But wonder about death is full of life; it keeps the imagination and the heart alive.

Another response is exactly the opposite. Intelligent and sincere people simply assert that there is a life beyond this one. Some even describe it in detail. Others look for hints and proofs in near-death experiences and the like. But this approach, too, seems to me a bit defensive. Like the materialist skepticism about immortality, this apparently more spiritual way often sounds anxious and too insistent. It tends to close discussion and therefore serve self-protection rather than wonder.

It seems clear to me, as I get older, that I am the same person I was as a child. My entire life circles me closely and intimately and is in some manner always part of who I am. I am also aware that my choices and experiences come from such a deep and mysterious place that even in the most concrete and timebound moments I am more than I could ever imagine myself to be. The eternal plays a constant role in my everyday life, and so it takes no intellectual stretch to imagine immortality.

If I feel life moving through me rather than always initiated by me, then I want to give more reverence to it. I can appreciate that same kind of life flowing through others and want to protect them as well. I can understand how others make mistakes and do irrational things, as I do, when they crave vitality. I know what it is like to desire a full life and at the same time fear its intensity. So empathy is yet another way to transcend the self and prepare for death.

If I can imagine that I am transparent and translucent, that a greater will passes through me, and that I am hollow and vacant, filled with the riches of a life I don't own or direct or understand, then death is not so strange and immortality is already familiar. But isn't this the condition of the Christian saint and the Indian bodhisattva and the tribal shaman? Religion is all about being fully in this life and in this body, and in that way fully engaged with the eternal mysteries and presences.

A spirituality imbued with soul takes us profoundly into, through, and beyond this life. It doesn't opt for avoidance or distraction. According to mythology, Krishna's mother looks deep into his mouth and beholds the universe. We can all do that—look into the simplest and most ordinary orifice, anything that opens up beyond itself, and behold the all. If a spiritual system shows us only our own egos, it is completely missing the point. But if it helps us look at the flesh and see the spirit, it is performing acts of religion on us, making us holy.

The eternal quality of the most ordinary things allows our souls to enjoy the eternity of a moment in time. Every object is potentially holy, and if we fail to see and employ its holiness, chances are it will become demonic. We live in a world of sacraments and fetishes, tools of holiness and instruments of evil. The difference is religion.

There is no end to this journey into eternity. The closer we get, the farther away it appears. Only those who avoid the eternal in the name of religion claim to have reached the end point. The rest of us remain in the rhythm of discovery and forgetfulness, achievement and loss. Given fully to life in all its particulars, we are ferried deep into eternity, like Dante after he passed through the portal in the woods. For everyday life is porous, full of holes that open onto the sacred.

And so there can be no end to these reflections. The alchemist might recommend throwing it all back into the pot to simmer more and gain in flavor. My end is my beginning, tradition says. The snake bites his tail: we circle around and around, getting dizzy in the cycles of our thoughts and our lives. But once in a while it may occur to us that this dizziness is the sensation of eternity, the soul fed by ongoing life and by occasional eruptions of emptiness where the sacred shows itself. This paradox, the interchangeability of the secular and the sacred, is the very stuff of religion and the goal of our spiritual craving.

Our job, then, is not to look for an end but rather to see the end, death and the eternal in everything we do. But this kind of vision requires a religious attitude and a spiritual outlook. We finish reading a book. It has ended. But now life begins anew. What we thought was ink on paper, a mere manual for getting on with life, a life raft, turns out to have been more like a window, a pool of water, and a mirror in which we may have glimpsed the inexpressible. This thing in our hands as well as the life we are trying to live wisely, so tangible and limited, are actually, like everything else, made of heavenly crystal. They are the spirit incarnating and flesh revealing its innate eternity.

All we have to do is live this life with openness, imagination, and a sense of paradox and wonder. Then it will be spiritually alive, with or without the formal language of tradition. But there is no escaping the wry paradox that has been the guiding principle of this book: Only by allowing the fool his place will we find the wisdom and holiness we seek. Only by giving ourselves fully to the puny task that life has offered us this day will we have access to the eternal and the infinite. Only by seeing through to the eternal and blissful soul of our neighbor will we catch a glimpse of the unnameable.

Index

⚏ Perennial

Books by Thomas Moore:

THE SOUL'S RELIGION
Cultivating a Profoundly Spiritual Way of Life
ISBN 0-06-093019-5 (paperback) • ISBN 0-694-52425-5 (audio)

Written as a companion to *Care of the Soul*, Moore offers a completely new interpretation of religion and spirituality.

"A thoughtful guidebook for seekers willing to go beyond instant messaging in their own religious journeys and do their own work." —*Publishers Weekly*

CARE OF THE SOUL
A Guide for Cultivating Depth and Sacredness in Everyday Life
ISBN 0-06-092224-9 (paperback) • ISBN 1-559-94603-2 (audio)

Drawing on ancient wisdom and modern in-depth psychology, this national bestseller examines how we can find deep satisfaction and pleasure in life.

"Thoughtful, eloquent, inspiring." —*San Francisco Chronicle*

CARE OF THE SOUL: THE ILLUSTRATED EDITION
How to Add Depth and Meaning to Your Everyday Life
ISBN 0-06-757511-0 (hardcover from HarperCollins)

THE RE-ENCHANTMENT OF EVERYDAY LIFE
ISBN 0-06-092824-7 (paperback)

A guide to finding wonder within common events and surroundings often taken for granted—food, home, business, politics, rituals, and more.

"[A] profound yet practical sequel to . . . *Care of the Soul*." —*Publishers Weekly*

SOUL MATES
Honoring the Mysteries of Love and Relationship
ISBN 0-06-092575-2 (paperback) • ISBN 1-559-94941-4 (audio)

Examining the rich idea of a soul mate, Moore offers guidance through the beginnings, the ups and downs, and the sometimes devastating ends of romances, friendships, and marriages.

"Moore moves love off the fast track and into the realm of mystery and imagination where it belongs." —*New Woman*

▊ Perennial

THE EDUCATION OF THE HEART
Readings and Sources for CARE OF THE SOUL, SOUL MATES,
and THE RE-ENCHANTMENT OF EVERYDAY LIFE
ISBN 0-06-092860-3 (paperback)

A selection of readings designed to educate the heart and mind,
and expand the soul.

ORIGINAL SELF
Living with Paradox and Originality
ISBN 0-06-095372-1 (paperback) • ISBN 0-694-52299-6 (audio)

Fifty heart-lifting meditations guide readers back to their God-given
personalities. This inspiring collection urges us to live with originality rather
than conformity, presenting multidimensional portraits of the creative self and
different angles from which to tap one's primal emotions and possibilities.

MEDITATIONS
On the Monk Who Dwells in Daily Life
ISBN 0-06-092700-3 (paperback)

Thomas Moore draws on the twelve years he lived as a monk in this insightful
book of one hundred meditations. Interspersed with glimpses of the beauty and
humor of the monk's life, each page suggests a way of finding spirituality and
nurturing the soul that can be applied in any walk of life.

THE SOUL OF SEX
Cultivating Life as an Act of Love
ISBN 0-06-093095-0 (paperback) • ISBN 0-694-51975-8 (audio)

Thomas Moore turns to religion, mythology, literature, and visual imagery to
explore the spirituality and profound mysteries of life bound up in sex.

**"Moore writes about sex with depth and intelligence, blending mythological
material with a caring, personal style."** —*San Francisco Chronicle*

THE THOMAS MOORE AUDIO COLLECTION
ISBN 0-694-51493-4 (audio)

Two of Moore's books in one collection: *Soul Mates* and *Care of the Soul.*
Read by Thomas Moore and Peter Thomas.

**Want to receive notice of events and new books by Thomas Moore?
Sign up for Thomas Moore's AuthorTracker at www.AuthorTracker.com**

Available wherever books are sold, or call 1-800-331-3761 to order.

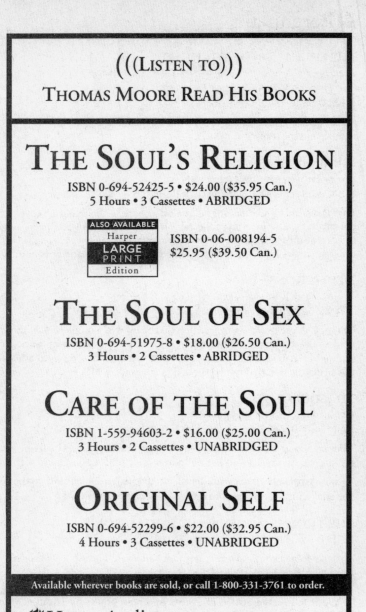